Economics in a
Business Context

Business in Context Series

Editors

David Needle
Currently Head of the Department
of Business Studies and Languages
The Polytechnic of East London*

Professor Eugene McKenna
Currently Director of the School
of Business and Management
The Polytechnic of East London*

Accounting Information in a Business Context
Aidan Berry and Robin Jarvis

Behaviour in a Business Context
Richard Turton

Business in Context
David Needle

Economics in a Business Context
Alan Neale and Colin Haslam

Law in a Business Context
Bill Cole and Peter Shears

Quantitative Techniques in a Business Context
Roger Slater and Peter Ascroft

* Formerly North East London Polytechnic.

Economics in a Business Context

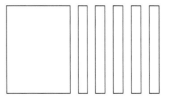

Alan Neale

and

Colin Haslam

Van Nostrand Reinhold (International)

First published in 1989 by
Van Nostrand Reinhold (International) Co. Ltd
11 New Fetter Lane, London EC4P 4EE

© 1989 Alan Neale and Colin Haslam

Typeset in Times 10 on 11½ point by
Photoprint, Torquay, Devon
Printed in Great Britain by
Richard Clay Ltd, Bungay, Suffolk

ISBN 0 278 00076 2

British Library Cataloguing in Publication Data

Neale, Alan
    Economics in a business context. – (Business
    in context)
    1. Business.   Management.   Economic aspects
    I. Title   II. Haslam, Colin   III. Series
    338.7

ISBN 0 278 00076 2

Contents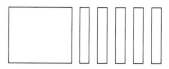

Series foreword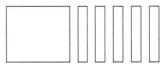

This book is part of the 'Business in Context' series. The books in this series are written by lecturers all with several years experience of teaching on undergraduate business studies programmes. For a number of years we have been aware that many of the books we were recommending to our students didn't cater specifically for business studies courses. Although there are some good books covering the different disciplines found in the business studies curricula, few of these texts are aimed specifically at the business studies student. Many of the best management texts assume a level of managerial experience and the worst take a simplistic and prescriptive view of business life. The interdisciplinary nature of business studies often means presenting students with a range of books dealing with various specialist topics, which can prove both daunting and expensive.

It is certainly not our intention to offer our individual texts as a panacea. Indeed our policy throughout this series is that the books are well referenced and the student guided to further reading on every topic. However, we do feel that our books provide a focus for the student attempting to seek some meaning in the range of subjects currently offered on business studies programmes.

Business studies has attracted a growing band of students for a number of years and is currently one of the most popular undergraduate courses. Whilst many books have emerged to feed a hungry BTEC market, the undergraduate business studies student has been somewhat neglected. One of the causes of that neglect has undoubtedly been the difficulty of many, academics and members of the business community alike, to define business studies, beyond a list of loosely connected subject headings. With this series we hope to make good some of those missing connections.

With the exception of the text Business in Context, which takes the series title as its theme, all our texts take the approach of a particular discipline traditionally associated with business studies and taught across a wide range of business studies programmes. The first books in our series examine business from the perspectives of economics, behavioural science, law, quantitative methods and accounting. However, whereas in traditional texts it is the subject itself that is the focus, our texts make business the focus. All the texts are based upon the same specific model of business illustrated in Figure 1. We have called our model 'Business in Context' and the text of the same name is an explanation and expansion of that model.

The model comprises four distinct levels. At the core are the activities which make up what we know as business and include innovation,

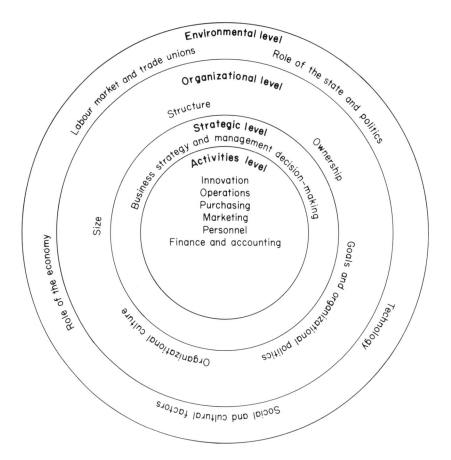

Figure 1 Business in Context

operations and production, purchasing, marketing, personnel and finance and accounting. We see these activities operating irrespective of the type of business involved. They are found in both the manufacturing and service industry as well as in the public and private sectors and constitute the first level.

The second level of our model is concerned with strategy and management decision making. It is here that decisions which influence the direction of the business activities at our core are made.

The third level is concerned with organizational factors within which business activities and management decisions take place. The organizational issues we examine are structure, size, goals and organizational politics, patterns of ownership and organizational culture. Clear links can be forged between this and other levels of the model, especially between structure and strategy, goals and management decision making, and how all aspects both contribute to and are influenced by the organizational culture.

The fourth level is concerned with the environment in which businesses operate. The issues here involve social and cultural factors, the role of the state and politics, the role of the economy, and issues relating to both technology and labour. An important feature of this level is that such elements not only operate as opportunities and constraints for business, but also, are shaped by the three other levels.

This brief description of the 'Business in Context' model illustrates the key features of the series. We see business as dynamic. It is constantly being shaped by and in turn shaping those managerial, organizational, and environmental contexts within which it operates. Influences go backwards and forwards across the various levels. Moreover, the aspects identified within each level are in constant interaction with one another. Thus the role of the economy cannot be understood without reference to the role of the state; size and structure are inextricably linked; innovation is inseparable from issues of operations, marketing and finance. The understanding of how the model works is what business studies is all about and forms the basis for the series.

In proposing this model we are proposing a framework for analysis and we hope that it will encourage readers to add to and refine the model and so broaden our understanding of business. Each writer in this series has been encouraged to present their own interpretation of the model. In this way we hope to build up a more complete picture of business initially through the eyes of an economist, a behavioural scientist, a lawyer, a statistician and an accountant.

The series therefore aims for a more integrated and realistic approach to business than has hitherto been the case. The issues are complex but the authors' treatment is not. Each book is built around the 'Business in Context' model and each displays a number of common features that mark out the series. Firstly we aim to present our ideas in a way that students will find easy to understand and we relate those ideas wherever possible to real business situations. Secondly we hope to stimulate further study both by referencing our material and pointing students towards further reading at the end of each chapter. Thirdly we use the notion of 'Key Concepts' to highlight the most significant aspects of the subject presented in each chapter. Fourthly we use Case Studies to illustrate our material and stimulate further discussion. Fifthly we present at the end of each chapter a series of questions, exercises and discussion topics. To sum up, we feel it most important that each book will stimulate thought and further study and assist the student in developing powers of analysis, a critical awareness and ultimately a point of view about business issues.

We have already indicated that the series has been devised with the undergraduate business studies student uppermost in our minds. We also maintain that these books are of value wherever there is a need to understand business issues and may therefore be used across a range of different courses covering BTEC Higher and some professional and Masters degree courses in business and management studies.

David Needle and Professor Eugene McKenna
March 1989

Acknowledgements

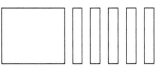

We would like to thank Angela, Rosemary and Paul for their support over the past year. Without this, the book could not have been written. In addition, we would like to acknowledge the roles of K. Williams and Professor L.J. Williams, of Aberystwyth University, in developing some of the ideas in this text.

Preface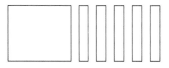

Students and managers of business enterprise who have encountered traditional economics courses often find it difficult to relate and apply what they have learnt to the realities of modern business. This is not surprising, since the traditional approach to economics (sometimes called neo-classical) makes a number of simplifying assumptions which limit its usefulness as a tool for business calculation and strategy. In this book we develop an alternative approach, in which relevant and available information and knowledge are applied to real problems associated with the allocation of resources and management of these resources.

The neo-classical approach takes as its basic framework the phenomenon of market exchange, under conditions of perfect knowledge and information. It focusses attention on market prices as instruments which determine the resources needed to satisfy demand at a given price. Within this framework, it is assumed that:

☐ market forces bring about an equilibrium where prices equate quantity demanded with quantity supplied; and
☐ firms respond immediately to changes in equilibrium price by continually re-allocating, in an optimal sense, the resources at their command, in the single-minded pursuit of maximum profitability.

The comments of Fritz Machlup, a leading neo-classical economist, reveal the abstract nature of the approach. The model of the firm, he wrote in 1967,

> is not . . . designed to serve to explain and predict the behaviour of real firms: instead, it is designed to explain and predict changes in observed prices . . . as effects of particular changes in conditions . . . In this causal connection the firm is only a theoretical link, a mental construct helping to explain how one gets from the cause to the effect.

While market exchange is an important feature of modern industrial life it is not the only one. Modern large firms dominate output and employment in the UK economy. These organizations are bureaucratic, and resources are allocated within them not by market exchange but by administrative procedure. For example, where a firm sub-contracts certain activities such as the supply of components to other firms, the price and product characteristics of these components will be the subject of negotiation, and are only indirectly influenced by market forces. Even final consumer demand is not straightforwardly determined by price alone, but by other so-called non-price factors such as quality, delivery, reliability and after-sales service etc.

The neo-classical framework for understanding firms' economic behaviour could be useful where we could also invoke, in practice, the very strict assumptions governing the model of perfect competition. However where production is dominated by large firms, and products are differentiated across and within market segments, neo-classical theory is less than illuminating. To understand how enterprise resources are allocated in a way which leads to some form of market advantage we need to ask a number of simple questions, to which the answers are often complex.

☐ How are resources allocated within firms?
☐ To what extent does the allocation of resources effectively meet the requirements of the market and meet with the firms' initial objectives?
☐ How are relationships between the firm and its suppliers and distributors structured?
☐ Why do some firms succeed and others fail, and what lessons can be drawn from this process of comparison?

In this text we will refer to the traditional neo-classical approach, identifying its uses and its limitations as an explanatory tool for business and resource management, although market exchange will not be our central focus. We shall, in contrast, be much more concerned about the calculations that business enterprises make with regard to market opportunities/threats, productive organization of labour and capital, and the financial outcome of the relation that exists between the market and productive performance of the organization. Our approach is an economic one, in that it does focus on how resources are allocated and managed both on a day-to-day and strategic basis. However, maximum efficiency in the management of resources is perhaps an impossible dream. In fact such an outcome could only be achieved under conditions of perfect knowledge, to which any approximation would require the application of massive resources dedicated both to gathering information and organizing the enterprise.

Our work in this text is an attempt to explore the nature of problems faced by the firm across the productive, market and financial boundaries of business organization. The operational and strategic relations we are considering cannot be represented in a unitary or stable way, because they are subject to constant change and controversy. The fact that we have suggested a model of business strategy does not mean that relations between different objectives will remain fixed over the planning time horizon. New objectives will need to be formed as and when new external or internal business conditions arise. Enterprise calculations must be set in a dynamic framework when the relations between different forms of enterprise calculation are rarely supportive and often contradictory.

We have been guided in our approach by the general model of the Business in Context series, of which this book is but one. However, we have adapted this to our own specific needs within the text. Our focus is on the nature and conditions under which enterprise, operational and strategic decisions are made. We consider the forms of calculation made by firms under three headings – the productive, market and financial. We are, however, not just concerned with these enterprise calculations in isolation, but with how they interact to produce either harmonious or contradictory relations. As a result the enterprise needs to pay attention to the changing nature and structure of the market, assessing how best to use available or potential labour and capital resources to meet market requirements, and considering the financial resource implications and possible financial outcomes of the firm's decisions.

In the first four chapters of this text we take a look at the economic calculations made within functional boundaries of the firm – marketing, production, personnel and finance. However, in each chapter we also illustrate, with the use of relevant case study material, how particular enterprise calculations can be privileged possibly at the expense of others. We use this material to encourage the student to consider positively the interrelationship between such things as for example, a decision to invest in new technology which requires either the retraining of labour so that it can be properly utilized, or its introduction in a balanced way into the production process so that it does not compromise the level of production and market share of the firm.

Finally we recognize that we cannot isolate the enterprise from an environmental context in which various institutional actors play a vital role in shaping and changing the environment for business. Even where the firm has successfully achieved a relation of balance between the productive, market and financial aspects of resource management, the firm's decisions will be affected by the constraints which are set by the banks, the stock exchange, the government etc. The conditioning role of these institutions in relation to enterprise performance is explored in the latter chapters of this text.

We have included at the end of each chapter a number of exercises. Some of these exercises take the form of data collection and analysis. This is to encourage you to develop those particular skills, and to find out for yourselves how the competitive environment of business is changing. We also make more frequent reference to recent research than is usual in introductory textbooks. This is not to convey a spurious academic 'respectability' for our approach, but to encourage you to check out the sources for yourselves, and to arrive at your own judgements.

Firms in the UK have not been doing particularly well in recent years, and they face the prospect of an increasingly competitive environment in the 1990s. We hope that students will be able to use this text and its case study material to obtain a positive insight into the problems of managing resources around the objective of securing competitive advantage in a changing environment.

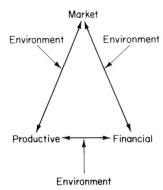

The decision-making context of the firm.

Bibliography

Machlup, F. (1967) Theories of the firm: marginalist, behavioural, managerial. *American Economic Review*, March.

Business organization and the market place 1

Introduction

One of the basic tenets of marketing specialists is that firms need to develop a 'marketing mix' for their products which is both internally consistent and appropriate to environmental conditions. In this chapter, we explore some economic aspects of that mix, and particularly the relationship between price, product, and promotion within different organizational and environmental contexts.

We start the chapter with the traditional, neo-classical, theory of the firm, which focusses on price as the most significant variable affecting the behaviour of consumers and suppliers. We argue that such an approach has limited applicability in the modern industrial world, because it is based on unrealistic assumptions about the organizational and environmental contexts of modern business, and because it fails to focus attention on the precise structures of demand which firms face in the real world. The chapter goes on to examine the marketing implications of changes in the organization of firms and industries and in the level and composition of demand, and to stress the economic importance for firms of continually adapting their marketing strategies to the changing market situations within which they operate.

Consumer demand

The neo-classical analysis of demand for a product divides the influences on quantity demanded (sales) into two categories.

☐ The product's own price.
☐ The conditions of demand (a catch-all concept which includes all the influences on demand other than the product's own price – e.g. income, taste, advertising, the prices of substitute or complementary products).

If the conditions of demand remain constant, there will usually be an inverse relationship between a product's own price and sales. This reflects its price elasticity of demand (Key Concept 1.1). One of the main uses of the elasticity concept is to estimate the effect of price changes on revenues. If demand is elastic (i.e. the price elasticity of demand is greater than 1), a rise in price will lead to a fall in total revenue, while a fall in price will lead to a rise in total revenue. If demand is inelastic (i.e. the price elasticity of

KEY CONCEPT 1.1

ELASTICITY

The term elasticity is used in economics to describe the relationship between a proportionate change in one variable and a proportionate change in a related variable.

The term price elasticity of demand describes the sensitivity of quantity demanded to changes in the product's own price, according to the formula

$$\frac{\text{percentage change in quantity demanded}}{\text{percentage change in price}}$$

Thus, if a 10% drop in price leads to a 20% increase in quantity demanded, assuming the conditions of demand remain constant, then the price elasticity of demand is two. (Strictly, it is minus two, but it has become conventional for economists to ignore the negative sign of price elasticity.)

Other elasticity concepts that are often referred to include the following.

1. Income elasticity of demand, with the formula

$$\frac{\text{percentage change in quantity demanded}}{\text{percentage change in income}}$$

2. Elasticity of supply, with the formula

$$\frac{\text{percentage change in quantity supplied}}{\text{percentage change in price}}$$

3. Cross elasticity of demand (between two different products) with the formula

$$\frac{\text{percentage change in quantity demanded of one product}}{\text{percentage change in price of another product.}}$$

demand is less than 1), the opposite will be the case. Only if the price elasticity of demand is exactly equal to 1 will a price change have no effect on total revenue.

Much empirical work has been done in quantifying the price elasticities of demand of different products, particularly in the agricultural sector. In measuring demand relationships it is important to separate out the influence of a change in price from a change in the conditions of demand, or from a change in supply. This involves the use of sophisticated statistical techniques, and is much easier to do with homogeneous products like potatoes than with differentiated products like cars, where it is hard to separate out the effects of price changes from those of product changes. In particular, we have in mind all the non-price characteristics of a product (design, quality, reliability, etc.) which affect the purchaser's decision to consume a particular product. These factors have made it difficult for firms to use traditional concepts of demand elasticity as a guide for price and output decisions.

The model of consumer behaviour on which neo-classical demand theory is based implies that consumers are perfectly informed about the price and quality characteristics of the products on offer, and are constantly altering their expenditure patterns in response to price changes, so as to maximize their total 'utility' (satisfaction). This model is unrealistic, as the range of products on offer in modern markets is immense, and no consumer has the knowledge or inclination to acquire the information which would be needed to make choices in this way. In addition, the model is misleading, as it encourages firms to focus on price as the most important variable influencing demand, instead of factors such as quality, design, reliability, delivery, and after-sales service, which, as we have said, may be more significant in practice.

More sophisticated economic analysis of consumer demand, based on the work of the behavioural economist Peter Earl (1983, 1986), suggests that the choices made by consumers take a different form from that suggested by neo-classical theory. In particular:

- [ ] Consumers have priority rankings of wants, some of which need to be satisfied before others can be explored. It follows that the main determinant of long-term changes in the structure of demand is not the pattern of relative prices, but the level of incomes.
- [ ] As their incomes rise, consumers are able to purchase new types of products, of which they have no personal experience. To make their choice more manageable, they will typically set a target price range, and confine their exploration to alternatives within that range.
- [ ] Within their chosen budget ranges, consumers will judge product alternatives across a range of characteristics. In purchasing an automatic washing machine, for example, a consumer might set a target price range of under £400, and want a fast spin speed, an economy programme facility, good reliability and after-sales service, and delivery within two weeks. If, say, there were three machines which shared these characteristics then the final choice might be made on the basis of what the machine looked like, or price.
- [ ] When making the transition from one stage of their life cycle to another, or one income bracket to another, consumers often have to make choices for which they have no direct personal experience, yet which they want to be appropriate to their new lifestyle. Here choices will often be guided more by the choices of others than anything else, and products will be chosen to complement each other.

The marketing implications of Earl's approach are clear. Firms would be better advised to research consumer perceptions than to attempt detailed estimation of price/quantity relationships. In particular, they need to discover consumers' target price ranges, and their preferred product characteristics, developing products and promotion strategies in line with their findings. Price-cutting may be useful in re-defining products to appeal to groups who would otherwise have rejected them as too expensive, but in most instances it would be better to price products near the top of the relevant price range, and build in extra features as standard to boost the potential number of consumers they appeal to. Good all-round performance will usually produce more sales than excellent performance in one attribute

CASE STUDY 1.1

SINCLAIR COMPUTERS

The Sinclair ZX 80 was the product which in 1980 launched the UK home computer market. By using only the cheapest components, and providing only limited memory, Sinclair was able to sell the ZX 80 by mail order for less than £100, drastically undercutting the existing competition. Over the next three years Sinclair introduced two new models (the ZX 81 and the Spectrum), set up retail sales through High Street outlets like W.H. Smith, and cut prices still further (in 1983, the ZX 81 was selling for less than £40). The Spectrum's colour graphics spawned a range of software based on simulations of arcade games, ensuring a buoyant market among male teenagers (and their parents, convinced that acquisition of a home computer would help their child's education). By 1983, Sinclair were selling 500 000 home computers per year in the UK, a market share of over 50%. Design limitations and poor reliability made the ZX range and the Spectrum unsuitable for serious computer applications, however, and in 1984 Sinclair introduced a new product, the QL, which they hoped would move them up market into the field of business applications.

The QL, like earlier Sinclair computers, was designed to a price target, and it sold for less than £400 (including business software). It incorporated a number of design innovations, including a Microdrive system which attempted to combine the rapid data storage and retrieval of a disc drive with the low cost of cassette storage. The new Microdrives created as many problems as they solved, however, and Sinclair's decision to stick with a keyboard design based on a touch-sensitive membrane made it totally unsuitable for sustained use as a word processor.

If the design of the QL was a disappointment, its marketing was a disaster. The QL was 'launched' before there was even a working prototype, and mail order adverts got customers to part with their money months before supplies were forthcoming. Whether the premature launch was an attempt to upstage the arrival of the Apple Macintosh, or to boost cash-flow in advance of a possible share flotation, is a matter of speculation. What is certain is that customer confidence in Sinclair products evaporated, and the QL flopped. Within 18 months of the launch, Sinclair had to halve the price of the QL, while Amstrad successfully opened up the bottom end of the business/professional market with the PCW8256, a reliable product based on tried-and-tested technology which included a monitor and printer in its low price of £399 plus VAT.

In 1985 and 1986, Sinclair's financial position was precarious. Its misguided attempt to break into the business computer market, and the competitive threat from Amstrad, coincided with its founder's failure to interest the public in purchasing electric tricycles (the C5). Salvation eventually came in the form of a deal with arch rivals Amstrad, who agreed to purchase all rights to Sinclair computer products, leaving Sir Clive Sinclair himself free to pursue new developments without the stigma of liquidation.

Further reading
Adamson and Kennedy (1986).

with poor performance in others, as Sinclair discovered to its cost in the low cost business computer market (Case Study 1.1).

Firms can influence consumer perceptions of their products, and thus demand, through their advertising, though this will be less relevant for firms whose products are already highly valued (Marks and Spencer, or the Body Shop, for example), or for firms whose customers are highly knowledgeable (capital equipment producers, for example), than for other firms. For adverts to be effective, however, they must be designed with a clear understanding of what existing perceptions are. It is no use, for example, emphasizing the maximum speed of a family car if its potential consumers are more interested in fuel economy and reliability. Where consumers feel anxious that an inappropriate purchase may undermine their self image, adverts can be designed to allay that anxiety. Amstrad, for example, has successfully stressed the advantages of its hi-fi, home computer, and TV/video systems for consumers who do not know how to make up their own systems from separate components. As Earl concludes (1983), 'If firms cannot succeed in moulding consumer thoughts to favour their products, they must discover the structures of the moulds that they should make their products fit.'

Pricing for profit maximization

In the traditional, neo-classical theory of the firm, all firms, irrespective of the different ways they are organized and the different environments in which they operate, are assumed to have a single aim – to maximize their profits in the short run. They do this in two ways.

☐ Expanding their output up to the point where marginal cost is equal to marginal revenue (see Key Concepts 1.2 and 1.3)
☐ Setting as high a price as the market will bear.

In the long run, as demand and cost conditions change, firms will move out of markets in which they can no longer operate profitably, and into those markets where the prospects of profits seem greatest. In markets where large numbers of firms compete with each other, the long-run tendency is for prices to equal average costs (including within those costs 'normal profit', that element of accounting profit which is necessary for the firm to remain in business). In markets where competition is less intense, long-run prices will be higher than average costs, and firms will be able to make 'monopoly profits'.

The formal neo-classical analysis of profit maximization is complex, and is elaborated in the Appendix to this chapter. Comparing it with the model around which this series is based, you will notice that it abstracts from all differences in the organizational context of business, and focusses exclusively on a single aspect of the environmental context, the extent of competition. As a result, its predictions are at a high level of generality, and theoretical elegance is achieved at the expense of a low level of realism. Three of its assumptions are particularly questionable.

☐ Objectives. The suggestion that all private sector firms aim to maximize

KEY CONCEPT 1.2

AVERAGE AND MARGINAL REVENUE

The total revenue received for a product in a given time period is its price, or average revenue, multiplied by the number of units sold, while marginal revenue is the contribution to total revenue which is made by the last unit sold. If a firm can increase sales of a product without changing its price, then average revenue and marginal revenue will be the same. If it can only increase its sales by dropping its price, however, then marginal revenue will be below average revenue, as the additional revenue earned from the last unit has to be weighed against the revenue which is lost by having to sell the existing output at a lower price. This is illustrated in the hypothetical example below.

Annual sales	Average revenue (price per unit, £)	Total revenue (per year, £)	Marginal revenue* (£)
			52
2000	52	104 000	
			44
4000	48	192 000	
			36
6000	44	264 000	
			28
8000	40	320 000	
			20
10 000	36	360 000	
			12
12 000	32	384 000	

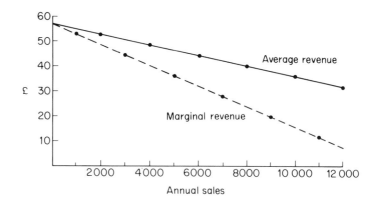

* Where demand estimates are available for only a limited number of possible prices, as in the above example, marginal revenue is calculated by dividing the increase in total revenue by the increase in sales, and plotting the result midway along the output range, as in the diagram below.

short-run profits is an oversimplification. Short-run profit is certainly an important objective, but it is not the only one. Business firms, like any organizations, are complex, and different groups within them have different interests. Key decisions in large corporations, for example, are taken by professional managers. These are not traditional entrepreneurs, but salaried employees who may be more interested in the growth of

In the short run, some costs are fixed, and some are variable (we leave discussion of the long run, when all costs are variable, to Chapter 2). Average fixed costs (AFC) fall as output is increased. Average variable costs (AVC) often remain constant over a substantial range of output. They may, however, rise when output falls below a critical level, if, for example, labour can no longer be organized as effectively. Average variable costs will certainly rise as output reaches the limits determined by the full capacity of the fixed factors. Average total costs (ATC, equal to AFC plus AVC) therefore fall, and then rise as output is increased.

Marginal cost (MC) is the increase in total cost (TC) when output is increased by one unit. Marginal cost will be equal to average variable cost where this is constant. Where average variable cost is falling, however, marginal cost will be below it, while where average variable cost is rising, marginal cost will be above it. Marginal cost is equal to average total cost where average total cost is at a minimum.

This is illustrated in a hypothetical example below, where a plant has a design capacity of 10 000 units per year, where fixed costs are £100 000 per year, and where normal variable costs are £20 per unit.

Annual output	AFC(£)	AVC(£)	ATC(£)	TC(£)	MC(£)
					75
2000	50	25	75	150 000	
					19
4000	25	22	47	188 000	
					16
6000	16.67	20	36.67	220 000	
					20
8000	12.50	20	32.50	260 000	
					20
10 000	10	20	30	300 000	
					50
12 000	8.33	25	33.33	400 000	

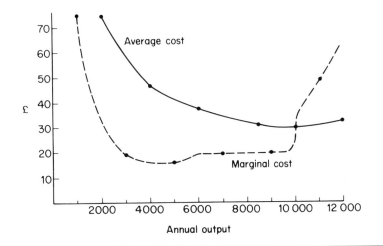

their firms (and their prestige) than in short-run profits. Even in small firms, objectives such as providing jobs for family members may be more important than making the maximum possible profit. In addition, most firms, whatever their size, give priority to their long-term survival. This may encourage the firm to initiate investments which have a depressing effect on short-run profits, or to remain in business despite current losses. Certainly, firms are more involved in processes of change over time than neo-classical theory, with its emphasis on static equilibrium, would allow. This is an important issue which we explore further in Chapter 4.

☐ Information. Few firms have the information which they would need to calculate their marginal costs and revenues, or even to estimate the price elasticities of demand for their products. It can, of course, be argued that neo-classical theory aims to predict how firms will adjust to changes in costs or demand, not to understand how they reach their decisions. As we shall see, however, lack of appropriate information makes a determinate profit-maximizing solution impossible in oligopolistic markets (markets dominated by a few firms). It also makes it difficult for any firms in competition with each other to make 'sensible' investment decisions, as they each have to make independent decisions about future capacity in response to current price signals. Where investment decisions are taken simultaneously, and there is a significant time-lag before they bring about changes in output, capacity may be expanded too much in response to an increase in demand, and contracted too much in response to a decrease in demand. It is not surprising, therefore, that unregulated 'perfect' markets, like many world commodity markets, are often characterized by wild swings in prices, rather than the smooth adjustment to equilibrium depicted in traditional textbooks.

☐ Uncertainty. The neo-classical world is a certain one, in which events never take firms by surprise. Managers have little to do except read correctly the price signals which their markets give them, and time is suspended while they respond to these signals and adjust to a new equilibrium position. In the real world, however, future demand and costs are surrounded with uncertainty and surprise, making optimum achievement of objectives impossible. Firms typically respond to this situation by making do with satisfactory rather than maximum achievement of objectives, or by suppressing competition to reduce the uncertainty (merging with a rival, for example). In addition, they may seek to incorporate flexibility into their planning. Flexibility costs money, and thus depresses short-run profits, but this may be a price worth paying if it enables a firm to respond quicker than its rivals to an unexpected change in market conditions.

Oligopoly

Profit maximization is particularly problematic in the context of oligopolistic market conditions. Under conditions of oligopoly, a few large firms dominate a market, and are able to make monopoly profits as they are protected by barriers to the entry of new firms. Oligopoly is the most common market structure in manufacturing, and is becoming increasingly prevalent in the service sector as well. Problems of information and uncertainty abound in this market structure, and it is extremely difficult for a firm to assess the effect on revenue of changing its price, as this depends on how its rivals will react. Because of this, it is impossible for an oligopolist to predict what its profit-maximizing price will be.

If, for example, a firm considers raising its prices, it does not know whether its rivals will keep their prices at the old level or raise theirs as well. If its rivals all raise their prices, each firm is likely to suffer only a small reduction in sales, and to raise its revenues (assuming the price elasticity of demand for the product is low). If only one firm raises its prices, however, it is likely to suffer a big drop in sales, and a fall in its revenue, as consumers switch to the close substitutes provided by its rivals.

When, on the other hand, a firm is considering cutting its prices, it does not know whether its rivals will drop their prices as well, or keep them at the old price. If its rivals remain at the old price, then the firm is likely to gain in sales, at its rivals' expense, and increase its revenues. Yet if all the firms drop their prices, their gain in sales is likely to be small, and revenues may fall. Even more seriously, the drop in prices may initiate a price cutting war, with potentially disastrous consequences for all firms in the industry.

The oligopolist's dilemma is illustrated in Figure 1.1. dEd′ represents the imagined demand curve for a firm's products if all its rivals match any price changes it makes (the shape of this demand curve is the same as that of the industry demand curve), and DED′ represents the demand curve for its products assuming its rivals' prices remain unchanged. E represents the existing price and output position of the firm, while the shaded area represents all the possible consequences for sales of a change in this price. As you can see, if a firm is uncertain about how its rivals are going to react to a change in price, it cannot predict the likely effect on sales, and therefore on revenue.

There are three broad possibilities for the price behaviour of an oligopolist within a neo-classical framework – collusion, price wars, or non-price competition.

☐ Collusion. It is possible for firms to agree to fix their prices and market shares. This has the effect of moving firms up the demand curve dEd′, and enabling them to boost their profits by charging higher prices. Such price fixing agreements were common in British manufacturing industry before 1956, but since the Restrictive Practices Court was established in that year, only a few such agreements have been allowed. (This aspect of competition policy is discussed further in Chapter 9.) It is possible for similar results to occur if one or two firms in an oligopolistic market are accepted as price leaders, with other firms following their price changes. The suggestion in neo-classical theory is that price leaders will set prices so as to maximize the joint profits of the industry, as if it were a monopoly, but the danger here is that prices would be set too high, attracting new entrants. This appears to have occurred in the UK petrol industry in the 1950s (Case Study 1.2).

☐ Price Wars. An oligopolistic firm will usually avoid straightforward

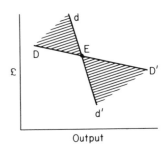

Figure 1.1 Equilibrium of an oligopolist.

CASE STUDY 1.2

**THE UK
PETROL MARKET**

In the 1950s, petrol supply in the UK was dominated by two firms – Shell/BP (then an integrated marketing organization), and Esso. These firms, who between them supplied about 80% of the UK market, were vertically integrated, with refining capacity, access to crude oil, and some retail outlets. Most independent retailers were tied to the big firms by agreements to take their petrol from a single supplier in return for a price discount. There was little price competition, and price rises took place more or less simultaneously, led by either Shell/BP or Esso.

In the 1960s, new oil reserves were developed in Africa and the Middle East, many of them by major international firms without retail outlets in the UK. Some of these firms were encouraged to enter the UK market for the first time (e.g. Gulf). Others sold surplus crude to new independent UK wholesalers (e.g. Jet), who boosted sales by undercutting the established firms. Initially, the price leaders tried to slow down new entry with price reductions, but they relied on customer brand loyalty to charge a premium over the new entrants. By the end of the decade, however, price differentials had narrowed. This reflected two factors.

1. Greater consumer awareness of the absence of quality differences between established brands and new entrants, following a 1964 report in the consumer magazine *Which?*, and the introduction of a star grading system for petrol in 1967, which made it difficult for established firms to continue to justify higher prices.
2. Supply shortages following the Six Day war in 1967, which pushed up the prices of new entrants in particular.

Leading firms started offering trading stamps and advertising their brands more intensively, in an attempt to maintain their market shares.

In the early 1970s oil prices rocketed, following the controls over supply instituted by the Organisation of Pertroleum Exporting Countries (OPEC). This made life difficult for the independent wholesalers, many of whom were taken over by the 'new majors', whose market share continued to rise. The retail structure of the industry also changed, with the emergence of a number of independent retailing 'chains' (e.g. Heron and Asda), whose superior efficiency and greater bargaining power enabled them to win substantial price discounts. By the late 1970s, the UK market was still dominated by Shell and BP (now separate) and Esso, but their combined market share had fallen to below 60%, and the price leadership system had broken down. Price variations were significant, with price reductions almost as frequent as rises. To some extent the price changes reflected changes in crude oil costs, but to some extent they were an expression of competition in the discounts offered to retailers.

Further reading
Penrose (1968); Shaw (1974); Lowe
(1976); Grant (1982).

price-cutting as a strategy to improve revenues, as it knows its rivals will respond by cutting their prices as well, hitting everyone's profits. It may, however, consider aggressive price cuts if it wants to expand its market share and it considers that a price war will drive one or more rivals out of business, or if it is suffering from cash-flow problems and needs a short-term injection of funds to survive.

☐ Price rigidity. Ironically, one of the bravest attempts to resolve the oligopolist's dilemma from within a basically neo-classical framework came from a Marxist economist, Paul Sweezy (1939). Sweezy argued that an oligopolistic firm will normally have pessimistic assessments of how its rivals will react to a price change. In other words, it will predict that if it raises its prices, its rivals will maintain theirs, but that if it drops its prices, its rivals will also drop theirs. In Figure 1.1, DEd' would be the firm's imagined average revenue curve, with a pronounced kink at the existing price, which is indeterminate. If DE is price elastic, while Ed' is price inelastic, then the firm will lose revenue both if it raises its prices or if it drops them. The result, Sweezy suggests, is price rigidity, based on an extreme unwillingness to risk possible negative consequences for revenue of any change in price. Competition between oligopolies then becomes non-price competition, focussing on product changes and expenditure on sales promotion.

Consumer sovereignty

Oligopolistic market conditions also pose problems for the neo-classical assumption that consumers in a market economy are sovereign. The notion of consumer sovereignty implies that the pursuit of profits by firms guarantees consumer satisfaction, and that what consumers want is the sole determinant of what firms produce. This can be understood most clearly in the context of the neo-classical analysis of the competitive behaviour of firms under conditions of perfect competition. Here, as you will see in the Appendix to this chapter, the assumptions of the model ensure that knowledgeable consumers choose between the identical products of large numbers of suppliers, while market forces drive firms who are not responsive to consumer wants out of business, and reward firms who satisfy those wants with survival.

Even in the idealized world of perfect competition, we cannot accept the idea that market forces guarantee the sovereignty of consumers without considerable qualification. In the first place, perfectly competitive firms must make investment decisions in isolation from each other. This means that adjustment to long-run equilibrium may be far from smooth, and that firms may often oscillate between oversupplying and undersupplying the market. Secondly, the market will supply only those wants which are backed by a willingness and ability to pay, giving the wants of the rich priority over those of the poor. This can sometimes produce grotesque results, as in famines, where people may starve because of a decline in their ability to purchase food even when there is plenty of food available (Sen, 1981).

The difficulties multiply if we attempt to extend the notion of consumer sovereignty to the real world situation of the UK economy in the late twentieth century. Here, most goods (and many services) are supplied in oligopolistic markets, and large firms spend considerable amounts of money promoting the sale of differentiated products in their struggle to enhance or maintain market share against their rivals. Consumers, meanwhile, have to make choices on the basis of incomplete information, much of it supplied by the producers themselves. In this situation, the neo-classical insistence that consumer wants are formed totally independently of any external influence is extremely misleading, and prevents us from even addressing important issues such as the role of corporate marketing policies.

The most prominent critic of the marketing policies of large corporations is J.K. Galbraith, in his books *The Affluent Society* (1958), *The New Industrial State* (1967), and *Economics and the Public Purpose* (1973). Galbraith suggests that the corporate economy is a planned economy, able to justify huge expenditures on modern capital-intensive technology only through doing everything in its power to suppress the uncertainty of market competition, including creating and managing demand for its products. In his view, the 'accepted sequence', where consumers determine what is produced, has been replaced by a 'revised sequence', where producers determine what is consumed.

Needless to say, marketing practitioners see things differently. T. Levitt, in his classic article *Marketing Myopia* (1960), accuses Galbraith of confusing marketing with selling. Selling, suggests Levitt, focusses on the seller's need to turn products into cash, while marketing concentrates on ensuring that products satisfy the needs of the customer. Indeed, many marketing practitioners see their activities as extending consumer sover-eignty, through researching what customers want, ensuring that product design incorporates the research findings, and providing consumers with information about the product.

Is Galbraith right in suggesting that the marketing departments of large firms manipulate consumer demand, or is the marketing profession correct in protesting that all it is doing is providing more effective methods for firms to seek out and meet consumer wants?

It is difficult to go all the way with Galbraith in asserting the power of producers to determine consumer demand for their products. In certain industries it may be the retailer who calls the shots – Marks and Spencer in the UK clothing industry is a classic example. (Interestingly, Galbraith himself analyses the 'countervailing power' of retailers in the Affluent Society, though this emphasis disappears in his later works.) More significantly, Galbraith's analysis gives insufficient weight to the combined impact of recession and intensified international competition, in weakening the power of individual corporations to dominate their environment. As many large firms in the US and the UK have discovered to their cost, expertise in promotion and packaging may have little effect in maintaining sales against the negative impact of mass unemployment on consumer expenditure, or against the tendency for consumers to prefer the more innovative products of Japanese firms.

If we recognize limits to the power of individual large firms to mainpulate consumers, we cannot accept the claims of some marketing practitioners that this power does not exist. Marketing has a dual function – to ensure that the firm makes products which conform more closely to what consumers are prepared to buy, and to make consumers more favourably inclined to the firm's products. In each case, its main aim is to

Infant formula is specially formulated milk powder. Made up with clean water, it resembles human milk, and can be fed to infants through a sterilized bottle. For mothers who don't want, or are unable, to breastfeed, bottle feeding with infant formula can be a satisfactory alternative.

For poor people in the less developed countries of the Third World, however, infant formula is often inappropriate. It is costly, so there is a temptation to over-dilute it, resulting in malnutrition for the infant. It also requires clean water, facilities for boiling water, and high standards of hygiene. These are rarely available, but without them there are considerable risks of infection. In an inappropriate environment, infant formula can kill.

Despite these dangers, infant formula is sold throughout the world. It has been marketed particularly aggressively in Third World countries, where multinational and local manufacturers alike saw a potential for enormous sales. Here, advertisements stressed the convenience and nutritional qualities of bottle feeding, but made no mention of the need for accurate measuring and scrupulous hygiene. In many countries, manufacturers ran extensive promotion campaigns, giving hospitals and doctors free samples in return for their recommending the companies' products. In Malaysia, company nurses, dressed in the same uniforms as hospital nurses, had unrestricted access to maternity ward patients. They discouraged breastfeeding, and recommended infant formula as the best way of ensuring the babies' health.

International campaigns against the abuses of infant formula promotion in the Third World resulted in the adoption of an International Code of Marketing of Breast Milk Substitutes by the World Health Organization in 1981. Under this Code, manufacturers are recommended to tone down their promotion of infant formula. The code is not mandatory, and violations continue to occur. A number of manufacturers do now adhere to it, however, thanks largely to the effects of consumer boycotts and adverse publicity by health campaigners.

CASE STUDY 1.3

THE MARKETING OF INFANT FORMULA IN THE THIRD WORLD

Further reading
Chetley (1979); Medawar (1979); Melrose (1981).

reduce the level of uncertainty surrounding the firm's revenue function. A marketing orientation may encourage firms to make products which are more in tune with what consumers are prepared to buy (though, as Levitt pointed out in 1975, obsessive segmentation of markets may price products beyond customers' ability to pay). Assessing consumers' willingness to buy is not the same as responding to their demands, however, particularly where they are not in a position to make informed choices.

The promotional aspect of marketing is the hardest to square with consumer sovereignty. It may be possible to argue, as Littlechild has done (1986), that advertising and other promotional activities can perform a positive function for consumers by attracting their attention to products of which they would not otherwise be aware. Yet it is difficult to deny the fact that much advertising works by taking advantage of consumers' lack of information – exaggerating the advantages of products (and neglecting to mention the disadvantages), and emphasizing (in some cases creating) anxieties which, it is suggested, consuming the advertised product will remove. On occasion, advertising promotes products which actually harm the consumer. As Case Study 1.3 shows, in such situations combined action by political authorities and consumer pressure groups may be needed before firms modify their policies.

Markup pricing

Most empirical studies of the pricing behaviour of oligopolistic firms conclude that selling prices do not vary significantly with demand, but that they do respond to changes in unit costs (for a comprehensive UK study, see Coutts *et al.*, 1978). While the first finding is compatible with Sweezy's theory of the kinked demand curve, the second is not, and for theoretical explanations which provide a realistic guide to business behaviour we have to move away from the marginalist framework of neo-classical theory. Two sets of contributions which are particularly relevant here are those of P.W.S. Andrews and Elizabeth Brunner (1949, 1964, 1975) and Alfred Eichner (1976, 1985).

Andrews and Brunner's work was based on extensive case studies of UK firms. These studies suggested that firms' pricing and output decisions were based on very different considerations from those assumed by neo-classical theory. Andrews and Brunner found that firms preferred not to charge the maximum price the market could bear, because this would encourage other firms with a similar technological base to enter the industry. Instead, they preferred to fix their prices just below the level they judged would attract new firms into the industry, and to change their prices only when costs changed. In the absence of price competition, regular customers tended to stick with the same supplier, unless they became dissatisfied with its reliability (over deliveries, for example). As a result, firms planned to run their plants at less than full capacity. This enabled them to take on new customers if demand conditions changed, without jeopardizing the goodwill of their existing customers.

Andrews and Brunner's theory is illustrated in Figure 1.2. Average Direct Costs (the costs per unit of output which are directly attributable to the product in question), are assumed to be constant over the relevant range of output, in line with the empirical evidence. Firms add a markup to these costs to cover average fixed costs, and earn positive net profits (limited by the need to avoid attracting new entry) at normal output levels. While the firm aims to maintain sales at or above target levels, it tends to maintain its prices even if sales fall below these levels, so net profits vary with the state of demand.

Eichner's analysis of the price and output decisions of large firms operating in oligopolistic markets shares many features with Andrews and Brunner's theory. What is distinctive in Eichner's work is his emphasis on the importance of growth as a prime objective of large firms, and on the signficance of retained profits in financing the investment needed to achieve this growth. Eichner suggests that the indeterminacy inherent in an

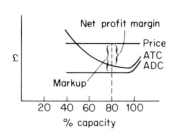

Figure 1.2 Price determination in relation to normal costs.

oligopolistic market is removed by firms in that market accepting one of their number as a price leader. In each industry, firms will apply a customary markup to average variable costs at normal levels of output (allowing a margin of spare capacity to meet fluctuations in demand). In such a situation, pricing is determined by accounting considerations rather than neo-classical economic concepts or marginal cost and marginal revenue. When the market leader judges that an increase in investment funds is needed to improve its long-run market position, it may decide to alter its markup, depending on its assessment of the risks of losing industry sales, attracting new entrants, or provoking state intervention. The change in markup initiated by the price leader, Eichner suggests, will be taken up by other firms in the industry.

In understanding the nature of business pricing and output decisions, the theories of Andrews and Brunner and Eichner represent a considerable advance on the neo-classical approach. In terms of the Business in Context model, they integrate into the determination of price environmental factors (the threat of entry by other firms if the price is too low, or of state intervention if the price is too high), organizational factors (the importance of growth objectives for large corporations), and strategic factors (the assessment by leading firms of the investment they need to enhance their market position). These newer approaches do, however, have important limitations, which stem from their assumption that firms correctly anticipate how much they should limit their markups to deter new entry, and that all firms are equally interested in pursuing, or able to pursue, long-term growth rather than short-term profits. These assumptions are behaviourally naive, and are becoming increasingly unrealistic in the face of intensified global rivalry between transnational firms and increased import penetration of national economies. In terms of the model, Andrews and Brunner and Eichner do not take sufficient account of the implications of increasing organization size for the *international* competitive environment, and the constraints this places on a firm's ability to set markups in relation to its own needs.

In deciding whether or not to enter a new market, a firm has to weigh the benefits of entry against its costs. These costs typically include higher unit production and distribution costs resulting from lack of experience or from the need to start operations at sub-optimal scale, and higher promotion costs resulting from a need to break down customer loyalties to existing brands. Yet what may be a significant entry barrier for a new firm, or for an existing firm of the same nationality based in a different industry, may be much less of a barrier for a transnational firm which is already established as a major supplier in its home economy. This was clearly a factor in the failure of the 'Big Three' to prevent new entry into the UK petrol market in the 1960s (Case Study 1.2). It has also been a significant factor in Japanese 'invasion' of European and North American markets for motorcycles, watches, cameras, consumer electronics, advanced machine tools etc.

A related issue is the conditioning effect of different national institutions on the time horizons of firms. As we shall see in Chapter 6, financial conditions (including the threat of takeover) encourage British firms to place greater emphasis in their investment and pricing calculations on short-term profitability than Eichner's theory would allow. Recent research by Doyle *et al.* (1986) suggests that this may be a significant factor in the failure of most British firms to respond effectively to the Japanese challenge. This study found that the marketing strategies of Japanese firms operating in UK markets tended to give priority to long-term market share over short-term profits. This enabled them to benefit from cost reductions and productivity improvements. Many British firms, in contrast, cut back on investment in an attempt to restore short-term profits. The result has often been a loss of market share, followed by a vicious circle of decline in which higher unit costs have led to reduced profit margins, and a consequent reduction in investment.

New product pricing

In the short run, the introduction of a new innovative product, for example the Sony Walkman personal stereo, may give the firm a window of opportunity in the market place. This may give the firm short-run temporary advantage even when competitors are free to operate in this product market in the longer term. In the short run, it may be possible for the business to price the product to do one of two things.

☐ Market skim. The firm can charge a high initial price to cream off the top end of the market, and then reduce its price when imitators start to appear. Market skimming maximizes returns at each stage of the product life cycle (see Key Concept 1.4), and is particularly appropriate for high quality products of firms who place a high value on short-run profitability.

☐ Penetrate the market. The firm can start with a deliberately low markup to encourage the rapid buildup of a mass market. This is particularly appropriate where significant reductions in production costs can be expected as sales build up, and where firms are prepared to forgo short-run profits in order to achieve long-run market dominance (Case Study 1.1).

Pricing strategies for new products need to be determined in relation to the competitive situation faced by the firm. In markets where international competition is speeding up the product development cycle, for example, the market skimming option would be a luxury few firms could afford.

Pricing in nationalized industries

Nationalized industries are state-owned corporations which produce marketed goods or services. Most of them are 'natural monopolies', where competition would be wasteful, but where the absence of market constraints might encourage exorbitantly high prices. In addition, it is often the case that nationalized industries involve significant externalities (Key Concept 8.1) with social costs and benefits diverging from private costs and benefits. It is not surprising, therefore, that successive governments have been particularly concerned with the pricing policies of nationalized industries.

The product life cycle is a concept, much referred to by marketing practitioners, which suggests that products, like people, have limited lives, and pass through distinct stages, as in the diagram below. At each stage, it is suggested, a different marketing policy will be appropriate.

1. Product development. When a new product is introduced, development costs are high, and sales uncertain. The main problem here is to tempt a minority of innovating consumers to try the product. Many new products fail – those that succeed go on to three further stages.
2. Growth. If a new product launch is successful, competitors enter the market with similar products, and the marketing emphasis shifts to improving the product and persuading consumers to choose one brand rather than another.
3. Maturity. When saturation of the product's potential market is achieved, the marketing emphasis shifts again to strengthening brand loyalty, and to persuading consumers to replace their existing products quicker.
4. Decline. Eventually, sales of a product fall off, and the firm must diversify into new products if it is to survive.

The main problem with the product life cycle concept is that not all products follow the same development path. Each product's life cycle can only be defined retrospectively, making it a poor guide to marketing strategy. In extreme cases, managers can be encouraged by the concept to misread a temporary slump in demand as evidence that decline has set in, spurring them to embark on costly new product development when simpler measures to extend the life of the existing product might have sufficed.

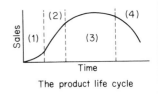

The product life cycle

In the 1950s, nationalized industries were instructed to charge uniform prices to consumers, and to break even. Cross subsidization was widespread, and in many cases low prices stimulated an increase in demand which could not be met by existing capacity. Because prices had been set without considering investment needs, there was insufficient internal finance to cover the new investment which was required, and the nationalized industries had to increase their borrowing.

Concern about the financial effects of nationalized industry pricing policies led to a series of government White Papers, in 1961, 1967, and 1978. In 1961 and 1978, the emphasis was on financial targets for each nationalized industry, usually expressed as a rate of return on assets. In 1967, however, the Government made detailed suggestions as to the pricing policies which should be adopted by the nationalized industries. Prices, it proposed, should both cover full accounting costs (including the service and replacement of capital) and reflect the marginal costs of each product provided. This, it was hoped, would improve resource allocation by providing a more realistic indication of investment needs. Some steps were made towards marginal cost pricing in the electricity industry, where there is now considerable variation in charges between different times of day, reflecting the higher marginal costs of meeting demand in peak hours. Progress elsewhere was slow, however, because of the practical difficulties in identifying marginal costs. Since 1978, detailed government guidance on pricing policy has given way to more generalized encouragement to relate price structures to cost structures, and to pay more attention to market circumstances.

One problem which nationalized industries periodically have to face is government interference in their pricing decisions, sometimes against the spirit of the government's own policy guidelines. In the early 1970s, for example, the Heath government prevented certain nationalized industries from raising their prices in line with costs, as part of its counter-inflation policy. The result, inevitably, was increased financial deficits and increased borrowing. In the early 1980s, however, the Thatcher government followed the opposite tack when it forced the electricity industry to raise prices above costs in support of its policy to reduce the Public Sector Borrowing Requirement. That government's emphasis on preparing nationalized industries for privatization, which we explore further in Chapter 9, has also encouraged them to accumulate financial surpluses.

Retail prices

With most producer goods and services, products are sold directly from producer to purchaser. With most consumer goods however, sales take place via a retailer (and in many cases a wholesaler as well). Prices to the consumer thus reflect not only production costs and the producer's markup, but distribution costs and the distributor's markup as well.

Before 1964, the retail prices of most consumer goods in the UK were determined by the manufacturer. Such resale price maintenance was outlawed in that year, except where it could be shown to be in the public interest. Resale price maintenance still exists, most notably with the supply of books, but in most cases the manufacturer now merely recommends a resale price, which the retailer is free to accept or reject.

The extent to which retailers undercut manufacturers' recommended prices varies with a number of environmental, organizational, and strategic factors.

- ☐ Environmental influences. Where a consumer chooses to shop depends on a number of factors, including his or her income, lifestyle, time available for shopping, and access to shops. There is considerable scope for variation here, and different market segments will have different shopping habits, and different price elasticities of demand.

  Take food shopping as an example. Some consumers will make weekly trips by car to a supermarket for their food shopping, and some will spend more time in a shopping centre visiting different shops and market stalls to compare products and prices, while others will make more frequent visits to a local shop. The pricing implications will be different in each case. A supermarket will, for example, aim to be price-competitive with other supermarkets for a basket of goods. It can afford, however, to charge a higher markup on certain items, while offering some others at a loss to tempt new customers into the store. A corner shop. on the other hand, can take advantage of the convenience it offers local shoppers (particularly those without a car) to charge higher prices across the board.

☐ Organizational influences. With the development of large shops like department stores and supermarkets, certain retailers can negotiate substantial discounts off manufacturers' list prices, while trimming their own margins through judicious selection of a range of quick-selling items to stock. Consumers (particularly those with cars) often benefit from the lower prices associated with large stores. But large general shops typically stock a much smaller range of products, within any category, than the specialist shops they divert trade from. If lower prices in the large stores drive specialist shops out of business, then consumers may have to pay in terms of a reduction in choice.

☐ Strategic influences. In the initial stages of the development of a new form of shopping, such as supermarkets or DIY superstores, pioneering firms may well adopt an aggressive price-cutting policy to boost their market share at the expense of their rivals. This is particularly the case where suitable sites (including a favourable attitude by the planning authority) are in short supply. As consumer tastes become more sophisticated, however, such firms may need to shift their emphasis away from cheapness towards improved product quality if they are to maintain their pre-eminence.

Product market structure and the composition of demand

So far in this chapter, we have considered those variables that determine the price and output decisions of firms and consumers' purchase behaviour in theory. We have argued that firms' pricing decisions are not based on the economic relation between marginal costs and marginal revenue, but that accounting rules form the basis for pricing of output. In addition to these accounting techniques price is also subject to strategic influence – that is price will also be determined by what the firm wishes to obtain by a 'price' at any moment in time. We have seen that price will be set differently depending on whether the firm is 'penetrating' the market or 'skimming' the market etc. Managerial skill at this level is choosing the price which best suits the firm's strategy for the 'market' at a particular time in the product's life cycle.

With regard to consumer choice we have also argued that this is not determined by price considerations alone. Although price is an important variable in the choice process, when considering a purchase its importance will also vary given the variety of circumstances that face a consumer. During this process of 'making a decision' the consumer will, of course, be affected in his or her choice by a multiplicity of what we summarize as non-price factors.

One thing is clear, within this complex set of continually shifting/ interacting relations the producer must actively seek to 'connect' the needs of the consumer with the output or product that is being sold. Here we also make the assumption that the objective of the firm is to stay in business although, as we shall see, this may not be the case where certain conditions operate to frustrate a firm's product investment strategy.

If the objective is to remain in a market place, the producer or enterprise needs to understand the nature of the market they are in. This market place will have both a structure and a composition which over time will be fluid rather than static in nature. An understanding of the dynamics of market structure and the composition of demand is crucial because it is this which sets the terms and conditions in which the firm's 'product market package' will be executed. In general terms a product market package will be designed to keep market share constant, increase market share or establish an orderly retreat from the market place for a particular product. This package must be determined by accurate assessments of the behaviour of the market in which the firm is operating.

Whatever else, a firm that is wishing to enter either an established market or a relatively new market for a particular product, needs to have a general appreciation of the market structure the firm is facing. It will be necessary for the firm to obtain volume trend sales for the particular product market it is facing, and the total value of that product market.

In addition it will be necessary for the firm to establish the share of the market (in volume and value terms) taken by imports, and the total number of competitors that are in the product market it is either *in* or wishing to *enter*. In this instance an assessment of the future or existing product market is made using simple or complex statistical tools for a general product or market trend analysis.

If the firm is already in a product market it will use the market statistics it has obtained to establish its position relative to competitors: in terms of market share (value and volume), rate of growth or deterioration in market share. Where the firm is wishing to enter a new or established market, the statistics will be used to judge the potential of the market in terms of sales revenue (and hence profit) against the resources that would have to be committed or invested to achieve market entry and the necessary market share. If the firm is already in the market for a particular product, the statistics will be used to assess the possibility of market expansion and/or contraction for the product being sold and the cost/revenue benefits of the decision made.

It is clear that the firm, whether a new entrant or an established firm, in the market place must have a clear understanding of the market it faces, or will face. As we shall see in Chapter 4, where a firm fails to get market estimates correct, or fails to execute its strategy to fill the expected market 'space', capital investment will not be recovered from sales revenue and the firm will suffer financial problems. Obviously the level of financial damage will be related to the level of resource commitment to the product strategy being undertaken, and its importance in the portfolio of investments being undertaken by the firm concerned. For example where the investment in new products requires 'strategic' changes to the business organization, market failure could well have a severe effect on the company's finances (Williams *et al.*, 1987).

Even so, whatever the level of resource commitment, it is necessary to have a good foundation on which to build and this will only be the case when the firm has made intelligent calculations concerning the nature of the overall product market position the firm is facing or would be expected to face. Although it is necessary to understand the general structure of a market place this in itself is not sufficient. It is also crucial that the firm understand and be aware of the *composition*, at a disaggregate level, of the market for a particular product or product range. In order to understand the composition of a market the firm will need to undertake a disaggregate market analysis. An enterprise can, as we have said, gather useful information from an aggregate product market analysis, but this may not and often does not represent what is happening in the specific product *segment* it is wishing to enter or develop in market share terms.

Market composition

In a simple immature product market we might well expect the composition of the market for a particular product to be relatively simple. That is, the product range would be relatively narrow, and the competition between producers relatively limited, in terms of numbers in a particular product market. However, as a product market develops over time the market a firm will have to face will become more complex in terms of its composition, for two reasons: firstly in terms of the model range of products or product variants (what we shall term product *segments*), and secondly in terms of increased competition within each product segment from an increased number of competitors both at home and from overseas in the form of imports to the home market (a process we shall term *fragmentation*).

A good example which illustrates the changing nature and composition of a product market is that for the electric toaster. In Case Study 1.4 below, we have illustrated three separate surveys undertaken by 'Which' magazine on the number and types of electric toasters that are available on the UK market in the years 1963, 1970 and 1986.

It is not easy or possible to prescribe one 'package' of price and non-price characteristics that will see a producer through a changing market environment. This would indeed be contrary to what we have developed so far, i.e. that there is no one way of marketing toasters because during different stages in the product's life cycle there will of necessity have to be a 'flexible' marketing strategy which adjusts price and non-price factors intelligently to meet changing product market structure and composition. In fact we could conceive of a variety of strategies that depend on the maturity and development of the product market the enterprise is in.

For simplicity we have outlined below four possible product market structures/scenarios which would require different price/non-price responses by the firm in order to preserve or maintain market share.

Possible product market structures and composition

Scenario A
Here your firm has a strong market share, in an environment where there is little or no import penetration. In addition there is a narrow product

CASE STUDY 1.4

ELECTRIC TOASTERS

Table 1.1 Types and source of electric toasters available to the UK consumer 1963 to 1986

Year	Non-automatic	Automatic	Automatic variants	No. of models supplied by:	
				Home	Importers
1963	4	5	A	6	3
1970	nil	11	A	2	9
1986	nil	29	B	5	24

Source: Which Magazine June 1963, Dec 1970, Dec 1986.
Notes: Number of models that are surveyed by *Which Magazine*. A = A two slot toaster model. B = Here the toasters were: two slice/single slot, two slice/two slot, four slice, cooled wall toasters, toasters that can take combinations of bread/crumpets/baps.

From the above table we can learn that even with a relatively simple product, the process of product market segmentation has been steadily developing over the last 20 years. What was a relatively simple product (or model) has developed into segments which deliver particular functions specific to consumer needs. By 1986 the product had become differentiated in a number of ways – slot sizes, convenience of use, technical specification, all of which can be combined in various permutations for the consumer.

In addition to the process of product market segmentation, the above table illustrates an increasing level of import penetration on the market for electric toasters, surveyed by *Which Magazine*, in terms of the number of importers on the UK market. In 1963 six out of the nine models surveyed were UK–produced (five producers) and three imported from three producers.

In 1986 five models were UK produced (by only two producers) while 24 models were imported from over a dozen producers. It is clear that within each different segment of the toaster market (two-slice/one slot, two-slice/two slots etc.), increased fragmentation of these segments is also taking place as the number of producers competing in each segment of the market also increases.

It is here that we have to return to our work on the aggregate structure of the market. If the market for toasters has been expanding in the UK then it may well be that even though increased segmentation/fragmentation has taken place, it is possible that an individual producer will be able to expand market share across a number of product segments or enter the product market in a particular segment.

In terms of unit sales, UK producers dominated the home market for toasters in the early 1960s. In 1960 most toasters sold in the UK were manufactured here. However, as the market for toasters segmented and fragmented the share of the market taken by UK producers falls.

The market opportunities available for the producer of toasters is no longer determined by how many standard specification toasters at a particular price can be produced, but by how many toasters of a particular specification (which in the current market structure we would

Continued over page

now need to develop or improve attributes such as design, reliability etc.) can be sold in the particular price/segment the firm is targetting with its product. The market has now become a complex environment in which many price and non-price factors determine the level of sales of a particular product across a number of market segments.

Continued from previous page

Table 1.2 UK market for toasters taken by UK producers and importers

	1960	1970	1986
British sales	179 000	181 000	439 000
Imports	n/a	311 000	1 661 000
Total market	179 000	492 000	2 100 000
Percentage share taken by UK producers	100%	42%	21%

Source: AMDEA statistics.

The above statistics represent the effects of a changing market structure/composition and the failure, over a period of time, of UK producers to adjust their products such that market sales shares are maintained.

range on offer and only a few firms are in competition so that there is little fragmentation of the product segments available.

At this stage the product market is relatively immature. That is, consumers have had little experience in using these products and non-price factors such as durability and reliability have not yet surfaced in the purchase decision. Given also that the purchase decision is limited to a few models, the tendency would be to decide on price grounds predominantly. Decisions to buy at a higher or lower price would depend on the level of expenditure incurred as a percentage of total income.

Few market segments for product – dominated by home market producers

Scenario B

Here again your firm is one of a number of domestic producers which dominate the market, but there is now an increasing level of import penetration. Your firm may well still have a narrow product range but fragmentation in a particular segment is increasing.

At this stage what might have been a relatively large product market segment is becoming increasingly fragmented by imports or increased domestic competition. Increased competition may well come in the form of increased or similar reliability/durability etc. as the existing products but the price of these may well be lower. It may well be that the prices of the products that are being sold are all roughly equivalent but that the newer products have improved non-price characteristics.

A classic example is that of British motor bikes, which in the early 1970s could not successfully compete with the Japanese in the smaller bike segments of the UK market. The Japanese product was found by users to

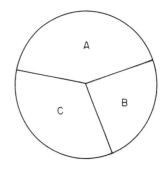

Domestic manufacturers dominate their home market

Figure 1.3 Market segmentation for Scenario A.

be easier to maintain, having fewer oil leaks and a convenient electric start (Boston Consulting Group, 1975).

Scenario C

Here domestic producers, including your own firm, are losing market dominance to imports (even though the market may be expanding) and we now have a much wider product range and the possibility that the number of product market segments is also increasing while some of the older-established segments in which your firm has a presence become more fragmented.

At this stage it may well be that domestic manufacturers are 'lagging' in terms of product development and the sort of innovation needed to establish a position in new product segments. The objective at this stage would be either to invest in new product lines and innovate products for these new segments, or to make improvements to non-price characteristics of the product mix the firm already has, and try to defend old product market segments while paying attention to new product market development.

Scenario D

In this case domestic producers suffer from very high import penetration in which the market is becoming saturated across and within market segments. As we shall see, if the firm is facing such a market it is likely that this will affect the full utilization of equipment and depress profits. At this stage the product market strategy becomes one of retreat, which can be managed in a disorderly or orderly way.

With these simple scenarios we have attempted to show that at each stage of the product market's development the firm must make the most effective use of the resources made available to it. Market strategy must be operationally fluid in order that it can react to the dynamics of changing market structure and composition. In essence this text is concerned with examining how, in differing market circumstances, the enterprise needs to organize its resources (finance, labour and capital) around the objective of maintaining or achieving 'competitive advantage' in the particular market targetted by the firm.

So far we have only considered the 'home market' for a firm's product and the 'market packages' designed for a domestic market. It is true that a firm must serve a characteristic market structure and a specific market composition. In Britain firms are generally heavily dependent on their home market, and it is generally this market which will serve both to condition and constrain the forms of marketing strategies a firm will wish to pursue. However, it is important to remember that firms also have to export, so they must enter foreign markets. This tends to be a gradual process, maybe one market at a time, and also requires the firm to 'match' the diverse needs of these markets with the product on offer. Again the markets faced will be at different stages of development, in terms of the price and non-price factors which determine consumption patterns. For example if the firm is selling in Europe, a mature set of markets where the interchange of manufactures is at a sophisticated and developed state, then the product market package will also need to reflect this sophistication. It

Domestic manufacturers dominate home market product segments

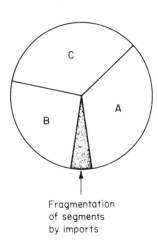

Fragmentation of segments by imports

Home market demand increases – imports take a small slice of segment A

Figure 1.4 Market segmentation for Scenario B.

is likely that these markets will also have product markets which are segmented within and across product ranges and that they have complex rather than simple compositions. As a result a firm must analyse its overseas markets in a detailed way, product by product, country by country. In a developing or relatively underdeveloped economy, product market structures may be less complex in terms of product segments/ composition. However, even here market analysis must be taken seriously if the firm wishes to invest resources in these markets against other potential competitors.

Export prices are determined by the exchange rate, and we will examine the mechanics of this in Chapter 7. It is sufficient here to say that the exchange rate determines the price of your firm's output in terms of the currency an overseas purchaser would have to pay for your output. If the exchange rate were to fall from $2 : £1 to $1 to £1 your exports to the United States would become cheaper because a citizen in the US would pay less, in terms of dollars for your product/service. However, and we will be coming back to this point later, although a fall in the exchange rate (a fall in the price of a firm's exports to a particular country) may be necessary for improving overseas exports, it is not a sufficient condition. We will be arguing throughout this text that so-called non-price factors are also critically important in determining the success of any product market strategy.

For example your firm may be selling, or wishing to sell, a product in an overseas market and the price determined by the exchange rate puts your product at a disadvantage relative to other competition in that market. What you require is clearly a fall in the exchange rate which 'prices in' your exports unless you wish to loss lead, in price and profit terms, to obtain a market beach-head. Although the price change through the exchange rate is necessary for increasing your product's overseas sales, it may well not be sufficient to either maintain market share or sustain and develop an entry into the overseas market. What is also needed is attention to non-price factors. For example with a favourable exchange rate a firm may not be able to increase sales because of a poor distribution network (Williams *et al.*, 1987) or because once the product is sold it might need a repairs and maintenance network or trade-in facility. We can see this product market philosophy developed at its best with the Japanese. As we shall see in Chapter 2, they see product market/marketing strategy as an extension of the active production process, not something that is separated from the production process.

It is clear that product markets develop and undergo constant change in terms of the mix of price and non-price characteristics of the output being sold. This must be so where the objective of the firm and its competitors is to move from simple low value-added products to higher (more sophisticated) value-added product sales. As we have seen, this process of change requires that the enterprise pay attention to both the price and non-price characteristics of the product being sold. Earlier in this chapter it would be clear to the reader that 'price' in economics has and still retains a dominant position – in that it determines the level of consumer demand and the level of output a firm is prepared to offer and supply to the market at that price. However, there are many non-price factors needed to supplement price,

Market for product matures with increased segmentation

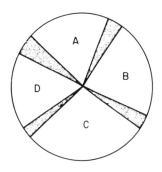

Within each segment importers now take a share of sales but their position is still not dominant in terms of overall product market sales

Figure 1.5 Market segmentation for Scenario C.

particularly where the objective is to win and hold on to market share and competitive advantage in the market place.

> There are many non-price factors which govern competitiveness. For example quality, design, reliability, delivery times, after-sales service and many other factors which influence the relative attractiveness of the product. (House of Lords Select Committee on Overseas Trade, 1985).

Summary

The traditional, neo-classical, theory of the firm overestimates the role of short-term profits as an objective of firms, and gives too much weight to 'getting the price right' as a key determinant of market success. Changes in the organizational context of modern business suggest that growth objectives have become at least as important as profit objectives, and that decisions about price need to be related to decisions about investment. At the same time, changes in the environmental context mean that firms need to have a much clearer picture of the product characteristics that customers want, and of the increasingly segmented character of markets. This is a particularly important lesson for business in Britain, as study after study highlights the role of non-price factors in explaining the current disastrous international trading performance of the UK manufacturing sector. Finally, there is no single 'right' pricing policy or product policy – if a firm is to survive the turbulent environment of modern business, it needs to adapt its policies to changing market conditions continually.

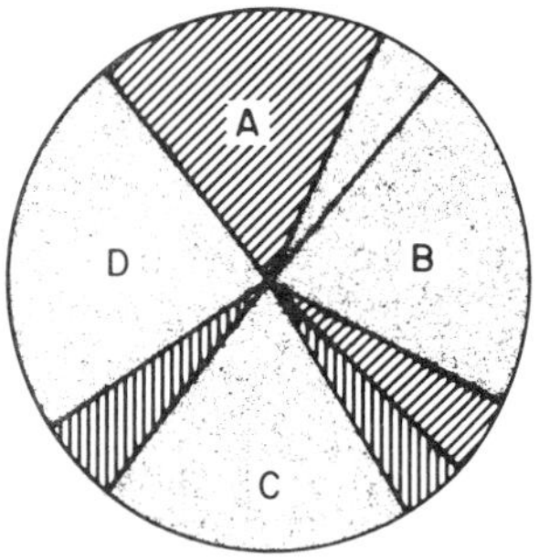

Imports now take a dominant share of most product segments

Domestic producers retreat to market segment niches in segments B, C and D but still dominate segment A. Overall, imports dominate home market sales

Figure 1.6 Market segmentation for Scenario D.

Further reading

Peter Earl provides the most comprehensive economic analysis of marketing, in his books *The Economic Imagination* (Wheatsheaf, 1983) and *Lifestyle Economics* (Wheatsheaf Books, 1986). These books provide both an accessible critique of the orthodox approach, and a constructive alternative which, unlike much economic theory in this field, is of practical use. For greater detail on the technicalities of pricing, Neil Dorward's *The Pricing Decision* (Harper and Row, 1987) is invaluable.

If you are interested in how economic theories of the firm have changed over time, it is a fascinating exercise to compare the 1933 text of Joan Robinson's *Economics of Imperfect Competition* with her 1969 Preface to its 2nd edition (Macmillan, 1969). On the marketing implications of the trade situation of the UK, there is no better source than the House of Lords *Report from the Select Committee on Overseas Trade* (HMSO, 1985).

Exercises

1. Using the data presented in Key Concepts 1.2 and 1.3, calculate the following.

(a) The price elasticity of demand at the profit maximizing output.
(b) The price that would be charged by the firm adding a markup of 100% to Average Variable Costs at a normal output level of 8000 units per year.

2. What would be the total profit per year at an output of 8000 units per year?
(a) Determining price as in 1(b).
(b) According to neo-classical theory.

3. What would be the effect on total profit per year of a drop in output from 8000 to 6000 units per year?
(a) Keeping price at the same level as determined in 1(b).
(b) According to neo-classical theory.

4. What options might be open to a firm in the situation described in Q.3 to restore its profits?

5. What differences would you expect between the actions of British and Japanese firms to restore their profits in such a situation?

6. Does price discrimination favour consumers or producers?

7. Why did the price leaders in the UK petrol market in the 1950s not set lower prices to deter new entry?

8. What could Sinclair have learned from Amstrad in the marketing of low-cost business computers?

9. Do the activities of the marketing departments of large firms extend or limit consumer choice?

10. 'British goods don't sell because they are overpriced.' Discuss.

11. What do you understand by the terms market segmentation and market fragmentation? Illustrate your answer with relevant examples.

Sources
April 1985 *Which Magazine* p 104–5.
June 1977 *Which Magazine* p 352.
Sept 1986 *Which Magazine* p 417.

12. From the *Which Magazine* reports on portable radios (see margin) you are asked to present a report on the following points.
(a) To what extent have importers increased their market presence in this product market?
(b) How has the product changed in terms of its sophistication and product characteristics.
(c) Calculate the average price of the radios surveyed in each year and then express these prices in terms of present money values.

Appendix

Profit maximizing output and price

Short-run profits (total revenue − total cost) are maximized at the output where marginal cost is equal to marginal revenue (providing marginal cost is not falling). At lower levels of output, marginal revenue is greater than marginal cost (so increases in output would add to total profits), while at higher levels marginal cost is greater than marginal revenue (so increases in output would diminish total profits). Figure 1.9 shows a hypothetical example, with the equilibrium output set at Q_1.

Neo-classical theory assumes that firms always maximize their short-run profits, so price will be set at the highest price the market will bear, which is determined by the position of the average revenue curve at the profit maximizing output (P_1 in Figure 1.9).

Long-run equilibrium and market structure

Neo-classical theory includes in its definition of cost *normal profit* – that element of accounting profit which is necessary to encourage firms to set up production, or to remain in business in the long run (when all factors of production are variable). If there are no barriers to the movement of firms from one industry to another, then firms will, in the long run, be attracted into industries where existing firms are earning super-normal profits (a positive difference between total revenue and total cost), and out of industries where they are making a loss. This movement should have the effect of increasing output and reducing prices and profits in industries where firms are earning super-normal short-run profits, and the opposite effect in industries where firms are making losses.

In many industries, however, existing firms have absolute cost advantages over new entrants, or benefit from economies of scale or customer loyalty to existing brands. These act as barriers to the entry of new firms, who have to weigh the cost disadvantages under which they would be competing against the attractions of the super-normal profits which are being made by the established firms.

In the long run, neo-classical theory suggests, movement of firms between industries tends to establish an equilibrium level of price and output in each firm. The nature of this equilibrium depends on the *market structure* in which the firms operate. This is defined in relation to the number of buyers and sellers, the degree of product differentiation, and the ease with which firms can enter or leave the industry. Four main market structures have been identified – *perfect competition, monopoly, imperfect* (or *monopolistic*) *competition*, and *oligopoly*. Figure 1.7 highlights the main points of difference between these market structures.

Characteristics / Market structure	Number of sellers	Extent of product differentiation	Ease of entry or exit
Perfect competition	Large number	None	Easy
Monopoly	One	Total	Difficult
Imperfect competition	Large number	Significant	Easy
Oligopoly	Small number	May or may not be significant	Difficult

Figure 1.7 Main characteristics of market structures.

Oligopoly is the most common business structure in the modern business environment, yet, as we saw in the main body of the chapter, its characteristics preclude strict profit maximization. The other three market structures fit better within the framework of neo-classical theory (which is why traditional textbooks spend so much time on them), yet they are analytical constructs whose relationship to the real world is a tenuous one.

Perfect competition

Under pefect competition, a large number of firms compete to supply identical products. This is not a common situation in manufacturing industry, but it is a feature of some agricultural markets (potatoes, for example). Here, no firm is powerful enough to influence price by altering its output, and the absence of product differentiation means that no firm can sell at a price higher than that charged by its competitors. Each firm, then, is a price taker, with both average and marginal revenue remaining constant at different levels of output. In the short run, the market price (P_1 in Figure 1.8(a)) may be higher than average cost, enabling firms to make super-normal profits (the shaded area in Figure 1.8(a)).

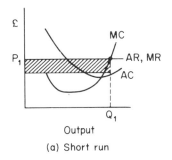
(a) Short run

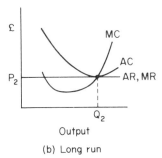
(b) Long run

Figure 1.8 Equilibrium of a perfectly competitive firm.

In the long run, new entrants will be attracted into the industry by the super-normal profits, increasing the total output of the industry. This will depress prices, and thus average and marginal revenue for each firm, because of the inverse relationship at the industry level between quantity demanded and price. Equilibrium will be reached where average revenue is equal to average cost, so there is no longer any super-normal profit, and no longer any incentive for further new entry. This equilibrium position is at price P_2 and output Q_2 in Figure 1.8(b). A special feature of perfect competition is that in long-run equilibrium, each firm is producing at the minimum point on its average cost curve.

Monopoly

A 'pure' monopoly is the sole producer of a product which has no close substitutes, and where entry into the industry is restricted. In the traditional theory of monopoly, the firm is free to set its own price, within the constraints imposed by the nature of demand for its product (newer developments, based on the work of Baumol *et al.*, 1982, emphasize that if

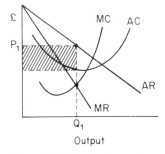
Figure 1.9 Equilibrium of a monopolist.

its market is 'contestable' by rivals, it is also constrained by the threat of new entry). Increases in output bring reductions in average revenue, so marginal revenue will be below average revenue. A typical equilibrium position might be as in Figure 1.9, with the monopoly able to obtain super-normal profits by restricting its output below the full capacity level, and able to maintain them in the long run because no new firms can enter to expand industry output and bring prices down.

Because a monopoly can control what is offered to consumers, it is able to practise price discrimination – selling the same product to different buyers at different prices for reasons unconnected with cost differences. This will be a profitable exercise whenever there are differences in the price elasticities of demand between different identifiable groups of customers. The firm will increase its revenues, and thus its profits, by charging a higher price to customers with a high price elasticity of demand than to customers with a low price elasticity of demand. In this way, it pays British Rail to charge Old Age Pensioners a lower price than business travellers, or British Gas to offer discounts to industrial consumers.

Pure monopoly used to be comparatively rare in the real world, except in the nationalized industries, which practise price discrimination, but which are not allowed to boost profits by restricting output. Private sector monopoly became more common in the 1980s with the privatization of organizations like British Telecom and British Gas, but even here prices have been held in check by government regulations.

Imperfect competition

An imperfectly (or monopolistically) competitive market, like a perfectly competitive one, has a large number of buyers and sellers, and free movement of firms into and out of the industry. Unlike perfect competition, however, each firm under imperfect competition sells a differentiated product – one which is different in some way from its competitors' products. Because of product differentiation, each firm faces a less than perfectly elastic demand curve, which means it can raise its price and not lose all its customers to competitors. In the short run, the equilibrium of an imperfectly competitive firm can look like that of a monopolist, with a downward sloping average revenue curve and super-normal profits, as in Figure 1.9.

In the long run, however, firms will be attracted into the industry by the super-normal profits, as under perfect competition. Equilibrium is again where average revenue equals average cost, but in this case the firm will be producing at below full capacity output, and at a price which is above the minimum level of average cost, as can be seen from Figure 1.10.

The emphasis on differentiated products in imperfect competition theory is an important one, but in many markets large numbers of differentiated products are produced by only a small number of firms (breakfast cereals, for example). Even in the service sector, where there are often large numbers of firms apparently competing with each other, considerations of customer convenience often limit the effective competition to other firms located nearby (corner shops, for example), and what at first sight seems to be an imperfectly competitive market turns out on closer inspection to be a linked chain of local oligopolies.

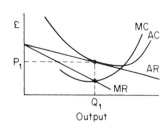

Figure 1.10 Long-run equilibrium of an imperfectly competitive firm.

References

Adamson, I. and Kennedy, R. (1986) *Sinclair and the 'Sunrise' Technology*, Penguin, Harmondsworth.

Andrews, P.W.S. (1949) *Manufacturing Business*, Macmillan, London.

Andrews, P.W.S. (1964) *On Competition in Economic Theory*, Macmillan, London.

Andrews, P.W.S. and Brunner, E. (1975) *Studies in Pricing*, Macmillan, London.

Baumol, W.J. *et al.* (1982) *Contestable Markets and the Theory of Industrial Structure*, Harcourt Brace Jovanovich, San Diego.

Boston Consulting Group (1975) Strategy Alternatives for the British Motorcycle Industry, HC Paper 532, HMSO, London.

Chetley, A. (1979) *The Baby Killer Scandal*, War on Want. London.

Coutts, K. *et al.* (1978) *Industrial Pricing in the UK*, Cambridge University Press, Cambridge.

Doyle, P. *et al.* (1986) Japanese marketing strategies in the UK. *Journal of International Business Studies*.

Earl, P. (1983) *The Economic Imagination*, Wheatsheaf Books, Brighton.

Earl, P. (1986) *Lifestyle Economics*, Wheatsheaf Books, Brighton.

Eichner, A. (1976) *The Megacorp and Oligopoly*, Cambridge University Press, Cambridge.

Eichner, A. (1985) *Towards a New Economics*, Macmillan, London.

Galbraith, J.K. (1958) *The Affluent Society*, Penguin, Harmondsworth.

Galbraith, J.K. (1967) *The New Industrial State*, Penguin, Harmondsworth.

Galbraith, J.K. (1973) *Economics and the Public Purpose*, Penguin, Harmondsworth.

Grant, R.M. (1982) Pricing behaviour in the UK wholesale market for petrol. *Journal of Industrial Economics*, March.

Levitt, T. (1960) Marketing Myopia. *Harvard Business Review*, July–August.

Levitt, T. (1975) Retrospective Commentary. *Harvard Business Review*, Sept.–Oct.

Littlechild, S.C. (1986) *The Fallacy of the Mixed Economy*, 2nd edn, Institute of Economic Affairs, London.

Lowe, J.F. (1976) Competition in the UK retail petrol market 1960–77. *Journal of Industrial Economics*, March.

Medawar, C. (1979) *Insult or Injury*, Social Audit, London.

Melrose, D. (1981) *The Great Health Robbery*, Oxfam, Oxford.

Penrose, E. (1968) *The Large International Firm in Developing Countries*, George Allen and Unwin, London.

Sen, A. (1981) *Poverty and Famines*, Oxford University Press, Oxford.

Shaw, R.W. (1974) Price leadership and the effect of new entry on the UK retail petrol supply market. *Journal of Industrial Economics*, Sept.

Sweezy, P. (1939) Demand under conditions of oligopoly. *Journal of Political Economy*.

Williams, K. *et al.* (1987) *The Breakdown of Austin Rover*, Berg, Leamington Spa.

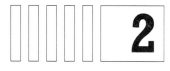

2 New technology and the organization of production

Introduction

The rate of technological change achieved through the use of micro-electronic systems has increased rapidly over the last twenty years, and the rate of obsolescence of existing products and production technologies has intensified. Firms in the 1980s therefore have to run faster in order just to keep abreast of their competitors. Where a competitor introduces a product which embodies certain new attributes in terms of its function or design then your firm may well, it it wishes to continue to stay in the manufacture of that product, introduce new technologies and manufacturing systems that can deliver a more up-to-date product.

In this chapter we will argue that the introduction of new technology may well be a necessary condition on which to maintain competitive advantage, but that it is not a sufficient criterion. As we shall see, the full potential benefits from the introduction of a new machine or new technology are not always easy to obtain in practice. This is because the introduction of a new technology rarely has unambiguous benefits for the firm or industry concerned.

Against this it must be said that those organizations that are able to capitalize fully the benefits of a particular technology may well be able to secure a competitive advantage in their domestic or overseas markets.

In this chapter we will initially consider briefly how the benefits of new technology are incorporated into the traditional micro-economic theory of production and costs. We will then argue that traditional theory fails to incorporate a number of important intra- and extra-firm considerations which can either contribute to or frustrate the possible advantages that a technology might deliver to the firm.

First we will discuss how the benefits of new technology are incorporated into the micro-economic theory of production and costs.

Technology and the theory of production and costs

In traditional micro-economic theory the 'production function' describes the physical relation between output and factor inputs (land, labour, capital and materials). That is, in any production process one or all of the above factors of production will be combined in order to convert raw materials into a finished saleable product (see Key Concept 2.1).

In economics the production function is a mathematical statement of the relationship between the output of the business and factor inputs required to produce that output.
Where

$$Q = f\,(K,L,L,M)$$

In production terms various combinations of factors of production are required (capital, land, labour and materials) to produce different product types. Factors of production are transformed in the production process into a final end product.

KEY CONCEPT 2.1

THE PRODUCTION FUNCTION

At this stage no costs have been attached to the factors of production used in the production process, although in practice we would attach costs to each of the inputs used in the production process. We are here only concerned with the physical unit inputs of land, labour, capital and materials. In addition to just using a physical measure of the factor inputs of the production process, we are also assuming that the production process we are using combines the factors of production in physically the most efficient way possible. At this point we are only concerned with the 'technical efficiency' of production and not 'economic efficiency', because in the latter case we would need to take the price or cost of factors of production into account. With this distinction in mind we can consider the following two production processes X and Y, both of which use the following labour and capital physical inputs.

Table 2.1 Inputs to processes X and Y

Process	X (units)	Y (units)
Labour input	100	75
Capital input	50	75

In this example both processes would be considered to be equally technically efficient, because both processes use the same number of labour and capital inputs namely 150 units to produce the same output. If process X were, in fact, to use say 120 units of labour and 50 units of capital then the 'rational' business would choose to operate process Y and not X because in physical input terms (with a given state of technology) process X now uses more resources than that of Y to produce the same output.

In practice managers make decisions about which production process is the most efficient in terms of the costs of production (physical inputs times unit costs). The decision about which production process is the more efficient becomes an 'economic' rather than 'technical' one. Using the above example we could allocate the following unit costs to capital and labour.

	£
Unit capital cost	4.00
Unit labour cost	1.00

The costs of producing a given output from process X and process Y now become as shown below.

Table 2.2 Costs of processes X and Y

Process	£ X	£ Y
Labour input × unit costs	100	75
Capital input × unit costs	200	300
Total labour and capital cost	300	375

In economic terms the decision as to which is the most efficient production process becomes complicated when we introduce factor costs into the calculation. It would now appear that Process X is the most economically efficient process because it produces a given output at lower cost than does process Y. Going back to our initial example we can see that the physical combinations of each factor of production differed between processes. If we then introduce differing factor unit costs it is likely that one process (in this case X) will be more economic because it uses relatively more of the cheaper factor input, which in this case is labour. It must also be said that the above is an oversimplication because it considers only a single process stage within the overall production process of a particular firm, and that in practice different firms will have a variety of variable and fixed inputs, because they are either of a different size or they are in a different type of business activity.

In the short run (see Key Concept 2.2) it is possible for a firm to vary labour input but not capital because to change machinery and equipment is by its nature a difficult and time-consuming process. If in the above example managers of process X have to use an extra 20 units more labour in order to produce its given output level, this process is now technically inefficient because it takes 170 units of capital and labour (50 + 120) to produce the same given output as process Y which is still using 150 units of

Table 2.3 Total costs of processes X and Y

Process	£ X	£ Y
Labour	120	75
Capital	200	300
Total Costs	320	375

labour and capital (75 + 75). However, in economic terms, taking into account the unit cost of labour and capital process X is still the more economic of the two by £55.

We have seen that with a given technology the decision about which production process to adopt is made more complicated when we introduce factor costs into the equation. For process Y it was the high unit costs of capital relative to labour coupled with the high physical input of capital relative to process X that were the cause of 'economic inefficiency'. In the long term it may well be possible for the firm to reduce capital input into process Y in order to become economic relative to process X.

So far we have made the assumption that the level of output from a production process remains fixed at a given level. However, over a period of time the output from a production process will vary and so the combinations of factors of production will also adjust to meet changes in the level of output. We could conceive of the following relationship between factor inputs (labour and capital) and output. That is as output from a production process doubles or halves so factor inputs have to double or halve.

In any production process the costs of production are split between those that can vary in the short run, namely variable costs and those that are fixed in the short run.

A firm may wish to increase the level of production output in the short run, but there are a number of constraints on this decision. Extra capacity will be needed which requires either additional plant or equipment. Increasing capacity in the short run would be difficult where capital equipment has to be produced and plant constructed.

In the short run capital is said to be fixed in relation to output. However, it may be possible for the firm to increase output by increasing the labour intensiveness of the production system and increasing out-sourcing from firms that can supply on relatively short notice those components that the firm requires. Paying more in wages and salaries through taking on more employees or by paying more for overtime working would increase variable labour costs. Similarly, an increase in the use of sub-contractors would also increase the level of variable bought-in materials and purchases of the organization. Both these actions may be possible in the short run and both would require an increase in variable costs.

Fixed Costs = Land and capital costs
Variable Costs = Materials and labour

In the long run it will be possible for the firm to add more capital in the form of plant and equipment and land for the construction of new facilities, so that in the long run capital and land are variable factor inputs or costs.

KEY CONCEPT 2.2

THE CONCEPT OF THE LONG AND SHORT RUN

KEY CONCEPT 2.3

CAPITAL AND LABOUR PRODUCTIVITY

Different firms may be able to obtain productivity levels that are at variance to those of similar competitors using similar technologies. Productivity is a concept that is used to demonstrate statistically how output behaves relative to factor inputs, notably labour and capital.

Productivity differentials arise either because firms are able to improve market share relative to their competitors, who, at the same time utilize similar levels of capital and labour input, or where the firm relative to competitors uses less labour and capital input to produce a similar output level.

In practice we can use a number of ratios to calculate the productivity of labour and capital.

Labour productivity

Labour input can be measured simply in terms of the number of employees at a given process or firm level. Output can be measured in terms of a physical or financial value (usually net output/value added or gross output)

(i)   Output per person employed   Total output/Total number of employees

(ii) Output per person hour   Total output/total hours worked

Capital productivity

Capital inputs are normally measured in terms of gross capital stock, as represented in the annual accounts of the business (i.e. fixed assets, plant and equipment, fixtures tooling etc. less disposals of assets but excluding depreciation).

Capital productivity is usually taken to mean Net Output/Capital stock, where net output is defined as *either:*

(1)   Sales
      − Bought in materials and services
                or
(2)   Labour costs (wages and salaries etc.)
      + Depreciation
      + Tax and dividends
      + Retained profit.

Sometimes, however, Gross Output/Capital stock is used as the measure of capital productivity, where Gross Output is

      Sales
      +/− Stock adjustments made during the year.

Total factor productivity

This measures the total contribution to productivity made by all the factors of production and is essentially an average productivity measure.

$$\text{Total factor productivity} = \frac{\text{Total output}}{\text{Inputs of all factors of production}}$$

Although productivity ratios can be a static ratio it makes much more sense to use productivity ratios in either a relative or dynamic framework. That is comparing one firm with another in similar activities or analysing changes in the firm's productivity performance over a number of years.

Table 2.4 Relationship of inputs to outputs

Output	50 units	100 units	200 units
Factor inputs			
Labour	5 units	10 units	20 units
Capital	20 units	40 units	80 units

Over the output range 50 to 200 units the productivity of labour (output/labour) and the productivity of capital (output/capital) remain constant at ten units of output per unit of labour and 2.5 units of output per unit of capital. That is, in the above example, as output increases or decreases capital and labour inputs adjust so as to maintain a constant pari passu relationship with output, i.e. 'constant returns to scale'. It is also possible to conceive of an example where output from a particular production process increases at a faster rate than the increase in factor inputs, i.e. 'increasing returns to scale'.

Table 2.5 Effect of increasing return to scale

Output	50 units	100 units	200 units
Factor inputs			
Labour	5 units	8 units	12 units
Capital	20 units	30 units	35 units
Output per unit of labour	10 units	12.5 units	16.6 units
Output per unit of capital	2.5 units	3.3 units	5.7 units

In theory increasing returns to scale are often used to represent a situation in which it is possible to increase output to a greater extent than

In the short run we show the average total cost curve to have a 'U' shape. In order to produce a particular level of output the firm needs to invest in both capital and labour resources. Over the output range OX_1 the firm will be able to reduce average costs of production because increasing returns to scale are said to be obtained. That is, as output expands average fixed costs fall. In addition, labour inputs expand but at a slower rate than output. A doubling of output is met with a less than two-fold increase in the use of labour inputs.

Around the point X_1 we could conceive that constant returns are achieved when output increases are just matched with the same proportionate increase in labour inputs. Beyond this point output increases are met with an even greater proportionate increase in the use of labour, possibly because the firm has reached the capacity limits of the capital investment made and therefore needs to increase the payments to labour.

KEY CONCEPT 2.4

RETURNS TO SCALE

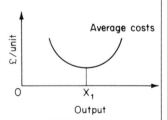

Figure 2.1 The average total cost curve.

the required increase in labour and capital input. Increasing returns to scale are often associated with methods of 'mass production' such as those applied in the steel industry or motor vehicles industry.

We can use the case of steel production in blast furnaces to illustrate the concept of increasing returns to scale. It is argued that the level of investment required to build a blast furnace is related to the surface area of the furnace. However, where you then decide to double the surface area (that is the capital input), the volume of the furnace (or output) will increase by a factor of three. This relation is founded on the engineering rule which relates the surface area of a cylinder to the volume of that cylinder. We can illustrate this with a simple example in which the capital input doubles but output increases threefold.

Table 2.6 Economies of scale in steel-making

	Capital input	Output
Small blast furnace	100	100
Large blast furnace	200	300

In the above example, if the market expands sufficiently, it would be rational for a firm to construct a larger blast furnace because in physical capital input-output terms, the larger furnace would be more efficient. That is output obtained per unit of capital input would increase from 1 unit to 1.5 units (100/100 and 300/200).

So far we have considered that with a given technology, decisions concerning the combinations of factor inputs to produce a particular level of output is complicated by the relative cost of each unit of capital and labour used in the production process. In addition, in the short run it is assumed in economic literature that we cannot easily change capital input in the production process (in the short run it is regarded as a fixed factor).

New technology and capital investment

It is clear that organizations exist and function in an environment which is subject to continuous technical change, and in such an environment it is open to a firm to plan and adjust its production processes as certain techniques become obsolete. In the early 1970s the British Steel Corporation wished to change from the old open hearth technology to the basic oxygen system (BOS) of steel production. The new technology of injecting oxygen into the furnace made it possible to increase the speed at which iron could be converted to steel. In the open hearth furnace it would take several hours to convert a tonne of iron to steel but in the new basic oxygen furnace this conversion time was cut down to 30 to 40 minutes. The introduction of the new BOS furnace would allow steelmakers to increase dramatically output from a furnace of similar volume to that of the open hearth system, because it would convert iron to steel at a faster rate. The introduction of this new technology would allow the steel industry to increase the amount of steel produced per unit of labour and capital.

Economies of scale refers to those factors which allow the organization to produce a large volume of output at lower average cost relative to the production of a small volume of output. Where the costs of labour and capital resources are constant a tenfold increase in output would lead to a less than tenfold increase in factor input.

KEY CONCEPT 2.5

ECONOMIES OF SCALE

Qty.	Labour costs £	Capital costs £	Unit costs £
10	10	20	3
100	50	100	1.50

At particular points in time (the economist would call this the long run) it is open to a firm to change the technology or production process techniques being used and take on board any changes that have taken place in production process technology. At this stage it is open to a firm to evaluate the future benefits that will arise from a change in technology either at a process stage level or at an overall plant or strategic level. In both cases, of course, it is crucial that the cost/benefit calculations of a particular investment in new technology reflect realistic expectations about future costs and revenues.

If, for example, a firm incorrectly estimates the benefits to be gained from the introduction of a new process stage, this may not seriously damage profitability. However, where the investment in new technology is of strategic importance and requires a substantial commitment of resources, it is essential that the business can obtain the fullest benefits from the investment. Failure at a strategic level may well compromise the financial future of the organization and lead to a fundamental misallocation of resources.

One of the more interesting economic calculations made by many managers and academics to support the rationality of large-scale strategic investment in new technology is that related to 'economies of scale'. In economic texts the theory of economies of scale expresses a relation between output over a given period and unit total costs of producing that output. That is, where output expands it is expected that unit costs of production tend to fall. In the next section we will examine the assumptions that are used to support this economic relation between output and unit costs and introduce a case study that illustrates some of the problems that can practically operate to frustrate obtaining any benefits from investments in economies of scale.

Economies of scale

In the long run it is open to the firm to plan the introduction of new technology which either replaces old process technology within existing facilities or establishes the need for an entirely new 'greenfield site'. The extent and level to which such new investments will be carried out very much depends on the capacity levels the firm requires to meet expected market demand.

At this stage let us assume that there are three plant sizes available to the firm (small, medium, large) and that these plants have the following output and cost profiles.

Table 2.7 Economies of scale with increasing capacity

Output p.a.	1 Labour input	Wage rate p.a. £	Total labour Cost £m	2 Capital cost £m	3 Average total cost per unit £
Small plant 1000 units	100	10 000	1.0	5.0	6000
Medium plant 10 000 units	500	10 000	5.0	25.0	3000
Large plant 100 000 units	1000	10 000	10.00	150.0	1600

From this table it is apparent that as we increase the size of the plant capacity from 1000 units to 100 000 units, we see that the average total cost per unit of production falls from £6000 to £1600. This average total unit cost of production is found by adding the total capital and labour costs together and dividing through by output from each plant. Why does the total average unit cost of production fall when output increases? The answer lies with the relationship between output and labour and capital factor inputs.

$$\text{Total costs} = \text{Fixed (Capital)} + \text{Variable (Labour)}$$

$$\text{Average total costs} = \frac{\text{Fixed} + \text{Variable costs}}{\text{Quantity}}$$

From the small to medium plant output increases by a factor of ten, while the total of labour and capital only increases by a factor of five in each case. That is, as output increases it is not necessary to increase the level of labour used to the same extent, because at higher levels of output the possibilities for the introduction of increased automation reduce the need for labour. With capital investment the same conditions operate in that capital investment need not double in order to double output (see the previous example on the blast furnace).

The relationship between average total unit costs of production and increases in output can be represented in the diagram shown below in Figure 2.2. In this diagram we illustrate how average total unit costs are expected to fall as output increases from a small to a large plant.

If we now assume that we have constructed the medium-sized plant with an average total unit cost of £3000 we are now, in the short run, stuck with this plant size. If output from the medium plant falls below 10 000 units to

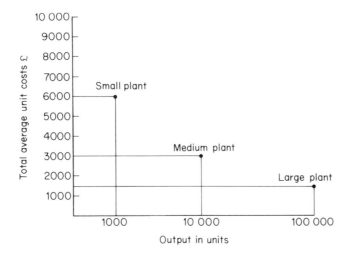

Figure 2.2 The relationship between costs and output.

say 8000 units then we move up and to the left on what is termed the Short-run average cost curve (in Figure 2.3 SRACCm) to where average total unit cost is £3750 (£30 million/8000 units). If we produce more than 10 000 units we are operating above the most efficient capacity of this plant (i.e. minimum point on the SRACC). We may well have to pay overtime or sub-contract out work so that average total unit costs start to increase for every extra unit we produce. It is for these reasons we show the SRACC to be 'U' shaped around the point of minimum average total unit cost for each plant.

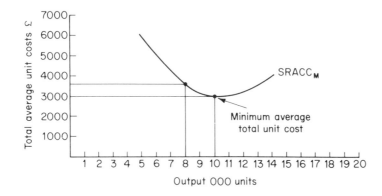

Figure 2.3 The short-run average cost curve.

In the diagram in Figure 2.4 we have illustrated the three short-run average cost curves, the shapes of which are determined by increasing and decreasing returns to scale (Key Concept 2.4).

However, in order to construct a long-run average cost curve (LRACC)/planning curve/economies of scale curve we have to make a number of very abstract assumptions, for example that over a given output range, there are, at the planning stage, an infinite number of plant sizes open to a firm. The long-run average cost curve is therefore a locus of points which

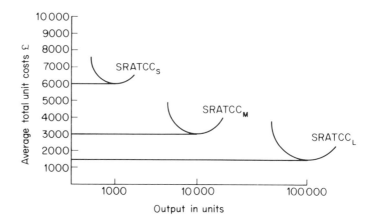

Figure 2.4 The effect of changing returns to scale on SRACCs.

describes the lowest cost of production when all factors of production vary. This is in contrast to the short-run average cost curve which illustrates the lowest cost of producing a range of output when one or more factors of production is fixed (capital and land for example). The long-run average total cost curve is assumed to be a continuous curve, as shown in the diagram below (Figure 2.5) and it is constructed by connecting the set of short-run average cost curves tangentially. We can see at the point * that both the SRACC minimum point and the LRACC are tangential; we call this point the minimum efficient scale (MES).

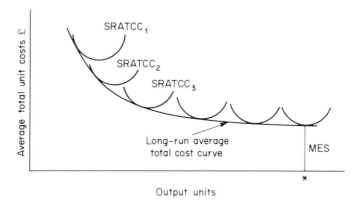

Figure 2.5 Long-run average total cost curve or economies of scale curve.

Generally the LRACC is shown to have the following characteristic shape. That is as output and plant size expand so average total unit costs fall up to a point at which unit average total costs reach a minimum termed the point of minimum efficient scale (MES). Beyond this point the curve is shown to have a flat portion illustrating that over certain ranges of output long-run average unit costs remain constant (X_0 to X_1) and are equivalent to the SRACC minimum average unit cost. Long-run average costs are shown to turn up eventually where the sheer scale of operations becomes too complex and unmanageable.

For a firm wishing to plan for an expansion in the level of output with a new technology or given technology, the above economies of scale curve

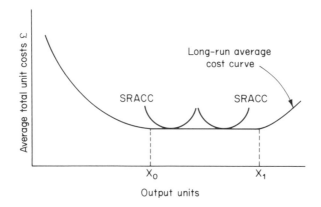

Figure 2.6 Long-run average cost curve illustrating constant total average unit cost range.

ECONOMIES OF SCALE AND THE CASE OF BRITISH STEEL

In the late 1960s the management of British Steel visited Japan steel producers who had by this time invested successfully in large 'giant' integrated steel-making systems with production capacities in excess of 10 million tonnes. At this time such plants were three to four times larger than those constructed in the UK.

After nationalization in 1967 the industry had access to the sort of funds necessary to bring the UK steel industry up to the standard of the Japanese systems. In 1972 the British Steel Corporation (BSC) had completed its corporate plan. This projected an increase in the level of production and demand for steel from 25 million tonnes to 36 million tonnes by 1983. This investment strategy involved the commitment of £3000 million over a ten-year period at the rate of £300 million per annum. In addition, and crucially, the BSC's corporate plan involved the development and construction of new large integrated steel facilities. The BSC's plan then involved the construction of new large-scale integrated steel facilities in order to obtain the benefits of economies of scale. Port Talbot in Wales would eventually have an ultimate capacity of 6 million tonnes while a new 'greenfield site' at Teesside would have an ultimate capacity of over 11 million tonnes.

The management of BSC were convinced that economies of scale were available to those who were prepared to take the risk of investing in large-scale facilities and that the subsequent benefits, in terms of lower averge unit costs of production, were too lucrative to resist.

> Japan is the most efficient producer in the world. There should be no doubt in anyone's mind that their large-scale plant, operating to a standard which we hope to achieve, is the most economic way of producing steel in bulk and at lowest cost (Accounting for British Steel p. 92).

At the time management were also supported by academic economists such as A. Cockerill (1974), whose evidence on reductions in unit average costs suggested that the construction of steel facilities up to 10 million tonnes capacity would reveal lower average unit costs. His evidence on unit steel production costs is reproduced in the table and graph overleaf.

Continued over page

Continued from previous page

Table 2.8 Index of unit average costs of production in steel plant

Plant size 000 tonnes	250	1000	2000	5000	10 000
Index of unit:					
Material cost	100	84	81	80	79
Operating costs	100	67	61	60	60
Capital charges	100	68	52	41	40
Total average costs	100	80	75	73	72

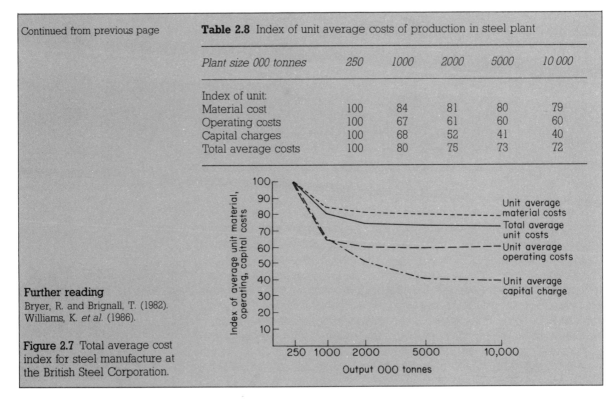

Further reading
Bryer, R. and Brignall, T. (1982).
Williams, K. *et al.* (1986).

Figure 2.7 Total average cost
index for steel manufacture at
the British Steel Corporation.

presents the decision-maker or planner with a powerful argument for
increasing the scale of operations. That is, mass production from large-
scale facilities will present your firm with a long-run average unit cost
advantage if you expand output to say Q2 in Figure 2.8 when your
competitors produce at Q1 or below. It is this calculation of cost advantage
through economies of scale which played a very important role in the
British Steel Corporation's plans to expand production capacity from its
basic oxygen steel-making facilities in the 1970s as you can see from the
case study of British Steel.

So far the discussion has been related to the 'static' framework of costs
and output under the long-run average cost curve. However, implicit in the
model and framework of the long-run average cost curve is a dynamic
relation between costs and output. It is the case that technical economies of
scale are traditionally assumed to result from the introduction of highly
specialized production processes, and the classic example of such a mass
production system has been the Ford Model T. In the 1980s the
development costs of a new car are very large, for example the new Fiat car
the Tipo has cost £1 billion to develop, and new high fixed cost equipment
is also required for its manufacture. All this investment requires a car
manufacturer to obtain, over a period of time, long, large production runs
to spread capital and operating costs over large volumes of output. If this
cannot be achieved then the firm will face a large cost penalty per unit
produced.

For a number of reasons the logic of economies of scale is problematic.
Firstly we have implicitly assumed that as output expands from the process

When firms invest in new technology they invest in new capacity (in the diagram Q_1 to Q_2) against a projected growth in market sales Gm. If growth continues at Gm then there will be excess capacity constructed (the area of triangle ABC) until time period T_2 when the investment is fully utilized. If output growth is below Gm at Go then the time period over which underutilization takes place is extended, to T_3, whilst a faster than expected growth rate will result in full utilization of the investment at a much earlier time period than expected. Investments are lumpy and when made against an uncertain market growth rate can result in extended periods of underutilization when market demand fails to materialize in the levels expected.

KEY CONCEPT 2.6

LUMPY INVESTMENTS IN NEW CAPACITY

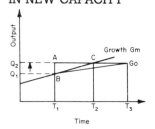

Figure 2.8 Underutilization periods.

Further reading
Scherer, F.M. (1975).

stage or plant we have installed this will, in the long run, lead to a reduction in unit average costs of production. At the now lower cost and price level, demand for the product will expand to either fill the facilities you have constructed or necessitate the construction of new facilities. However, the most alarming effect of massive 'lumpy' investment against an uncertain market is that in periods of slow market growth for the product being produced, the investment will be in overcapacity until and unless growth in the market operates to utilize fully process investment and plant constructed. A misreading of the nature of the market place can have serious consequences for those who hope to benefit from economies of scale.

> Overoptimism and other judgemental errors that frequently may escape serious penalty in times of prosperity may turn out to be catastrophically costly in a period of economic stagnation.
>
> *K. Ohmae, 1982, p 167*

It is clearly very important to consider the nature and composition of the market place before launching an investment project, and more particularly an investment strategy which commits large amounts of the firm's resources. In the case of British Steel, McKinsey Management Consultants were drafted in to assess the BSC's future market sales potential. They concluded that the firm would need to be producing at most 23 million tonnes of steel by 1983. It was against this background of market uncertainty that the BSC went ahead with a major strategic investment programme.

Secondly, as we have seen, the investment in larger facilities is designed to move the firm down the long-run average cost curve. This as we have seen is typically shown as a smooth curve, in which adjustments down the curve to new ever-larger plant are shown as being unproblematic. However, 'unless the slate is wiped clean and production begins anew on a greenfield site, the enterprise must operate a collection of old and new plants and processes' (Williams *et al.*, 1986).

KEY CONCEPT 2.7	Firms rarely have production processes that are characterized as having a single product or single process stage. In practice firms operate a collection of processes and produce a range of different products. As a result balancing these systems requires the firm to pay attention to process cycle times, and the complex scheduling of production flows. Firms use complex statistical tools as a means for sequencing and optimizing production flows so that the best use of capacity can be made.
PLANT AND PROCESS OPTIMIZATION	Failure to carry out these calculations can result in bottlenecks where the best equipment is run at the rate of the slowest because imbalances between and across process stages are not corrected for.

In the case of British Steel, investments in new steel-making technology had to be set against older technology such as ironmaking which provided the raw material for the steel furnaces, and the finishing facilities, which roll and shape the finished steel. It is clear that in any overall production process technological change is, more often than not, uneven in its effects and it is necessary to 'match' the output of the new production stage with the old production stage. It is of no use investing in new technology which cannot be fully used because the previous stage was not of a sufficient capacity to balance up the process throughput. In this case the most efficient stage of the production process is constrained by the least efficient stage.

We could, for example, envisage a production process with three stages using different technologies.

Table 2.9 Three-stage production process.

	Stage 1	*Stage 2*	*Stage 3*
Minimum efficient scale (units)	2000 $\longrightarrow$	10 000 $\longrightarrow$	5000 $\longrightarrow$ Finished output

At each stage we have different minimum efficient scales (points at which the most efficient or lowest level of unit costs is reached). In this above example the production process balanced would simply consist of five machines at stage one, one at stage two and two at stage three.

$$(5) - - - - - - - - - - (1) - - - - - - - - - - (2)$$

Some reserve capacity is assumed to exist at each stage in case of breakdown or demand variation. However, if we assume that a new machine is introduced at stage two which can produce 15 000 units with a minimum efficient scale which significantly reduces unit costs at this stage, we would also need to increase the number of machines at stage one and three if there has been no corresponding improvement in the technology at these other stages. It may well be that there are space constraints which prevent you from putting an extra two or three machines at stage one.

Whatever else, the decision to invest in new technology has had 'network' effects throughout the production process, and these other constraints need to be considered.

At the BSC this problem emerged at Scunthorpe where the basic oxygen steel facilities could produce more steel than could be processed by the finishing plant. (R. Pryke, 1981, p 186.)

Investment in new technology cannot be considered in isolation from the market place or in isolation from other parts of the production process. Investment, if it is to be strategically beneficial, must be incorporated into existing vintages of technology in a balanced and not disruptive way. If a new investment results in imbalance and bottlenecks in the process, this may well cancel out any cost advantages revealed by the introduction of new technology at a particular stage of the process. It may be necessary to increase buffer stocks in order to compensate for imbalances introduced across process stages. Equipment may have to be run at or above its designed capacity to balance up the system with increased problems of breakdown and increased unproductive time. The firm will be constrained by the lowest capacity of the production system.

Finally there are a number of external factors that may operate to frustrate the attainment of economies of scale. We have already discussed in relation to the British Steel case study that the realized level of market demand can operate to undermine seriously the investment strategy of the firm. It is not possible to rely on the simple relation that as output expands, lower unit costs/prices increase the level of demand. This relation is circular and we have to break into it somewhere. In our chapter on the nature of the market we argued that this is done by minimizing market miscalculation by sensible disaggregate market segment analysis in both the home and overseas market you are operating. Investigation may well reveal that competition is based on better quality materials, finish of the product and the sales service given to the customer. It may well be that non-price factors are much more important than the price at which it is sold relative to close competitors.

One thing is clear, where the market fails to deliver the volume necessary to utilize the capacity of the process or plant constructed, it is not possible to make an instantaneous adjustment to plant capacity to match this lower level of demand. Rather you must underutilize existing plant. At this stage the firm is caught in a vicious circle whereby market failure exacerbates productive imbalance. In addition the business cannot reveal positive financial results because underutilization of investments results in financial losses, which will further compromise the ability of the business to balance up investments.

Another external constraint which could operate to frustrate the firm's realization of internal economies of scale may well be the relationship with suppliers or its relationship with the distributor of the final product. In the Japanese manufacturing system coordination between the supplier and the user firm is seen as essential. Any disruption in supply or imbalance between the capacity of your supplier, and your own firm will generate bottlenecks beyond your control and lead to underutilization of your own production facilities. Firms like Marks and Spencer have, like the Japanese, developed strong 'active' involvement rather than 'passive' involvement with their suppliers for good reasons of production control and planning. In Japan 'active' involvement involves making sure that products are delivered in time and in the right quantity and quality required. Kenichi Ohmae presents this behaviour as one of *value analysis* and *value engineering*.

> The purpose of these techniques, which are now employed by practically every Japanese manufacturer as part of a routine control of business operations, is to investigate and analyse purchased materials or components from the point of view of price so that results can be incorporated into planning in such areas as cost reduction and development of new products. Studies of purchased goods are carried out to examine whether their quality and reliability are right for a particular product design and function (value engineering) and whether their costs are reasonable for the product price (value analysis).

For UK firms, such a strategy of direct involvement should be of vital importance when we consider that bought-in components and purchases typically account for 50 to 60% of the total costs of a manufactured product, whereas direct labour costs typically account for 20% of manufactured costs. Many firms in the UK are undertaking a more active role with their suppliers, but in many cases there is still a lot of work to be done in this area.

In addition to the constructive relationship with suppliers, the firm will also need to consider the forward linkage to the distributors. Any

KEY CONCEPT 2.8

ACTIVE SUPPLIER AND DISTRIBUTION ARRANGEMENTS

Firms should consider wherever possible that the production process extends backwards to suppliers and forwards to the distribution network of the firm. Close linkages need to be established with suppliers to improve the nature of input quality and reliability. This is of particular importance when 50 to 60% of the total costs of production relates to bought-in components and services. Active linkages are needed with the distribution channel in order to ensure that output 'matches' demand in the market place otherwise the firm will be left carrying excess stocks.

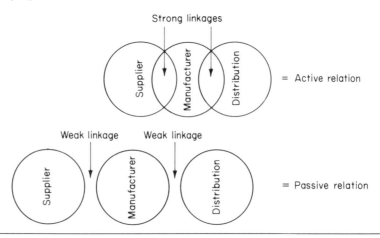

Figure 2.9 Supplier and distribution linkages.

manufacturing process will only approach minimum efficient scale if the output is pulled from the factory gates into the market place. More often than not the manufacturer may consider that the job is done when the product leaves the factory gate. However, the distribution network should be viewed as an extension of the production process and not isolated from it. In order for a mass production system to work the distribution network of the firm must tap into the mass consumption environment. Where dealerships are few and distribution channels inadequate then the firm will suffer from underutilization cost penalties, even though there may well be a substantial enough market for the firm's production capacity to be fully utilized.

Summary

In summary, 'economies of scale' in theory represent the unit cost advantage to be gained from a growth in output which takes the firm down the long-run average cost curve. As we move down the economies of scale curve, it is necessary to increase the size of operations and possibly introduce new technology. In practice the benefits of economies of scale are very difficult to reveal and sustain because it is necessary to pay attention to a number of other essential factors related to the organization of production which are not considered in the conventional economic theory of the firm. New investment must be set against the constraints of existing equipment and plant layout. Economies of scale are market-determined, and attention needs to be paid to the market structure the firm is operating in at home and abroad. The failure of suppliers and the underinvestment in distribution channels may all operate to frustrate the achievement of economies of scale.

It is the case that one of the most commonly used examples of the 'mass' production system is that of the Ford Model 'T'. Ford's corporate investment strategy made use of a mix of existing technologies in a way which was unbeatable in the market place of the early 1900s in the US. His strategy was to delivery a utility vehicle at a price people could afford. In real terms the price of a Model T fell by almost 60% over its production period, and demonstrated that economies of scale could be passed on in the form of lower prices to the customer (Halberstam, 1987). However, as the market for cars developed, individuals were predisposed to purchase a product which could be differentiated from the model T in terms of design and function. They no longer wanted 'any car so long as it was black'. In a market where replacement was the determinant of market demand, the consumers' choice changed and so did the composition of demand for cars. When the market for the product changes, the manufacturer with the more inflexible facilities or dedicated facilities is at a disadvantage relative to the competition. General Motors was able to take advantage of the changing nature of the market place because it offered a variety of cars in the market which appealed to the now developing market segments.

For Ford the crisis of mass production was related to the changing nature of market demand for cars. The market place of the 1980s has indeed become a much more complex place as competition from domestic and more importantly overseas producers operates increasingly to segment and fragment the market place. It is argued that product life cycles are becoming progressively shorter because firms tend to overlap product life cycles so that as one product phases out the other is being phased in.

New technology and the market place

Against the background of the complex market of the 1980s it is argued that new technology can offer the manufacturer or service enterprise a number of advantages, which in essence allow the firm to 'match' the now more competitive structure of the market place with the output produced by the firm. Goldhar and Jelinek (1983) describe the possibilities of new technology as 'economies of scope' rather than economies of scale. That is, it is necessary for the firm to produce a variety of output in volume, not standard output in volume. However, this is not to argue that economies of scale are dead because in many circumstances, such as the manufacture of standard components or products where market demand is sufficient, economies of scale still operate.

However, with new computer technologies utilizing computer aided design (CAD), and computer aided manufacturing (CAM), it is becoming possible for the firm to manufacture in volume a variety of output for the now more complex market structure. Where computer aided design and manufacture are integrated then we have what is termed computer integrated manufacture (CIM). The future, it is argued, now lies with automation and not inflexible giantism of the old-fashioned kind. Here the firm can alter its product mix more rapidly than in the past and so adjust to the needs of the market in a more 'flexible' way. An enterprise that is successful with new technology can, it is argued, now maintain throughput by changing the output mix to the requirements of the market without suffering the penalties of underutilized 'dedicated' equipment at low volume. This idea is illustrated with a simple example below.

Production process	*Market share 10%*	
Dedicated technology	Product A 1000 units	
Flexible technology	Two product types	A 500 units
		B 500 units

With old dedicated technology the firm can obtain a market share of 10% selling 1000 units. However, consider a situation where the market place becomes more competitive such that with dedicated equipment and a standard product the firm will steadily lose market share and incur increased unit costs of production. With flexible technology it is possible to produce, say, two products A and B, so that where demand for say A falls below 500 units it may well be possible to produce more of product B to compensate and still maintain throughput. This sort of flexibility exists at the Ford Dagenham car production facility. Here it is possible to shift the product mix from Fiestas to Sierras or from a small to a medium car and as a result maintain the level of plant utilization by adjusting the product mix.

We will firstly review some of the advantages that are commonly used to justify the introduction of new technology in the firm.

Reduced development lead time

It is argued that the use of powerful computer technology by firms now allows manufacturers to design products with the use of computer aided design (CAD) software. In areas of product design the use of computer technology can drastically cut the lead time from product conception to construction of prototypes and then final versions of the new product. CAD eliminates the use of traditional engineering and drafting jobs and may also allow the designer to incorporate changes in structural properties, and to make rapid design adjustments. According to Freeman and Jones (1986)

> The designer can analyse for stress, check for compliance with codes, and test for linkages with other modules in a complex system in a matter of seconds. He can modify the design and test out the effects in a variety of ways, without the need for whole sets of new drawings. CAD already facilitates a much closer integration between design, production planning and orders for tooling.

Strategically this technology can allow the firm to react to changing market needs more rapidly by shortening the lead time from design to final manufacture. For industries that operate in rapidly changing markets (Hi-Fi, TVs, VCRs etc.) the potential of such equipment is obvious. The benefit of new CAD technology is that it can if properly utilized cut the turnaround time from old to new product lines significantly. However, it is of no use designing and redesigning products if this design flexibility is not matched with manufacturing flexibility. In addition, for some products design and development costs are very high and as such the product life cycle has to be, for financial necessity, longer.

Design changes to a product or production process often have 'network' effects elsewhere in the production process. Changes in the product's specification may well require changes in plant layout, the purchase of new machinery and as a result more heavy financial expenditure. If the firm is financially constrained, design changes need to be set against and accommodated within existing capital plant and equipment and/or require minimal adjustments to plant layout. Where the firm has the necessary financial resources it is important that 'design flexibility' be matched with the capabilities of the 'Flexible manufacturing system' (FMS) itself.

Flexible manufacturing systems (FMS)

According to Shah (1987)

> Flexible Manufacturing Systems (FMS) are being implemented at a fast rate in Japan. The driving force behind this development is the priority given to improving productivity rates in a production and market environment characterized by rising costs, decreasing product life spans, increasing numbers of product variants and the resulting shift from rigid production lines to adaptable, computer controlled set ups.

KEY CONCEPT 2.9

FLEXIBLE MANUFACTURING SYSTEM

A flexible manufacturing system is one which uses computer software and hardware to establish a production system that can react quickly to the changing requirements of the market place. Such a system uses advanced manufacturing systems that can automatically transfer and process materials for use in final products. Such a system is said to be more flexible than a mass production environment in which standardized products are made on dedicated inflexible equipment.

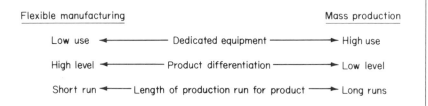

What then is the difference between a computer-aided manufacturing system (CAM) and a flexible manufacturing system? and what are some of the perceived benefits for the firm when it invests in FMS technologies?

It is clear that the difference between CAM and FMS is related to the *extent* of automation and the *diversity* of the parts/products that can be produced. A computer-aided manufacturing system might well consist of a number of machines producing one or more parts where manufacturing operations are controlled by a computer, but the raw material drawn from stores is transferred from one machine to another using manual handling. However, an FMS is defined as essentially one in which materials are handled and processed automatically. Thus an FMS is defined as:

> An integrated, computer controlled complex of automated material handling devices and numerically controlled (NC) machine tools that can simultaneously process medium sized volumes of a variety of part types.

We could also use this definition for 'flexible' services and use automatic cash dispenser machines as an example. Here a variety of cash dispensing amounts can be obtained as well as a variety of services, where the cash taken out is automatically debited against the account with minimal or no manual operations in between.

It is 'flexibility' that is the main characteristic of FMS. In this sense, flexibility is thought of as the ease with which adjustments to the firm's product mix, to meet changes in demand, take place. Strategically, therefore the most important perceived benefit of FMS technology is that it can deliver variety in volume. FMS, then, it is argued, sits somewhere between traditional mass production of a very few products/variants and manufacturing systems of a conventional nature that undertake 'job lot' production. The position of FMS is illustrated in the diagram below.

In practice it may not be possible for the firm to invest in either a 'greenfield' site in which new technology can be incorporated in a totally new plant layout or in a re-organization of existing facilities. The firm in

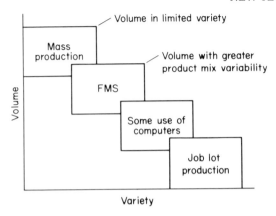

Figure 2.10 The position of FMS.

Source: ECE
Recent Trends in Flexible Manufacturing.

practice will encounter resource constraints (for example the lack of necessary finance on the right terms and conditions or the necessary labour skills, see Chapter 3). As a result of these constraints the firm must introduce flexibility where it is necessary and where it can plausibly contribute to some form of strategic/market advantage. In addition the organization will need to ask itself the question 'flexibility for what purpose?'. As a recent study on flexible manufacturing systems (FMS) has shown, there are a number of levels of flexibility that the firm may wish to obtain from new technologies.

Machine flexibility
This describes the ease with which new machines can be reset with respect to tooling, fixturing and positioning. Although the machines can be repositioned more easily than say, conventional machines, the business will still need to pay attention to the costs of resiting or repositioning and then subsequent running in of the newly-located fixtures.

Process flexibility
This is the ability to produce a given set of parts but using different material types.

Expansion flexibility
With new technologies such as FMS it is possible to adjust the level of throughput either positively or negatively through the addition or subtraction of modular units of the FMS, namely the FMC (flexible machining cell or centre).

Operational flexibility
At an operational level it is now possible, through the use of computer control, to develop systems that allow different parts to be delivered to a particular point in the production process for assembly into different products or variants of the same product.

Product flexibility
Here the firm is able to obtain (a) product mix variability from the technology it is operating or (b) rapid changeover from one product type

CASE STUDY 2.2

**NEW TECHNOLOGY
AND AUSTIN ROVER**

During the late 1970s and early 1980s Austin Rover undertook an investment programme which involved the introduction of more 'flexible' assembly operations at its two production plants. This technology would allow the firm to build cars that would meet the requirements of the market place.

At Austin Rover's Longbridge plant where the Metro is built the firm invested in the old-style dedicated technology designed to build only one type of small car. At Cowley the firm had the opportunity to invest in new flexible manufacturing systems. When completed the Cowley plant was able to cope with identifying, welding and manufacturing up to five different body types. At Cowley it was recognized that 'the planning of the next generation of cars ... will require much more flexible facilities'. At Cowley two models, the Maestro and the Montego were to be built in the one plant including their variants. At Cowley over 100 robots were installed and for the first time new 'portal' robots were used.

However, when completed the Cowley works was much less 'flexible' than had been anticipated – 'the new plant was laid out such that the line, which could deliver more flexibility than the company wanted, delivered less product mix flexibility than the company needed'. The inferiority of the production process at Cowley can be demonstrated by an examination of the Ford Dagenham plant which was constructed at roughly the same time as that at Cowley. At the Dagenham plant the new robotic finishing line could, in the late 1980s, process two entirely different models, the small car Fiesta and the medium car Sierra, whereas the Cowley plant at Austin Rover sends down the line two related models the Maestro and the Montego which are roughly 60% the same car. In addition, on completion of the production facilities at Cowley the Maestro and the Montego were sent down two separate lines which only served to duplicate equipment needs. The resulting difference in *product mix* flexibility is considerable.

The Ford system by way of contrast was designed to deal with variations in the mix of demand for the Fiesta and the Sierra, whereas at Austin Rover the system of manufacture involved a 50/50 mix, so that where one model was failing in the market this line became increasingly underutilized because the firm could not shift from one model mix to another on the one production line.

Fundamentally the point raised by the Austin Rover case study is that the potential of new flexible manufacturing technologies is complex, and much depends on how and for what purpose that new technology is exploited by the organization. At Austin Rover the firm invested in new technology but this only delivered more inflexible manufacturing systems and hence product mix. This was indeed contrary to what the company needed, and, when the demand for the Maestro did not materialize at anything like the level expected the *fixity* of the new capital intensive way of building cars became a financial liability for Austin Rover.

Further reading
Williams, K. *et al.*, (1987).

to another when a particular product mix is becoming outdated and losing market share. With regard to both of these points new flexible manufacturing technologies can allow the firm to adjust its product mix operationally to suit the pattern of demand on a week-by-week basis. Rather than obtain economies of scale – the mass production of a standard product, the firm can aim for economies of scope – the mass production of a range of product types for the market place.

Strategically, it is argued that product mix variability can give the firm a positive advantage over the firm or competitors that can only produce one particular product targetted at one particular segment. As we have seen it is possible for the firm to adjust the product 'mix' to meet the requirements of the market which has increasingly become more segmented and fragmented.

In the case study on Austin Rover we examine just how successful the firm was in obtaining 'flexibility' from investments in new FMS type technologies.

The case study on Austin Rover serves to illustrate how expectations from a particular investment in new technology can diverge from actual experience in practice. It is clear that some degree of flexibility was achieved at Austin Rover (namely the ability to produce variants of say a Maestro on the one line). However, this is not the sort of model mix variability achieved at Ford Dagenham where two entirely different cars have been produced on the same line. For Austin Rover, successful execution of investment in product mix flexibility was crucial for a firm that was trying to survive in an increasingly fragmented and segmented market place.

These arguments are all the more pertinent when we realize that advanced technology is indeed very costly. A European survey of FMS in Europe estimates that on average an FMS system costs over $3 million. Large investments in such technology make it imperative that the firm manages to do the following.

☐ Produce a large enough product family (in terms of both the number of parts and volume of each part) over a sufficient length of time so as to ensure a sufficiently high degree of utilization and hence cost recovery of the FMS investment outlay. This point has already been made in the section on economies of scale. The more capital intensive the system of manufacture becomes, the greater the need to ensure that growth in output is sufficient to utilize fully the investments made.

☐ Balance up the production process so that investments in FMS technology at one stage in the process are not constrained by design constraints or capacity limitations of downstream or upstream processes. A business may have improved productivity in one location of the overall system, but these gains will be cancelled out where other locations have a lower productivity potential. The most efficient stage in any system will be constrained by the least efficient stage in the overall system where each stage is interlinked. More importantly, planned labour and capital productivity gains from a new investment will not be realized if this is the case.

☐ Establish a relationship with suppliers which is constructed such that they are able to deliver the quality and variability of parts mix that is necessary for the flexible manufacturing system installed. Here it is necessary to be 'actively' rather than 'passively' involved with suppliers. Active linkages of the type promoted by Japanese and some UK firms with their suppliers allow the firm to have greater control over the quality and reliability of the parts and bought-in materials that account for between 50 and 60% of total manufacturing costs (De Meyer *et al.*, 1986; Ingersoll Engineers, 1987; New and Myers, 1986).

☐ Invest in a sufficient degree of re-skilling of the workforce so that advanced FMS machinery is run 'flexibly' rather than as if it were a conventional piece of equipment (Jaikumar, 1986). Many systems are not sufficiently utilized because the employer has not invested sufficient time and effort in training the workforce to operate equipment effectively.

☐ Construct forward linkages to distributors in the market place so as to establish a closer linkage between the manufacturing function and the requirements of the market. The Japanese have designed their KANBAN stock and manufacture control system with this in mind. Orders for the products being manufactured are fed back to the manufacturing process as a signal for more production. Output is 'pulled' through the system and components and materials are bought-in just in time for manufacture. Such systems are seen as an obvious way of controlling balanced manufacturing operations such that the maximum value is added to throughput in shortest possible time with a minimum of stocks.

☐ Finally, with all mass production systems, producing more or less variety, the benefits of investing in new technology can only be realized when the market for the finished or intermediate product sold is sufficient to utilize capacity to its fullest extent. According to Verdoorn's Law, productivity is positively related to the growth in output. Any investment in new additional capacity must be made on the premise that market demand will be sufficient to fill this space. Failure to anticipate the market correctly will result in a reduction in productivity which can then only be defended by reductions in labour and capital inputs – redundancy and the closure of plant capacity.

In summary we have seen that academics, production engineers, management and politicians have all in the past argued for and sponsored technological change. We have looked at two examples of how the benefits of new technology can be represented – namely through economies of scale or economies of scope. In both cases the decision, to invest in new capital to realize economies of scale or economies of scope, must be supported with other considerations. On their own these concepts cannot help us. In an uncertain market environment where firms typically run complex multi-plant, multi-product, multi-process systems, management must be aware of the many real conditions and actions that must be taken in order to realize fully the benefits that new technologies promise.

Further reading

It is well worth reading the article in the *Economist* (May 30th, 1987) entitled 'Factory of the Future'. This will provide you with a good understanding of the changes that are taking place in manufacturing systems and a good introduction and background to this chapter.

Also have a look at A. Griffiths and S. Wall *Applied Economics* (Longman) on economies of scale, or T. Hill *Manufacturing Strategy* (Macmillan, 1985), pp. 82–9, and Chapter 4 on economies of scale and flexible manufacturing systems.

There are a number of important articles which cover some of the main points in this chapter. J. Goldhar and M. Jelinek 'Plan for economies of scope' (*Harvard Business Review* Nov/Dec, 1983). R. Jaikumar 'Post industrial manufacturing' (*Harvard Business Review* Nov/Dec, 1986) and K. Williams *et al.* 'The end of mass production?' (*Economy and Society*, Sept. 1987).

Exercises

1. What do you understand by the term economies of scale? Illustrate your answer with relevant examples.

2. What are the differences between technical and economic concepts of efficiency?.

3. Compare and contrast the terms 'economies of scale' and 'economies of scope'. Illustrate your answer with relevant examples.

4. In the early 1970s the British Steel Corporation believed it could obtain the benefits of economies of scale. What other factors needed to be considered in order to obtain the benefits that economies of scale promised for the BSC?

5. What are the different types of flexibility offered by flexible manufacturing systems? Are there any market advantages available to a firm that successfully invests in this type of new technology?

6. What do you understand by the terms labour and capital productivity? What are some of the difficulties associated with measuring capital and labour productivity?

7. 'Investments in new technology usually require a substantial commitment of financial resources. As a consequence it is necessary that the firm correctly estimates growth in future demand and fully integrates the new technology within existing systems'. Discuss this statement.

References

Bryer, R. *et al.* (1982) *Accounting for British Steel*, Gower, Aldershot.
Cockerill, A. *et al.* (1974) University of Cambridge Occasional Paper no. 42.
De Meyer, A. *et al.* (1986) *Flexibility the Next Competitive Battle*, INSEAD, Fontainebleau, France 86/31.
European Commission for Europe (1986) *Recent Trends in Flexible Manufacturing*, UN, New York.
Freeman, C. and Jones, D. (1986) *Technical Trends and Employment in Engineering and Vehicles*, Gower, Aldershot.

Goldhar, J. and Jelinek, M. (1983) Plan for economies of scope. *Harvard Business Review*, Nov./Dec. pp. 141–8.

Halberstam, D. (1987) *The Reckoning*, Bantam Books, New York.

Ingersoll Engineers (1987) *Procurement, Materials Management and Distribution*, Ingersoll Engineers, Rugby.

Jaikumar, R. (1986) Post industrial manufacturing. *Harvard Business Review*, Nov./Dec.

New, C. and Myers, A. (1986) *Managing Manufacturing Operations in the UK 1975 to 1985*, Cranfield Institute of Management, Bedford.

Ohmae, K. (1982) *The Mind of the Strategist*, McGraw Hill, New York.

Pryke, R. (1981) *The Nationalised Industries*, Martin Robertson, Oxford.

Scherer, F.M. (1975) *Economics of Multi-Plant Operation*, Harvard University Press.

Shah, R. (1987) Manufacturing operations. In *Manufacturing Systems*. (ed. V. Bignell), Blackwell, Oxford.

Williams, K. *et al.* (1986) Accounting for the failure of nationalised industries. *Economy and Society*, May.

Williams, K. *et al.* (1987) *The Breakdown of Austin Rover*, Berg, Leamington Spa.

The organization of labour $\boxed{3}$ ||||||

Introduction

At the heart of the personnel function in modern business is a recognition that workers are people, and that management has to win their support for the achievement of company goals. Yet traditionally, labour economics has gone to considerable lengths to deny the human attributes of labour, treating workers as a 'factor of production', a commodity whose behaviour, like that of any commodity, is determined by the impersonal forces of supply and demand.

This chapter starts with an outline of the traditional neo-classical approach, and the problems that arise from its exclusion of the human element. It goes on to explore a variety of environmental and organizational influences on labour demand, labour supply and pay, drawing on alternative and more realistic approaches. Finally, we examine some of the labour market strategies pursued by British firms in recent years, and assess their wider economic implications.

The neo-classical theory of the labour market

The neo-classical theory of the labour market elaborates the profit-maximizing theory of the firm in the context of the hiring of labour. It consists of three main elements.

☐ A theory of the firm's demand for labour, based on the concept of marginal productivity.
☐ A theory of labour supply, based on the concept of utility maximization.
☐ A theory of labour market competition, based on the idea that wages vary to equate labour demand and labour supply.

A firm's demand for labour is determined by the demand for its products and by the productivity of its workforce. If other factors of production can be substituted for labour as they become relatively cheaper, then, neo-classical theory suggests, there will be an inverse relationship between the quantity of labour demanded and the wage level (other things being equal). To maximize profits, a firm will hire workers up to the point where the value of the output produced by the last unit of labour exactly equals the cost of hiring it. More formally, the firm will equate the marginal revenue product of labour (its marginal physical product multiplied by the

KEY CONCEPT 3.1

SUBSTITUTION AND
INCOME EFFECTS

In the neo-classical theory of consumer choice, a price increase has a
depressing effect on quantity demanded for two reasons:
1. Relative prices will change, encouraging consumers to substitute
other commodities for the commodity in question (the substitution
effect).
2. Real income falls, causing demand for all commodities, including the
commodity in question, to fall (the income effect).

   In the field of consumer choice, substitution and income effects
combine in most cases to establish an inverse relationship between
price and quantity demanded. In the field of labour supply, however, the
effects pull in opposite directions, so that the relationship between wage
and hours of labour supplied is indeterminate.

marginal revenue the firm obtains from the sale of an extra unit) to its
marginal cost.

   On the supply side of the labour market, neo-classical theory assumes
that individual workers choose between time spent in paid work and time
spent at 'leisure' (including unpaid work!) so as to maximize their utility, in
much the same way as individual consumers are assumed to choose
between different purchases. A wage increase will have a contradictory
effect on labour supply. On the one hand it will raise the cost of leisure, in
terms of pay opportunities forgone (the substitution effect) (Key Concept
3.1). On the other hand, it will increase income, and with it the demand for
leisure (the income effect). For some individuals, the substitution effect
will outweigh the income effect, and a wage increase will increase labour
supply. For others, the opposite may well be the case.

   Finally, having related labour demand to marginal productivity, and
labour supply to the allocation of time between paid work and leisure, neo-
classical theory suggests that competitive forces operate in labour markets,
just as in commodity markets, to establish an equilibrium price (wage)
which rises and falls to equate the quantity of labour demanded with the
quantity of labour supplied. In the short run, market imperfections like
geographical immobility might allow pay differentials to emerge, but in the
long run free access of workers to job vacancies would ensure pay equality
between workers who generate the same productivity. Persistent pay
differentials will reflect different investments in 'human capital' (Key
Concept 3.2), and are needed to match the supply and demand of 'quality'
labour. At the level of the economy as a whole, wages would rise or fall to
ensure that there was no involuntary unemployment.

   For a formal, diagrammatic analysis of the neo-classical approach to
labour markets, you are referred to the Appendix at the end of this
chapter.

Limitations of the neo-classical approach

You will remember from Chapter 1 that there are a number of problems
associated with the neo-classical theory of product markets, which limit its
usefulness as a tool for understanding modern business reality. In

Neo-classical theory sees individuals as embodying not just the capacity to work, but 'human capital', the product of deliberate 'investment' in education, training and on-the-job experience. The acquisition of human capital involves an immediate cost in terms of pay and other opportunities forgone, but it also involves a subsequent return in terms of higher pay. In choosing between different types of human capital investment, individuals, it is suggested, will be influenced by the rate of return they can expect. Changes in demand for 'quality' labour will affect pay and thus expected returns, bringing about appropriate adjustments in human capital investment and thus supply.

KEY CONCEPT 3.2

HUMAN CAPITAL

particular, the theory oversimplifies the objective functions of modern business, and underestimates the difficulties posed by lack of information in an uncertain environment. These problems are also shared by the neo-classical approach to labour markets. Here we highlight three additional problems which are specific to labour market theory.

Variable productivity

Neo-classical theory assumes that, if capital equipment and technical knowledge are both given, there is a fixed relationship between labour input and output. Labour productivity will, accordingly, change only if there is a change in capital equipment, or in technology. In practice, however, there are enormous differences in labour productivity between firms, even where the capital equipment and technology are similar. Employment contracts give an indication of the tasks workers are expected to perform, but these can be specified precisely only when product demand is stable, and where production methods do not change. In the more usual circumstance where there is an element of uncertainty about future product demand, and where new production methods are periodically introduced, employment contracts will be more specific about the hours which are worked than about the work which is done within those hours.

Imperfectly specified contracts provide an essential element of flexibility for management to be able to respond to changed circumstances, but they also open up considerable potential for conflict between managers and workers as to how much work is actually performed within the contracted hours. Even more significantly for productivity, however, there are considerable differences between firms in how effectively managers do the following.

☐ Coordinate different work tasks.
☐ Make full use of the technologies which are available.
☐ Develop products with sufficient sales potential to make best use of plant capacity.

In short, it is dangerous to assume, as marginal productivity theory does, that the relationship between time and effort is unproblematic, or that all employers are equally competent in utilizing the capacities of their workforce.

Structured labour markets

Central to the neo-classical approach is a picture of labour markets which are open, in the sense that all jobs are continuously open to all potential workers on the same terms. This, it is suggested, results in an equitable distribution of rewards and opportunities between comparable workers, with pay being determined in each case by the value of the marginal worker's product. The only differences between workers which are recognized in this theory are those relating to skill, monopsony and union organization. In the first case, it is suggested that wage differentials based on skill will encourage appropriate investments in human capital, bringing about a new equilibrium between pay and marginal product. In the second case, where a local labour market is dominated by a single employer, it is allowed that workers may be paid less than the value of their marginal product. In the third case, it is argued, trade unions can boost pay by influencing the supply of labour, but their capacity to do this without destroying jobs is limited by the degree of competition in the local labour market. (These last two points are elaborated further in the Appendix to this chapter.)

The evidence is, however, that differences between workers in modern labour markets are much more significant than neo-classical theory allows. In particular, different groups of workers are compartmentalized into different segments of the labour market, with only limited competition between these segments. As a result, significant differences in pay and working conditions emerge between workers who otherwise share similar attributes, and competitive forces are insufficiently powerful to remove these differences.

Ceteris paribus assumptions

Ceteris paribus is a Latin phrase, frequently used by neo-classical economists to mean 'other things being constant'. If we say, 'a rise in price will lead to a fall in quantity demanded, *ceteris paribus*', we are isolating the effect of a price change from the effects of other changes (in income, for example). While in real life other things rarely remain constant, *ceteris paribus* assumptions are frequently useful in isolating the effects of different independent variables (price, income, etc) on a dependent variable (quantity demanded). If the variables we are comparing are not independent of each other but linked in some way, however, then *ceteris paribus* assumptions may be positively misleading. This is, in fact, the case with the neo-classical theory of demand for labour.

In positing an inverse relationship between the price of labour (the wage) and the quantity of labour demanded, neo-classical theory assumes that other influences on quantity demanded, such as labour productivity, are constant. Yet there is considerable real world evidence to suggest that where wages are low, labour is used inefficiently, and firms find it hard to motivate their existing workforce or to attract higher quality workers. In such a situation, a rise in wages will often stimulate improvements in labour productivity. If the increased labour productivity enables a firm to increase its sales, the firm could, in many circumstances, concede increased wages without having to lay off workers.

Some neo-classical economists have concluded from the micro-economic theory of labour demand that, at the macro level, wage cuts would increase jobs. Again, there is a misuse of *ceteris paribus* assumptions here. Any inverse relationship between wage and quantity of labour demanded assumes that product demand remains constant. Yet, at the macro-economic level, wages are positively related to product demand, and in certain circumstances a general wage cut could increase unemployment, via its negative impact on product demand. This point was at the heart of Keynes's critique of the neo-classical approach to unemployment (1936), as we shall see in Chapter 9.

Environmental and organizational influences on labour demand

To understand the complexities of labour market behaviour in the real world, we have to take explicit account of the environmental and organizational influences which neo-classical theory tends to ignore. We consider some of the most important of these influences in this and the following two sections. On the demand side, we focus on the level and composition of demand for labour, and the demand for skills.

The level of demand

A firm's demand for labour is derived from the demand for its products, which depends fundamentally on its success in anticipating and satisfying consumer wants as expressed in the market place. As we saw in Chapter 1, this means understanding the variety of (mainly non-price) characteristics that modern consumers require, and competing successfully with other firms in selling products which incorporate these characteristics.

At the national level, governments can stimulate (or contract) consumer spending through their fiscal and monetary policies, and this will have a direct effect on demand for labour in retailing and other services. In a closed economy, there would also be a substantial impact on demand for labour in manufacturing, but in an open economy this effect is spread over a number of different national economies. In Britain in recent years, as we shall see in Chapters 7 and 9, government stimulation of consumer demand has been associated more with an increase in manufacturing imports than with an increase in manufacturing jobs.

An important subsidiary influence on demand for labour is the effect of technological and other changes on labour productivity. In British manufacturing industry, output per person hour has been rising on a long-term trend path of about 3% per year for the past couple of decades (Marris, 1987). This means that for manufacturing employment to remain constant, manufacturing output has to rise by around 3% per year. If manufacturing output falls (as it did, dramatically, in 1973–75 and 1979–81) – then the fall in manufacturing jobs will be even more severe.

The current generation of new micro-electronic technology has an enormous capacity to displace labour, in a range of different occupational fields. A recent survey suggests that on average there has been a net loss of about 45 000 UK manufacturing jobs per year associated with the use of micro-electronics over the period 1983–7 (Northcott and Walling, 1988). Against this, however, there are indirect job creation effects elsewhere in the economy, particularly where product applications are involved. In addition, any job losses from the introduction of new technology have to be weighed against the job losses associated with the loss of competitiveness which results from a failure to innovate.

Neo-classical theory assumes that there is a strong inverse relationship between the price of labour and the quantity of labour demanded. In practice, however, price will be just one of many factors influencing the ratio of labour to other factor inputs, not least of these being calculations which management make independently of price movements. Where, for example, there are rigidities in the way production is organized, it can seem that the factor mix which is needed to produce a given output is fixed, even when factor prices are changing. Where, on the other hand, management is actively seeking to reorganize production to reduce labour costs, the factor mix will change, even when factor prices stay the same. A rise in direct labour costs will, of course, usually be passed on to consumers in the form of higher prices, and this might have a negative effect on product demand and thus demand for labour. However, it should be noted that direct labour costs account for only 18% of total manufacturing costs (Table 3.7), and the resulting price changes will in many cases have only a negligible effect on product demand, given the greater significance of non-price factors which we identified in Chapter 2.

The composition of demand

It is sometimes argued that it does not matter if demand for labour in manufacturing is declining, so long as demand for labour in services is rising. The implication is that increases in one sector can compensate for declines in another, both quantitatively and qualitatively, and that workers who are displaced from manufacturing are taken on in services. Recent experience in Britain does not bear this out, however.

While it is true that service employment in Britain has been rising throughout the post-war period (except in 1980–82), a high proportion of

Table 3.1 Employees in employment, June 1977 and 1987 (GB, thousands)

| | Manufacturing | | Services | |
	1977	1987	1977	1987
Males	5058	3570	6035	6639
(of which part-time)	(na)	(53)	(na)	(790)
Females	2114	1501	6663	7888
(of which part-time)	(499)	(290)	(3029)	(3859)
Total	7172	5071	12 698	14 527

Source: Employment Gazette.

the gains have been in part-time jobs for women. Most of the losses in manufacturing, however, have been in full-time jobs for men. Table 3.1 presents the basic data for the decade since 1977. You should note that both male and female employment in manufacturing declined by 29% in this decade. Male employment in services increased by 10%, while female employment in this sector increased by 18% (most of the increase being part-time).

The spatial composition of demand for labour has also changed dramatically in recent years (Massey, 1984). Again, there seems to be little match between jobs lost in manufacturing and jobs gained in services. Indeed, many of the gains in service jobs seem to be associated with relative manufacturing success. The few areas of actual job growth – in the Outer South East region and parts of the South West and East Anglia, for example – have combined large job gains in services with lower than average losses in manufacturing. The areas suffering the most serious losses in manufacturing, however – Greater London, the West Midlands, the North and North West – have seen only a weak gain in service jobs (Hall, 1987).

The demand for skills

To use any technology effectively, a firm needs an appropriate mix of skills in its workforce. In choosing which products to make, and how to go about making them, the firm will be constrained by the capacities of its existing workforce, and by the prospects of recruiting new workers with the requisite skills. Changes in technology will have effects on productivity and company profits, not only directly through changes in productive efficiency, but indirectly through changes in work organization.

KEY CONCEPT 3.3

LABOUR PROCESS

The term 'labour process' was coined by Karl Marx in 1867, to describe the way raw materials are transformed by human activity into useful objects (Marx, 1976). The capitalist labour process, Marx suggested, differs from other labour processes in two ways.

☐ Workers work under the control of the capitalist.
☐ Their products belong to the capitalist.
   Because capitalists aim to produce commodities whose value exceeds that of the commodities used in their production, they are encouraged to develop production methods which subordinate workers to their direct control.
   Contemporary academic interest in the labour process has been stimulated by Harry Braverman, who extended Marx's analysis to cover twentieth century developments (1974). Doubts have been expressed about the validity of Braverman's tendency to reduce all production decisions to a desire on the part of management to de-skill the workforce, but Braverman has successfully drawn attention to the fact that they involve considerations of control as well as of technical efficiency.

Harry Braverman, in his influential book *Labor and Monopoly Capital* (1974), presents a mass of historical evidence indicating that, with mechanization, jobs have become fragmented, and workers de-skilled. This, he suggests, is due more to a desire on the part of management to take control over the labour process (Key Concept 3.3) away from craft workers than to considerations of technical efficiency. Subsequent research suggests, however, that Braverman has underestimated both the ability of skilled workers to resist de-skilling and the extent ot which some new technologies might create new skills as well as destroy old ones (Wood, 1989).

Fragmentation of jobs and the replacement of craft workers by machines and machine minders have certainly been characteristic of work processes involving the mass production of standardized products, though in some cases (notably the Swedish car industry in the 1970s) employers have allowed autonomous group working in an attempt to cut down the absenteeism and turnover costs resulting from worker dissatisfaction with repetitive jobs. When flexible manufacturing systems are used to produce differentiated products for fragmenting markets, however, de-skilling may be a totally inappropriate strategy for management. Effective use of micro-electronic systems requires at least a core of the workforce to have well-developed hybrid skills, combining, for example, craft and technician skills, engineering and design skills, mechanical and electronic skills, or operator and diagnostic skills (Burgess, 1985 and Northcott, 1986). Where these systems are being continuously developed, management may need employees to update their skills continually, and to be able to identify and rectify faults rapidly (Buchanan, 1987).

When the capacities of new manufacturing systems to produce a flexible product mix are exploited, the levels of skill and training required may be very high indeed. Mostly, this effect occurs at the top of the occupational hierarchy. Jaikumar, in a study of flexible manufacturing systems in Japanese factories (1986), points to the crucial role of engineering teams, and notes that 'engineers now outnumber production workers three to one'. It is nonetheless the case that firms in Britain which have been unwilling to train and retrain their production workers are not able to take full advantage of the flexibility of modern manufacturing systems. Where firms try to make full use of this flexibility, unforeseen problems may occur on the shop floor, and because workers are not sufficiently skilled (or not allowed) to solve them the resulting delays can be extremely disruptive and costly (Senker and Beesley, 1986). Alternatively, some firms may make operational decisions which result in less flexibility than was expected at the planning stage.

Environmental and organizational influences on labour supply

In this section, we focus on four aspects of labour supply where environmental and organizational influences are particularly significant – labour force participation, hours worked, the supply of effort, and the supply of skill.

Labour force participation

There are a number of cultural and political factors which limit labour force participation (the proportion of a population who are in paid employment or seeking it). There are, for example, extensive legal restrictions on child labour, while at the other end of the age spectrum provision of retirement pensions limits the need for older adults to seek paid employment. Some young adults delay entry into the labour market by staying on in the education system, while some adult family members (usually women) withdraw from the labour market to spend time looking after dependants and maintaining the family home.

There have been many changes over the years in labour force participation by different social groups. The school leaving age has been raised, for example, and more young people are staying on in the education system, encouraged by the growing use of educational qualifications by employers as a screening device in selecting applicants for high-paid jobs. Some older people are retiring earlier, encouraged in some cases by government schemes to ease the burdens of redundancy and unemployment for younger workers. By far the most significant trend in recent decades, however, has been increased labour force participation by women, who by 1987 constituted 46% of all employees in employment (compared with 34% in 1951).

As Table 3.2 shows, labour force participation by women has risen particularly dramatically amongst the over-30s, and this is associated with an increasing tendency for married women with children to return to the labour market when their children are old enough to go to school.

Table 3.2 Percentage of women aged 20–59 who are in the labour force, GB 1951–87

Age	1951	1961	1971	1981	1987
20–24	64	62	60	69	70
25–29	44	44	43	56 ⎫	64
30–34	38	41	45	56 ⎬	
35–44	39	47	56	68	73
45–54	40	50	59	68	71
55–59	30	40	49	53	53
20–59	42	48	54	63	67

Sources: Joshi and Owen, 1987; *Employment Gazette.*

In seeking to understand the labour supply decisions of married women with children, the basic neo-classical model is particularly inappropriate. The use of the term 'leisure' to describe time not spent in paid employment is, as Shirley Dex has noted (1985) 'a peculiarly male choice of label', ignoring as it does the enormous amount of unpaid work done in the home, by mothers of young children in particular. In fact, family life requires a series of interrelated decisions about labour force participation (to provide income which is needed to purchase consumption goods), unpaid work (to maintain the home and bring up the children), and consumption patterns (involving the allocation of time as well as money). In these circumstances, it is more appropriate, for married men as well as married women, to focus on the household rather than the individual as the main locus of decision-making about labour supply. This requires an understanding of the different positions of women and men within the family as well as in the labour market.

In Britain, as in most industrial countries, men have traditionally taken on few of the responsibilities for childcare and housework, and women have been discriminated against in access to higher-paid jobs. It is not surprising, therefore, that women with children have lower labour force participation rates than other groups. What has changed is that their withdrawal from the labour force has become temporary rather than permanent, and a number of interrelated developments on the supply and the demand sides of the labour market have helped bring this about. The following are particularly significant.

☐ The high level of aggregate demand in the 1950s and 1960s encouraged employers to recruit new sources of labour.
☐ The changing composition of demand away from heavy industry and towards services has expanded many jobs which have traditionally been done by women, while many traditionally 'male' jobs have declined.
☐ New products such as vacuum cleaners, washing machines, convenience foods, freezers, and microwave ovens have reduced the time which needs to be spent on unpaid housework.
☐ The expectations of married women have changed.

Intensified efforts to recruit more married women returners can be expected into the mid-1990s, as employers attempt to counteract the impact of declining numbers of school-leavers.

Hours worked

The growth in female employment in post-war Britain has been almost entirely a growth in part-time jobs, as Table 3.3 indicates. Part-time employment is much more significant in Britain than in other industrial countries (Beechey and Perkins, 1987), and a quarter of all employees (female and male) are employed part-time.

Table 3.3 Percentage of female employees who are employed part-time, GB 1951–87

1951	1961	1971	1981	1987
13	23	36	42	44

Source: Joshi and Owen, 1987; Employment Gazette.

In explaining the growth of part-time employment, both supply and demand factors are again significant.

☐ It is easier for women with children to combine part-time jobs with domestic responsibilities, particularly where community childcare facilities are underdeveloped.

☐ Where jobs require unsocial hours to be worked, or where there are considerable fluctuations in demand, employers value the flexibility that part-time jobs can bring (e.g. evening or Saturday work in retailing).

☐ Where employees work less than 16 hours per week, employers are exempt from the provisions of the Employment Protection Act, making it easier for them to lay off workers when demand is slack.

☐ Employers can pay part-timers at lower hourly rates than full timers, and save on National Insurance contributions.

For most workers who are employed on a full-time basis, basic working hours are fixed. There have, however, been a number of reductions since the mid-nineteenth century (when a 60-hour working week was common), and recent negotiations in the UK engineering industry suggest that a 37½-hour working week may become standard by the early 1990s. Changes in the level of economic activity have been one of the most significant environmental influences on the basic working week. In periods of rising unemployment, as in the early 1980s, trade unions often shift their emphasis from pay bargaining to bargaining over hours, in an attempt to protect jobs and reduce unemployment. Employers, however, are resistant to changes which adversely affect their profitability, and are more willing to accept reductions in hours if these are accompanied by improved labour productivity. The end result, as White (1986) and Curson (1986) have shown, is often an increase in work intensity or a change in working patterns, rather than an increase in jobs.

Traditionally, the main element of flexibility within full-time employment is overtime working, paid at premium rates. The extent of overtime working tends to vary with changes in the level of economic activity. When demand expands, employers often prefer to offer increased overtime rather than recruit extra workers. There are two basic reasons for this.

☐ They can meet increased demand without having to expand overhead labour costs.

☐ If the increase in demand proves to be short-lived, it will be easier to cut back again on overtime working than to declare workers redundant.

Since the recession of the early 1980s, many UK employers have made a determined effort to cut back on overtime working. As we shall see later in the chapter, some have preferred instead to introduce greater flexibility in working hours.

The supply of effort

There is widespread evidence that labour productivity (output per employee) in manufacturing industry is significantly lower in Britain than in other industrial countries (Table 3.7). An idea which has been promoted extensively in the media is that these productivity differences occur because British workers don't work as hard as workers in other countries. More thorough investigations carried out in the 1970s drew attention to the role of outdated plant and machinery in low British productivity, but suggested that there was a residual element which could best be explained

CASE STUDY 3.1

**LABOUR
PRODUCTIVITY
IN METAL WORKING**

International comparisons of labour productivity are notoriously difficult to interpret. Different industries use different production methods, so comparisons of national aggregates (involving different industry mixes) have little meaning. Even where the study is narrowed down to a particular product, there may be variations in the quantity and quality of labour, in the choice of technique, in work patterns, and in plant utilization. The effects of these variations are difficult to disentangle from the effects of any differences in the expenditure of effort.

One study which avoids most of these potential pitfalls was done at the National Institute of Economic and Social Research in 1983–84 (Daly *et al.*, 1985). The National Institute researchers compared simple matched metal products (screws, springs, hydraulic valves, and drill bits) made by six British and six West German firms. The choice of simple products reduced the need to take account of quality variations, and made it possible to measure output in physical terms. It also enabled the researchers to isolate the contribution of operator efficiency to productivity from that of design and technical staff.

In each of the comparisons, the German firms had higher levels of labour productivity, ranging from 10% to 130%. There were no significant differences in direct labour levels between the two countries (though there was some evidence of inefficient use of indirect labour in feeding materials to machines in British plants), and there was little difference in machine running speeds. The machinery used in the British firms was no older than that in the German firms, though technically it was often less advanced, because of a lack of technical competence among British decision–makers, and an unwillingness to contemplate long payback periods. Machine breakdowns were more frequent in Britain than in Germany, and took longer to put right, due largely to a failure to employ sufficient numbers of appropriately skilled fitters and maintenance staff.

About half of the German shopfloor workers had apprenticeship-type qualifications, whereas the British proportion was only a quarter. These differences were most apparent at the supervisory level. Few of the forepersons in the British plants had formal qualifications, while in the German plants nearly all had been trained not just in routine setting and maintenance of machines, but in staff supervision, work organization and light repair work as well. Absence of appropriate skills at all levels, reported one numerically-controlled machine tool manufacturer, meant that 'almost half the machines sold in Britain are not used as they might be, because their full capacity is not understood'. German users, in contrast, were better able to diagnose faults when machines broke down, and to undertake repairs themselves – a major factor in their superior maintenance record. As Daly *et al.* conclude about low British productivity, 'lack of technical expertise and training ... is the main stumbling block.'

Further reading
Daly *et al.* (1985);
Nichols (1986), Chapter 11;
Steedman and Wagner (1987).

by poor 'attitudes to work' (Central Policy Review Staff, 1975; Pratten, 1976).

Theo Nichols, in a careful analysis of research into international productivity differences (1986), shows that most of this research does not explore attitudes to work in any systematic manner, and fails to allow for differences in the way work is organized. As a result, there is little evidence to substantiate the assertion that different national attitudes to work have a significant effect on productivity. A growing body of research, however, of which Case Study 3.1 is a major example, suggests that labour productivity in Britain is adversely affected by low levels of training and poor maintenance standards, factors which reflect more on management competence in organizing work than on workers' attitudes to work.

It is sometimes suggested that the tax and benefit systems operate in such a way as to discourage effort. High income tax rates, it is argued, discourage workers from working as hard as they might, while levels of unemployment benefit discourage some potential workers from seeking employment at all. The evidence suggests that the significance of these effects is much less pronounced than is often claimed. Tax changes have little or no effect on the labour supply decisions of male employees, for example, though they have affected the labour force participation of married women (Brown, 1983). For low-paid married workers with children, however, the tax and benefit systems interact to generate a poverty trap. Here, a rise in gross earnings produces no rise in take-home pay, because of the combined effects of paying standard rate income tax and losing entitlement to income-related benefits. It would not be surprising, in this case, if some workers were discouraged from working longer hours, or seeking higher-paid employment, though there is little evidence of this taking place to any significant extent.

Where pay is low in relation to unemployment and supplementary benefit entitlements, there may in addition be an unemployment trap which discourages unemployed people from seeking a job. Calculations made by Layard and Nickell (1985) suggest that increases in the replacement ratio (the ratio of benefit paid per recipient to post-tax earnings) may have been responsible for about a tenth of the increase in male unemployment between the early 1960s and the late 1970s. None of the increase in unemployment since the late 1970s can be blamed on benefit levels, however, for in the 1980s the replacement ratio has fallen dramatically, as a result of changes in government policy. By 1982, DHSS calculations suggested that only 3% of unemployed men would have had a higher income out of employment than in employment.

The supply of skill

Skills can be acquired informally (at home, or through relevant on-the-job experience) or formally (through the education system, or through training schemes). There is evidence that skills which are acquired informally are insufficiently recognized and rewarded by British employers. In a survey of four manufacturing and two service industries carried out in 1980–81, for example, it was found that a significant number of jobs done by women were not classed as skilled, yet required at least six months on-the-job experience and particular qualities such as manual dexterity and sharp eyesight. Yet women who did such jobs were paid no more than inexperienced casual workers (Craig *et al.*, 1985).

Skill differences between Britain and other industrial countries are most pronounced at the level of intermediate formal qualifications (apprenticeships, City and Guilds certificates, and secretarial qualifications, for example). S.J. Prais, Karin Wagner and Hilary Steedman have done a series of surveys which explore the differences between Britain and West Germany, France and Japan in some detail (Prais, 1981, 1987; Prais and Wagner, 1983, 1985; Prais and Steedman, 1986; Steedman, 1987, 1988). While the variations revealed in these surveys are complex, three findings stand out as particularly significant.

□ International differences in the number of qualified personnel and in the quality of the qualifications are more significant at intermediate than at degree level.
□ Mathematical attainments by average and below-average pupils are significantly lower in British than in West German or Japanese schools, limiting their opportunities to go on to vocational courses.
□ Both the numbers undergoing vocational education and training and the standards required are significantly lower in Britain than in West Germany, Japan, or France.

As Case Study 3.1 shows, even with simple products higher productivity depends on a workforce that is technically skilled at all levels. With the technically more advanced industrial and office systems that are becoming increasingly more commonplace in the modern business world, and the growing need to provide differentiated products for fragmented markets, the implications of deficiencies in the British education and training systems are even more serious. It is disturbing, in this context, to note that British firms spend on average only 0.15% of their sales turnover on adult training, and that the number of trainees in UK manufacturing industry declined from 450 000 in 1967 to 180 000 in 1982. The conclusion that most British firms treat training as an expense rather than an investment is hard to avoid. Government initiatives to improve the quality of the Youth Training Scheme and Employment Training could have a positive role to play here, but the suspicion remains that many firms see such schemes as a source of cheap, 'flexible' labour rather than as a resource for the future, and that the government sees them primarily as a way of bringing down the unemployment figures.

Skill deficiencies are also important among British managers. Fewer than one in seven British managers have received an education in management, and in their jobs they receive on average only one day's formal training per year (Constable and McCormick, 1987). This contrasts with a much greater emphasis on management education and training in other industrial countries, and is part of the explanation of the poor record of British firms in adapting to changed market conditions and in making effective use of the opportunities provided by new technology.

It is not, however, sufficient just to improve the formal qualifications of British managers. One of the most important lessons of an influential study of Japanese firms in Britain is that Japanese managers are more effective because they combine qualifications with detailed knowledge of their company's products, processes and systems (White and Trevor, 1983). The British custom of rapidly promoting qualified managers to senior non-operational positions, while entrusting operational decisions to managers with practical experience but few technical qualifications, is inappropriate to the modern business environment.

Environmental and organizational influences on pay

We have suggested that labour markets are more complex than is assumed in neo-classical theory, and nowhere is this more apparent than in the field of pay determination. In this section, we examine the influence of trade unions on pay, and the organizational and environmental factors which structure labour markets into distinct segments. We also look at the role played by labour market segmentation in determining the extent and nature of low-paid jobs in a modern economy.

Trade unions

Slightly less than half of UK employees are members of a trade union, but around three quarters are in jobs where pay and working conditions are determined by collective bargaining between their employer and a trade union. Current research suggests that unionization adds about 10% to pay levels in an industry (Blanchflower, 1986).

A trade union's ability to improve pay stems basically from its influence over the supply of labour. In the old craft unions, this influence was direct. Skilled printworkers, to take a classic example, effectively controlled access to apprenticeships, restricting entry to their jobs in such a way as to raise significantly the price their labour could command.

Recent changes in work organization made possible by the introduction of new technology have, however, eroded this power, and direct control of entry to jobs is nowadays more common among professional associations than trade unions. What unions retain is an indirect influence over labour supply, through being able to threaten to withdraw labour if their demands are not met.

The effectiveness of a trade union in winning a pay claim reflects its bargaining strength relative to that of the employer. This depends on a number of factors, including the following:

☐ Trade union density (the proportion of employees who are union members).
☐ Trade union militancy (the preparedness of union members to take effective action in support of a claim).
☐ The potential cost to the employer of disruption to output and sales in the event of a strike.
☐ The cost to the employer of conceding the claim.

The strength of these factors will vary as underlying environmental conditions change over time. Trade union membership in the UK, for example, peaked in 1979 at 13.5 million (55% of all civilian employees plus registered unemployed). In the 1980s, however, trade union membership and bargaining power have been weakened by the combined effect of the following.

☐ The economic recession, which has destroyed jobs in highly unionized sectors of the economy, and created a pool of unemployed labour who might be prepared to work at below union rates.
☐ Legislative changes such as the criminalization of secondary picketing (see our companion volume, *Law in a Business Context*), which have weakened the power of a union to pursue a dispute with an employer effectively.
☐ The adoption of a tougher negotiating stance by certain employers (such as Hitachi in South Wales, who were only prepared to recognize a union like the EETPU which would sign a no-strike agreement).

Labour market segmentation

Discussions of 'the' labour market are often premised on an assumption that all workers have equal access to all jobs. This is, however, an oversimplification, and it is more fruitful to start by recognizing the organizational and environmental factors which create distinct segments within labour markets, and limit the movement of workers between those segments. Labour market segmentation, of one form or another, is the source of most pay inequalities and differentials, and in analysing it, we may find it useful to distinguish between those factors which operate on the demand side and those which operate on the supply side of labour markets.

Writers from the USA tend to emphasize labour demand factors, involving the development of internal labour markets (see Key Concept 3.4), as the main driving force behind labour market segmentation.

KEY CONCEPT 3.4	With external labour markets, the pricing and allocation of labour are controlled by economic variables. Pay is determined by the interaction of labour supply and labour demand, and all jobs are open to all potential workers on the same terms.
INTERNAL LABOUR MARKETS	With internal labour markets, on the other hand, the pricing and allocation of labour are controlled by administrative rules. Employers who have significant labour turnover costs, or who want to check out the extent to which individual workers comply with company requirements, will often prefer to develop internal labour markets rather than rely totally on the external market.
	In extreme cases, as with those Japanese workers who are offered lifetime employment, internal labour markets can be totally insulated from the external labour market, except at the basic entry grade. Thereafter, posts will be filled solely by internal promotion, depending on length of service and/or reliability. In Britain, the career structures in the police force and in banking would be good examples of internal labour markets.

Employers, it is suggested, offer certain workers relatively privileged conditions, either to retain the firm-specific skills they have acquired through on-the-job experience (Doeringer and Piore, 1971), or to divide the workforce in order to weaken union capacity to challenge management prerogatives (Gordon *et al.*, 1982). Maintaining such internal labour markets is, however, costly for employers. In sectors where job stability is not required, therefore, jobs continue to be allocated by competitive forces in the external market. Here unstable work behaviour is permitted, and even encouraged, and labour turnover is high. The result, it is argued, is a dual labour market – with one sector characterized by relatively high pay, good working conditions, and promotion ladders; and another sector characterized by low pay, poor working conditions, and no prospects of promotion.

European writers tend to emphasize, in addition to demand factors, the role of labour supply factors, both in segmenting jobs and in allocating workers between 'good' and 'bad' jobs. Trade unions, for example, have in many cases used their bargaining power to initiate internal labour market conditions for their members, seeing this as partial compensation for de-skilling of their jobs. To protect these privileges, however, they have adopted policies which exclude new entrants. As a result, 'outsiders' (particularly women, migrants, and ethnic minorities) have been confined to low-paid and insecure segments of the labour market, and to jobs which are defined as unskilled, regardless of the actual skill content of their work (Rubery, 1978; Phillips and Taylor, 1980; Cockburn, 1983).

The family is another 'supply side' institution which has a major impact on the structure of labour markets. As we have seen, the unequal division of work and responsibilities within the family constrains the job choices of married women, channelling them to low-paid jobs. 'Women's work' in the labour market often involves firm-specific skills acquired through on-the-job experience, yet these skills are unrewarded because employers can retain their women workers through a lack of alternative job opportunities rather than by developing an internal labour market for them (Craig *et al.*, 1985).

On a global scale, labour markets are profoundly segmented by national boundaries. Wages and working conditions vary greatly between different countries, and movement of workers between countries has, particularly since the 1970s, been severely limited by immigration and nationality laws. This has opened up the possibility for employers to take advantage of the insecure status and low expectations of 'illegal' migrants (Castles, 1984), and, as we shall see later on in this chapter, to relocate production facilities overseas to take advantage of cheap labour.

Low pay and government labour market policies

A number of definitions of low pay have been proposed, but most of them converge on a level of around 2/3 of median male earnings, or £132 per week (£3.50 per hour for part-timers) in 1987. The total numbers and proportions involved are shown in Table 3.4. As the figures show, low pay affects women more than men, and part-timers more than full-timers. Low pay is concentrated in industries such as agriculture, retailing, clothing manufacture, hairdressing, and catering – industries with a predominance of small firms, and low levels of unionization.

Table 3.4 Numbers and proportions of low-paid adult employees (GB, April 1987)

	Millions	%
Female full-timers	2.7	52
Male full-timers	2.4	23
Female part-timers	3.4	81
Male part-timers	0.7	78

Source: MacNeill and Pond (1988).
Note: figures exclude overtime pay.

Given the predominance of women in the ranks of the low-paid, equal opportunities policies obviously have a major role to play, not just in promoting greater equity of treatment between women and men, but in solving the low pay problem as well. The main legislation here is the Equal Pay Act (1970), which, as amended in 1984, makes it illegal for men and women workers to be paid different rates within a firm for doing the same or similar work, or work of equal value. (You are referred to our companion volume, *Law in a Business Context*, for details of this and other equal opportunities legislation.)

As the figures in Table 3.5 show, the period 1973–76, when the main provisions of the Equal Pay Act were implemented, was associated with a significant rise in the relative earnings of women. Contrary to the predictions of some neo-classical economists, however, the full-time employment of women relative to men did not fall as a result – indeed it has continued to rise.

Table 3.5 Relative earnings and employment of women and men in the 1970s (GB)

Year	Relative hourly earnings[a] Female as % of male	Relative employment[b] Female as % of male
1970	58	44
1973	60	47
1976	68	51
1980	67	52

Source: Zabalza and Tzannatos, 1985.
a New Earnings Survey data for all employees (full- and part-time).
b The ratio of female over male employees in employment multiplied by the ratio of female over male average weekly hours worked.

Since implementation of the Equal Pay Act, women's hourly earnings have remained at around ⅔ of those of men. This reflects the following:

☐ A continued high level of job segregation, which limits the scope for establishing comparability of job content.
☐ Grading structures which continue to undervalue jobs done mainly by women.

☐ Continued inequality in access to high-paid jobs, promotion, bonuses, etc.

☐ A high proportion of women in part-time jobs which pay lower hourly rates than their equivalent full-time jobs.

More effective equal opportunity policies, though highly desirable in their own right, would not be sufficient to solve the low pay problem, given the significant (and increasing) proportion of men in low paid jobs. Demands are therefore growing, particularly within parts of the trade union movement, for a national minimum wage, such as exists in many other industrial economies. National minimum wage legislation would make it illegal for firms to pay any employee at a rate below a specified hourly level – it would, in effect, be an extension of the Wages Council system which since 1909 has fixed legal minimum wages in certain industries characterized by low pay and weak collective bargaining machinery.

The government, in its 1986 Wages Act, weakened the Wages Councils by removing young workers from their protection, and it is opposed in principle to the idea of a national minimum wage. Neo-classical theory has been influential here in suggesting that minimum wages create unemployment, and that wage cuts are needed to price 'marginal' workers into jobs. This reflects an idealized view of how labour markets operate, and ignores the segmentation which confines certain groups of workers to low paid jobs irrespective of their productivity (Craig *et al.*, 1982). Using a segmented labour market perspective, it should come as no surprise that British employers did not reduce female employment in response to the Equal Pay Act (Zabalza and Tzannatos, 1985), or that other countries, such as Canada, the United States, and France, have introduced a national minimum wage without any noticeable loss of adult jobs (Starr, 1981: Pond, 1983).

Management strategy, worker organization and labour market structure

In this final section we shall be considering management strategies in relation to labour. We pay particular attention to how these strategies affect the structure of labour markets, and how they relate to other aspects of management strategy.

Who controls the labour process?

In Braverman's analysis of changes in the labour process (1974), a key role is ascribed to the influence on management of the ideas of F.W. Taylor. Before Taylor, management set work tasks only in general terms, leaving to workers control over how those tasks were to be performed. This raised problems for management, especially with craft workers who could use their specialized knowledge to restrict output for their own ends. Accordingly, Taylor recommended that management observe the fastest and most efficient work methods workers have evolved, reduce them to a set of rules, and specify precisely how work tasks are to be performed and who should perform them. These recommendations, Braverman suggests, have been adopted by management ever since, with only minor modifications to suit local circumstances.

A number of critics, though, have suggested that Braverman, an American writer, underestimates the ability of a strong organized labour movement to resist management attempts to increase work intensity, and that as a result he overstates the importance of Taylorian methods to modern management, particularly in a European context. Andrew Friedman (1977, 1986) develops a more complex and, we would argue, apposite approach to management strategy. Management, Friedman suggests, attempts to achieve more output in one of two ways – either by detailed specification and close supervision of what workers do (direct control), or by encouraging workers to contribute more than is laid down in their employment contract (responsible autonomy). The appropriate strategy for management to adopt will depend on the situation facing each firm, and this will change over time. However, sudden changes in managerial strategy are difficult to achieve without severe disruptions to the organization of work and production.

From management's point of view, direct control strategies achieve flexibility in labour costs (because labour is a variable cost of production), but this can be at the expense of flexibility in the performance of work tasks (so that managers cannot depend on workers to sort out unforeseen problems). Such a labour process control strategy may be effective in situations where product demand and technology are stable over time, and where the workforce is poorly organized, but it will be less appropriate in a more turbulent environment.

With a responsible autonomy strategy, workers are given limited amounts of responsibility and status, to encourage a creative response to changing market or technological demands, or to buy off potential resistance. This approach to labour process control may achieve greater flexibility in the performance of work tasks. A possible cost for the organization, however, is that to win cooperation, management might have to offer workers an element of job security, which would make for less flexibility in labour costs, although, as we have seen, direct labour costs form a relatively small proportion of total costs of production for most manufacturing firms.

In practice, Friedman suggests, management will attempt to combine the advantages of each strategy by differentiating between central and peripheral workers. Central workers, who have skills which are in short supply, or who have a high potential to disrupt output, can be bought off with higher pay, status, and an element of job security. Peripheral workers, on the other hand, can be laid off when product demand is weak without jeopardizing the security of central workers. In differentiating between central and peripheral workers, management can take advantage of (and perpetuate) gender and racial inequalities in the workforce.

Cultural, political, and institutional differences are significant here. In Japan, traditional notions that large firms should provide lifetime employment are breaking down, but management are encouraged to respond to recession by developing new markets rather than by laying off workers. Amongst 'seasonal' workers in large firms and the part-time women who constitute most of the labour force in the small subcontracting sector, on the other hand, job security is low. In West Germany, the legal obligation of employers to provide generous redundancy terms has made many firms unwilling to lay off German workers in a recession, though the jobs of 'guest' (migrant) workers have been notoriously insecure. In Britain, short-term business financial calculations have encouraged management to respond to recession by laying off even 'central' workers – to the extent that skill shortages would be a significant constraint on any industrial recovery (Lewis and Armstrong, 1986).

One problematic feature of responsible autonomy is how far the measure of autonomy which workers may win through their collective organization will be exercised 'responsibly' from management's point of view. It has been suggested, for example, that British industrial performance has been adversely affected by trade union defence of 'custom and practice' inherited from a pre mass production era, slowing down the rate of introduction of new innovation (Kilpatrick and Lawson, 1980). Such concerns can, however, be exaggerated. As a recent comparative study shows, shopfloor opposition to new micro-electronic technology is considerably lower in Britain than in France or West Germany, largely because of greater consultation (Northcott et al., 1985).

Senker (1984) and Rolfe (1986) have argued that one of the main aims of British management is to improve productivity and short-term profits by de-skilling labour and saving on wage and training costs. Where new technology is introduced merely to improve an existing process by which a product is made, a de-skilling strategy might be effective for the management of mass production. Yet the biggest opportunities for long-term market success occur in product applications, where new products are developed which incorporate technological innovation/design. In these situations, it is often necessary to enhance skill levels, and a de-skilling strategy would be positively counter-productive.

Management obsession with problems of labour process control can also serve to divert management attention away from other, more important operational and strategic issues. As we saw in the previous chapter, Austin Rover in the late 1970s failed to take advantage of the product-mix flexibility which new technology could provide. Part of the reason for this failure was that management were more concerned with using new technology as an instrument of labour process control and to displace workers than to tackle fundamental problems in the marketplace (Williams et al., 1987).

The industrial relations context

While it is easy to exaggerate the extent of trade union opposition to new technology in Britain, there is no doubt that the industrial relations system plays a significant role in determining the limits to which changes in technology or work organization can take place. Just-In-Time (JIT) production systems are a good recent example. The Just-In-Time concept of stock control is based on the possibility of reducing stocks and the associated overhead burden of their management. The key element of JIT, as we shall see in Chapter 5, is the reduction in stock requirements when output is pulled through the system. JIT places greater responsibility on shop-floor workers to rectify problems immediately, and reduces 'idle' periods within working time in order to create dramatic increases in labour productivity. However, improvements in the way work is organized have also been accompanied, in Japan, by an intensification of work itself, with oppressive effects on assembly line workers which have been graphically described by Kamata (1984).

The structure of trade unionism in Japan plays an important facilitating role in this process of work intensification. In the early 1950s, employers allied with the government to destroy militant industry-wide unions in the private sector, and replace them by tamer, company-based unions. This profound change in the industrial relations environment of Japan weakened worker resistance to worsening working conditions.

In the different industrial relations context of the UK, management attempts to establish JIT in conjunction with work intensification have proved more problematic (Turnbull, 1988). Lower stock levels make production systems more vulnerable to industrial disputes, and trade unions are able to halt output, at little cost to themselves, with limited actions like overtime bans. In this context, management can essentially choose between three possible courses of action:

☐ To abandon attempts to improve the organization of production.
☐ To force through changes in the industrial relations system so as to weaken the power of trade unions to resist work intensification (e.g. via 'no strike' agreements with compliant unions).
☐ To negotiate, with trade unions, ways of implementing improvements in production organization which do not involve a worsening of working conditions on the shop floor.

In the mid 1980s, the latter avenue was the one which was least explored in the UK. It is, however, arguably the approach which would be the most appropriate to the industrial relations environment of the UK, and which would offer the greatest opportunities of mutual benefit for management and shop floor workers alike.

The search for flexibility

In the early 1980s, employers faced with increased pressure from the global recession and from intensified international competition defended profit through a drastic reduction in the level of employment. In the medium term, recent research suggests that some employers, stimulated by the additional pressure of reductions in the basic working week, have attempted to pursue greater flexibility in working patterns (NEDO, 1986; Curson, 1986).

Flexible working practices, Atkinson suggests (1985), involve a conscious attempt by employers to achieve greater numerical flexibility by creating a group of 'peripheral' workers whose activities can be expanded or contracted at fairly short notice. For 'core' workers, who employers see as central to the future of the organization, the emphasis is on increasing functional flexibility, so that workers can be re-deployed more easily between different tasks and locations. The aim in each case, Atkinson suggests, is to develop competitive advantage through increased ability to respond to changes in the product market environment.

The Atkinson model has been described by Anna Pollert (1987) as resting on 'an uncertain basis of confused assumptions and unsatisfactory evidence.' While there have undoubtedly been moves in the direction of greater job flexibility in recent years, their significance should not be exaggerated. In many cases, Pollert suggests, they represent not so much a radical break with the past as a continuation of long-established trends (such as overtime working by men in manufacturing industry, and part-time employment of women in service industries). The motive is often to cut short-term costs rather than to improve a long-term market position. Indeed, moves to greater 'functional flexibility' are constrained by limited budgets set aside for retraining, and a preoccupation with 'numerical flexibility' can serve to divert attention from the negative impact of skill shortages on UK industrial performance.

In order to match the hours of core workers more closely to output and capacity utilization requirements, without the cost penalities of overtime working, attempts have been made in recent years to introduce flexible working hours, where the hours worked vary from one week to another, or from one day to another. Union opposition to these schemes has been well publicized (for example, ASLEF's resistance to British Rail's plans to introduce flexible rostering for train drivers in 1981), and as yet there have been few private sector applications other than for part-time employees.

Perhaps the most radical departure from customary practice has been the replacement of employment contracts by commercial contracts, through practices such as franchising and sub-contracting. More and more organizations, particularly in the public sector, are concentrating resources on core activities, and devolving to outside organizations activities which are not firm-specific. One advantage for the core organization is greater financial security. This is achieved, however, by shifting the burden of risk and uncertainty to the subcontractor or franchisee, a process which involves high levels of dependence for the latter, and employment which is frequently insecure and low-paid. As part of this process, the 1980s have seen a revival of homeworking, in many cases under highly exploitative working conditions. This has been a feature not just of traditional spheres such as the clothing industry, but of high-tech areas such as computer programming and systems analysis as well (Huws, 1984: Mitter, 1985).

There is nothing inherently anti-worker in the idea of job flexibility. Functional flexibility could, for example, lead to more varied and rewarding jobs – significantly, many trade unionists are now beginning to demand that new technology be used, not to control workers, but to enhance their skills and their opportunities for creative work (Cooley, 1987). Flexibility in working time could, in appropriate circumstances, offer workers more choice, and make it easier for women and men to share childcare and well-paid employment. Indeed, writers such as André Gorz (1985) and James Robertson (1985) see greater flexibility in working time as the key to a more satisfying, equitable and sustainable future. At present, however, such scenarios seem remote. Brian Towers has observed

CASE STUDY 3.2

**INTEGRATED
CIRCUITS**

At the heart of the micro-electronic revolution are tiny devices called integrated circuits (chips), whose components are all made from a single piece of semiconducting material. Production of integrated circuits involves four distinct stages, each with their own distinctive locational requirements.

1. *Circuit design.* Scientists and engineers produce complex, multi-layered circuit patterns which are then photographically reduced and incorporated into masks. This work is highly knowledge intensive, and much of it is done in California, though newer centres have emerged in Japan and Western Europe.

2. *Wafer fabrication.* Layers of silicon are 'doped' with chemical impurities, to control the flows of electrical current through the circuit. These semiconductors are then etched with the patterns in the masks, baked, and tested. This stage requires both technical and assembly workers, a 'pure' production environment, and good access to raw materials such as silicon. Initially wafer fabrication was also centralized in California, but recently there has been a shift to peripheral areas of West Europe. Central Scotland has, over the past decade, become a major wafer fabrication centre.

3. *Chip assembly.* Circuits are bonded to external electrodes, using extremely fine wire, and then baked to seal them in a protective coating. This is a low-technology, labour-intensive process, and most of it is done by low-paid women workers in South East Asia.

4. *Testing.* Finally, reliability is tested by dipping components in chemicals and applying electrical currents to them. Traditionally, this involved shipping the chips back to the US, but recently testing has also been carried out in South East Asia.

While it is significant that integrated circuits have heralded a new stage in the internationalization of production, it is ironic that they have also brought into being working conditions which hark back to the nineteenth century. Young Asian women are chosen for chip assembly because their high levels of manual dexterity are learnt informally at home, because they have few alternative opportunities for paid work, and because their governments restrict their rights to organize in a trade union (all of which limit their ability to win pay rises). Health and safety problems abound, from peering through microscopes for hours on end and using hazardous chemicals.

The new international division of labour which has emerged is far from static. Wages in Singapore have risen in response to labour shortages, and firms there have begun to diversify into new areas like testing and sub-systems assembly. Routine assembly work has been further decentralized to economies such as Malaysia and the Philippines, where wages are even lower. Meanwhile, developments in Computer Aided Manufacturing have encouraged some firms to automate chip assembly, so that it can be shifted back to the US to improve delivery times without increasing inventory costs.

Further reading
Mitter (1986);
Dicken (1986);
Pearson (1986);
Sanderson et al. (1987);
Scott (1987).

(1987) that 'employers enthusiastically advocating labour flexibility are mostly looking for short-term means of reducing labour costs'. The negative consequences, for peripheral employees above all, are considerable. As the research workers who carried out the NEDO study conclude, 'The entire "flexibility debate" has been conducted in terms of what flexibilities capital requires from labour; labour's own needs for flexibility have been squeezed off the agenda' (Atkinson and Meager, 1986).

The new international division of labour

The post-war period has seen enormous growth in the power and significance of transnational corporations – firms who straddle national boundaries. Initially, transnational corporations operated as loose federations of relatively autonomous national units, but since the 1960s many of them have developed structures which enable them to integrate production and distribution on a global scale. Global organization makes it possible for transnational corporations to exploit national differences for their own advantage. Through direct foreign investment, or through international subcontracting, transnational corporations can now restructure their activities to produce where costs are lowest, and sell where profits are highest.

Labour market considerations have played an important role in these calculations. One of the pioneers here was Ford, which integrated its European operations as long ago as the late 1960s. One of the principles adopted at that time was that of 'dual sourcing'. To achieve economies of scale, each plant specialized in only a limited range of activities. To bypass possible disruption from labour disputes, key activities were duplicated at plants in two different countries. If, for example, there was a strike affecting the production of Capri bodies at Halewood, then output at Saarlouis could be stepped up to compensate.

Another consideration is labour costs – low wage levels were an important factor in encouraging Ford in the 1970s to set up a new assembly plant for the European market at Valencia, and a new engine plant for the North American market at Mexico City. Labour cost considerations have been particularly significant in the clothing industry and in assembling electrical goods and electronic components. In industries such as these, important elements of the production process are both labour intensive and highly standardized, and here transnational corporations have relocated or subcontracted production to developing economies which can provide cheap disciplined labour and appropriate industrial inputs. In cases where labour requirements vary significantly at different stages of the production process, the resulting flows of components and final products can become extremely intricate (Case Study 3.2). Alongside the old international division of labour, where rich countries specialized in manufacturing and poor countries in primary products, a new international division of labour has emerged where certain developing countries have become major manufacturing exporters. As Case Study 3.2 indicates, however, changes in technology and in labour markets can be de-stabilizing, as they encourage continual shifts in the location of this type of production.

How important are labour costs?

A consistent refrain in both management and government circles over recent years has been that labour costs should be brought down if UK manufacturing industry is to become more competitive. Leaving aside the point that competitiveness in sophisticated product markets is about much more than just price, the evidence to support the criticality of labour costs in the relative prices of British products is distinctly shaky. There are two possible ways of approaching the problem – to look at relative labour costs in Britain and other industrial countries, and to look at relative labour costs in relation to other costs.

The Swedish Employers' Federation collects data annually on international comparisons on labour costs, and results for the seven major OECD economies are shown in Table 3.6.

Table 3.6 Hourly labour costs in manufacturing (GB=100)

| | Hourly earnings | | Total hourly labour costs* | | |
	1980	1984	1980	1984	1986
USA	126	205	126	194	161
Canada	122	193	113	173	134
Japan	92	132	80	109	129
France	91	90	121	114	122
W. Germany	127	122	165	153	173
Italy	77	90	108	117	127
Great Britain	100	100	100	100	100

* includes social charges.

Source: Ray (1987).

As the figures show, hourly earnings are higher in Britain than in France and Italy, but lower than in the other major industrial countries. When one takes social charges (employers' contributions to pension funds, etc.) into account, however, then total hourly labour costs are lower in Britain than in any of the other major industrial countries. British firms are unable to reap the competitive benefit of low labour costs, however, because their productive efficiency is so low. As Table 3.7 shows, labour costs per unit of

Table 3.7 Unit labour costs in manufacturing, 1986 (GB=100)

	Total hourly labour costs*	Labour productivity (Output per hour)	Unit labour costs
USA	161	265	61
Japan	129	173	75
France	122	179	68
W. Germany	173	206	84
Italy	127	153	83
Great Britain	100	100	100

* includes social charges.

Source: Ray (1987).

output are higher in Britain than in other industrial countries, but this is because labour productivity in Britain is low, not because hourly labour costs are high.

When employers seek to reduce their labour costs, they usually focus on direct labour (labour directly involved in the production process), not indirect labour (which they treat as an overhead cost) or the labour component of bought-in items and materials. According to a British Institute of Management study of British manufacturing plants, direct labour accounts, on average, for only 18% of total factory costs (Table 3.8).

Table 3.8 Average structure of factory costs of manufactured products (GB, 1985)

	Percentage of total
Bought-in items and materials	52
Direct labour	18
Overheads	30
	100

Source: New and Myers, 1986.

Only in one out of twenty plants in the British Institute of Management Study did direct labour account for more than 40% of total costs. As New and Myers stress, their findings place considerable doubt on the wisdom of management fixation on control of direct labour costs: 'In most plants the amount spent on purchased items is about three times that spent on direct labour, yet nothing like three times the management effort is directed towards purchasing efficiency.' This is supported by another recent report on UK manufacturing industry, by Ingersoll Engineers (1987), which argues that:

> In recent years, by most measures, the competitiveness of British industry has improved dramatically . . . And yet . . . demonstrably an even sharper competitive edge is demanded in many markets. In looking at ways to achieve it, we noted that one area – procurement, logistics and materials – appeared to be continuously neglected by UK industry. This despite the fact that materials usually account for over 50% of the manufactured cost of engineering products.

The adverse consequences of this misplaced effort are likely to become even more significant as British manufacturers begin to explore flexible automation. Fixed costs frequently account for 70% of total costs for Computer Integrated Manufacturing, and, as Nicholas Valery has argued, this 'exists uncomfortably in an environment where 80% of the accounting effort goes on tracking 20% of the activity; where all efforts are geared to cutting costs rather than boosting revenues' (Valery, 1987).

Williams *et al.*, in their study of Austin Rover (1987), suggest that where managers need quick results, they will prefer to attack direct labour costs rather than pay attention to components costs, because the latter are not

**SUBCONTRACTING
AT PORT TALBOT**

Further reading
Fevre (1986)

In 1980, the British Steel Corporation (BSC) instructed its plants to cut their employment levels in order to trim expenditure within government-imposed cash limits. At Port Talbot, in South Wales, nearly 6000 workers were made redundant. Much of the work they did was subcontracted to outside firms. Tendering procedures resulted in contracts being awarded to new firms which could undercut established contractors by paying lower wages and, in some cases, ignoring health and safety regulations. Local unemployment did not rise as much as had been predicted, but the pay and working conditions of the transferred steelworkers deteriorated.

These measures undoubtedly cut direct labour costs, but they have increased subcontracting costs, and there has been widespread suspicion that the new system has resulted in lower maintenance standards, contributing to more frequent plant breakdowns. Ralph Fevre, in a study of the Port Talbot redundancies, suggests that managers were more concerned with the distribution of costs than their volume. Their 'success' was measured in terms of their ability to reduce BSC's wage bill, regardless of the resulting increases in payments to subcontractors and in other costs, many of which could not even be separately identified in the BSC accounts.

under their immediate control. This is a fairly general problem, as the Ingersoll report we quoted earlier bears out. Fewer than half the firms surveyed in that report had an active supplies certification programme, and only 16% certified more than half their supplies. In addition, communication with suppliers on scheduling and requirements was both inadequate and slow (Ingersoll, 1987). In this sort of context, the enthusiasm which British management is currently expressing for increased sub-contracting of activities which were formerly undertaken 'in-house' seems inappropriate, because what at first sight appears to be cost saving, may, in the long run, prove to be cost escalating, if it results in a loss of quality control. Failure to develop an appropriate control system for subcontractors can generate problems even for routine activities like maintenance, as Case Study 3.3 illustrates.

As we saw in Chapter 2, the record of Japanese firms suggests that if subcontracting is to be effective, in terms of component quality and reliability, then the purchasing firm has to develop a much closer relationship with its suppliers than is traditional in Britain (with the partial exception of Marks and Spencer).

Conclusion

Traditional (neo-classical) economic theory greatly exaggerates the capacity of market forces to match workers and jobs, to pay everyone in accordance with their productivity, and to ensure an effective organization of work. In reality, a number of organizational and environmental influences interact to divide labour markets into relatively self-contained segments, and to render the labour process indeterminate. As a result, mismatches between workers and jobs are endemic, and there is often little relationship between pay and productivity. In this situation, market forces frequently perpetuate rather than remove inefficiencies and inequalities.

Organized labour, in pursuing the interests of its members, can sometimes frustrate the achievement of management objectives, and it is understandable that management should devote effort to attempting to minimize that potential. Such effort is often self-defeating in terms of other management goals, and it can, and often does, divert management attention away from what are more fundamental problems.

Further reading

The Economics of Labour edited by J. Creedy and B. Thomas (Butterworth, 1982) provides a good introduction to the neo-classical approach, while for information on current trends and research in the UK labour market the Labour section of *Prest and Coppock's the UK economy*, edited by M.J. Artis (Weidenfeld and Nicolson, new edition published every two to three years) is invaluable.

Paul Thompson's *The Nature of Work* (Macmillan, 1983) provides a comprehensive overview of recent debates on the labour process, while the segmented labour market approach is best outlined by Christine Craig and others in Chapter 5 of *New Approaches to Economic Life* (B. Roberts *et al.*, eds, Manchester University Press, 1985).

Shirley Dex's *The Sexual Division of Work* (Wheatsheaf, 1985) and Swasti Mitter's *Common Fate, Common Bond* (Pluto, 1986) both explore the significance of gender differences at work, while the latter provides, in addition, a succinct summary of recent trends in the international division of labour and in work organization.

Exercises

1. It is sometimes suggested that overall job losses from new technology will be less with product applications than with process applications. Why might this be the case?
   What are the implications of this for trade union bargaining strategy?

2. Using the current issue of *Regional Trends* (HMSO), choose two UK regions, and compare their recent experiences of changes in manufacturing and service employment.
   How would you explain your findings?

3. White and Trevor suggest that the British response to the example of Japanese management 'must come from the systems of management training and development within the leading British companies' (rather than from the formal education system).
   What would you suggest the main features of such a response might be?

4. Choose a recent industrial relations dispute, and compare and contrast the bargaining strengths and weaknesses of the employer and the union.

5. In what circumstances might an employer consider creating an internal labour market?

6. Why might a neo-classical economist have predicted that implementation of the Equal Pay Act would encourage employers to reduce female jobs?

7. Implementation of the Equal Pay Act was in fact accompanied by increased female employment.
How would you explain this?

8. To what extent do management strategies of direct control over the labour process inhibit the introduction of new technology?

9. What factors have brought about a new international division of labour in manufacturing?
How might trade unions appropriately respond to these developments?

10. If direct labour accounts for only 18% of manufacturing costs, why does so much management time and effort go into trying to find ways of reducing it?

Appendix

The neo-classical analysis of perfectly competitive labour markets

In perfectly competitive labour markets, there are so many buyers and sellers of labour that each has to accept as given a wage rate which is determined by the interaction of demand and supply in the labour market as a whole. Figure 3.1 (a) shows an upward sloping labour supply curve, indicating a positive relationship between hours of labour supplied and the wage rate offered. The labour demand curve is downward sloping, reflecting a decline in the marginal product of labour as the quantity of labour inputs increases. The elasticity of demand for labour (the sensitivity of quantity demanded to changes in the wage rate) will be lower:

□ The lower the proportion of labour costs in total costs.
□ The lower the ease of substitution of other factors of production for labour.
□ The lower the price elasticity of demand for the product.

As Figure 3.1(a) shows, there is a unique wage, W_1, where the quantity of labour supplied equals the quantity demanded, and this is the equilibrium wage.

Trade unions (or legally established minimum wages) alter the supply curve for labour by ensuring that no labour is supplied at below the union rate (or minimum wage). This is shown in Figure 3.1 (b), where the labour supply curve becomes perfectly elastic at the union rate W_2. The analysis

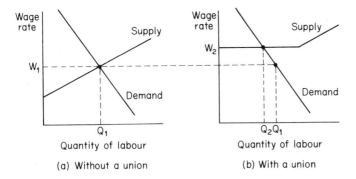

Figure 3.1 A competitive labour market.

suggests that if the union wage (W_2) is above the perfectly competitive level (W_1), there will be a loss of jobs (from Q_1 to Q_2). The extent of the fall in employment will depend on the elasticity of demand for labour.

The neo-classical analysis of monopsony

Monopsony exists where a single purchaser dominates a market. In a monopsonistic labour market, the employer can attract extra labour by increasing wage rates. Here the supply curve of labour represents its average cost, but the marginal cost of labour exceeds the average cost, because the wage increase needed to attract extra workers has to be paid to existing workers as well. This is shown in Figure 3.2(a).

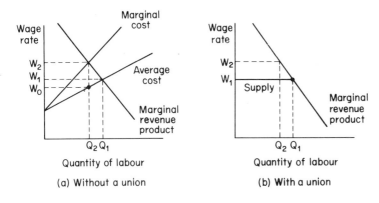

Figure 3.2 A monopsonistic labour market.

The profit maximizing monopsonist will hire labour up to the point where the contribution of the last unit of labour to total revenue just covers its contribution to total cost. This is at Q_2 in Figure 3.2(a), where marginal revenue product (the marginal physical product multiplied by the marginal revenue) is equal to marginal cost. The employer only needs to pay a wage of W_0 to attract this amount of labour, however, and this equilibrium wage is less than the marginal revenue product.

In a monopsonistic labour market, the effect of a union wage on jobs is less clear cut than in a competitive one. A union can again make the labour supply curve perfectly elastic at the union rate, and this makes the marginal cost of labour the same as its average cost. If a trade union boosts wages from W_0 to W_1 (the level that would obtain in a perfectly competitive labour market), jobs would increase from Q_2 to Q_1, as shown in Figure 3.2(b). If it boosts wages to W_2 in Figure 3.2(b), it will achieve a bigger increase in pay, and jobs will neither increase nor decrease. Only if wages are raised beyond W_2 will there be a loss of jobs.

References

Atkinson, J. (1985) The changing corporation. In *New Patterns of Work*, Ch.2 (ed. D. Clutterbuck), Gower, Aldershot.

Atkinson, J. and Meager, N. (1986) Is flexibility just a flash in the pan? *Personnel Management*, September.

Beechey, V. and Perkins, T. (1987) *A Matter of Hours*, Polity Press, Cambridge.

Blanchflower, D. (1986) What effect do unions have on relative wages in Great Britain? *British Journal of Industrial Relations*, July.

Braverman, H. (1974) *Labor and Monopoly Capital*, Monthly Review Press, New York and London.

Brown, C.V. (1983) *Taxation and the Incentive to Work*, Oxford University Press, Oxford.

Buchanan, D. (1987) Job enrichment is dead: long live high-performance work design! *Personnel Management*, May.

Burgess, C. (1985) Skill implications of new technology. *Employment Gazette*, Oct.

Castles, S. (1984) *Here for Good*, Pluto, London.

Central Policy Review Staff (1975) *The Future of the British Car Industry*, HMSO, London.

Cockburn, C. (1983) *Brothers*, Pluto, London.

Constable, J. and McCormick, R. (1987) *The Making of British Managers*, British Institute of Management, London.

Cooley, M. (1987) *Architect or Bee?*, Hogarth Press, London.

Craig, C. *et al.* (1982) *Labour Market Structure, Industrial Organisation and Low Pay*, Cambridge University Press, Cambridge.

Craig, C. *et al.* (1985) Labour market segmentation and women's employment: a case study from the UK. *International Labour Review*, May-June.

Curson, C. (ed.) (1986) *Flexible Patterns of Work*, IPM, London.

Daly, A. *et al.* (1985) Productivity, machinery and skills in a sample of British and German manufacturing plants. *National Institute Economic Review*, Feb.

Dex, Shirley (1985) *The Sexual Division of Work*, Wheatsheaf Books, Brighton.

Dicken, P. (1986) *Global Shift*, Harper and Row, New York.

Doeringer, P. and Piore, M. (1971) *Internal Labour Markets and Manpower Analysis*, Lexington (also extracted in *Readings in Labour Economics*, Ch. 2 (ed. J. King), 1980, Oxford University Press).

Fevre, R. (1986) Contract work in the recession. In *The Changing Experience of Employment*, Ch. 2 (eds K. Purcell *et al.*), Macmillan, London.

Friedman, A. (1977) *Industry and Labour*, Macmillan, London.

Friedman, A. (1986) Developing the managerial strategies approach to the labour process. *Capital and Class*, Winter.

Gordon, D. *et al.* (1982) *Segmented Work, Divided Workers*, Cambridge University Press, Cambridge.

Gorz, A. (1985) *Paths to Paradise*, Pluto, London.

Hall, P. (1987) The anatomy of job creation. *Regional Studies*, April 1987.

Huws, U. (1984) *The New Homeworkers*, Low Pay Unit, (also summarized in *New Society*, 22 March 1984).

Ingersoll Engineers (1987) *Procurement, Materials Management, and Distribution*, Ingersoll, Rugby.

Jaikumar, R. (1986) Postindustrial Manufacturing. *Harvard Business Review*, Nov.–Dec.

Joshi, H. and Owen, S. (1987) How long is a piece of elastic? The measurement of female activity rates in British censuses, 1951–1981. *Cambridge Journal of Economics*, March.

Kamata, S. (1984) *Japan in the Passing Lane*, Unwin, London.

Keynes, J.M. (1936) *The General Theory of Employment, Interest and Money*, Macmillan, London.

Kilpatrick, A. and Lawson, T. (1980) On the nature of industrial decline in the UK. *Cambridge Journal of Economics*, March. (Also reprinted in *The Economic Decline of Britain* (eds D. Coates and J. Hillard), Wheatsheaf Books, Brighton 1986).

Layard, R. and Nickell, S. (1985) The causes of British unemployment. *National Institute Economic Review*, February.

Lewis, J. and Armstrong, K. (1986) Skill shortages and recruitment problems in West Midlands engineering industry. *National Westminster Quarterly Review*, Nov.

MacNeill, K. and Pond, C. (1988) Britain can't afford low pay. *Low Pay Unit*, Nov.

Marris, R. (1987) Does Britain really have a wages problem? *Lloyds Bank Review*, April.

Marx, K. (ed.) (1976) *Capital*, vol. 1, Penguin, Harmondsworth.

Massey, D. (1984) *Spatial Divisions of Labour*, Macmillan, London.

Mitter, S. (1985) Industrial restructuring and manufacturing homework: immigrant women in the UK clothing industry. *Capital and Class*, Winter.

National Economic Development Office (1986) *Changing Working Patterns: How Companies Achieve Flexibility to meet new Needs*, NEDO, London.

New, C.C. and Myers, A. (1986) *Managing manufacturing operations in the UK 1975–85*, British Institute of Management, London.

Nichols, T. (1986) *The British Worker Question*, Routledge, London.

Northcott, J. *et al.* (1985) *Microelectronics in Industry: An International Comparison*, Policy Studies Institute, London.

Northcott, J. (1986) *Microelectronics in Industry*, Policy Studies Institute, London.

Northcott, J. and Walling, A. (1988) *The Impact of Micro-electronics*, Policy Studies Institute, London.

Pearson, R. (1986) Female workers in the first and third worlds. In *The Changing Experience of Employment*, Ch. 5 (eds K. Purcell *et al.*), Macmillan, London.

Phillips, A. and Taylor, B. (1980) Sex and skill. *Feminist Review*, **6**. (Also reprinted in *Feminist Review, Waged work: a Reader*, (1986), Virago, London.

Pollert, A. (1987) The 'flexible firm' : a model in search of a reality, *Warwick papers in industrial relations*, no. 19, December.

Pond, C. (1983) Wages councils, the unorganised, and the low paid. In *Industrial Relations in Britain*, Ch. 8 (ed. G.S. Bain), Basil Blackwell, Oxford.

Prais, S.J. (1981) Vocational qualifications of the labour force in Britain and West Germany. *National Institute Economic Review*, Nov.

Prais, S.J. (1987) Educating for productivity: comparisons of Japanese and English schooling and vocational preparation. *National Institute Economic Review*, Feb.

Prais, S.J. and Steedman, H. (1986) Vocational training in France and Britain: the building trades. *National Institute Economic Review*, May.

Prais, S.J. and Wagner, K. (1983) Aspects of human capital investment: training standards in 5 occupations in Britain and Germany. *National Institute Economic Review*, Aug.

Prais, S.J. and Wagner, K. (1985) Schooling standards in England and Germany: some summary comparisons bearing on economic performance. *National Institute Economic Review*, May.

Pratten, C.F. (1976) *Labour Productivity Differentials within International Companies*, Cambridge University Press, Cambridge.

Ray, G.F. (1987) Labour costs in manufacturing. *National Institute Economic Review*, May and Nov.

Robertson, J. (1985) *Future work*, Temple Smith/Gower, Aldershot.

Rolfe, H. (1986) Skill, de-skilling, and new technology in the non-manual labour process. *New Technology, Work and Employment*, Spring.

Rubery, J. (1978) Structured labour markets, worker organization and low pay. *Cambridge Journal of Economics*, March. (Also printed in *The Economics of Women and Work* (ed. A. Amsden), Penguin, Harmondsworth.)

Sanderson, S. *et al.* (1987) Impacts of computer-aided manufacturing on offshore assembly and future manufacturing locations. *Regional Studies*, April.

Scott, A.J. (1987) The semiconductor industry in South-East Asia. *Regional Studies*, April.

Senker, P. (1984) Engineering skills in the robot age. In *New Technology and the future of work and skills*, Ch. 9. (ed. P. Marstrand), Frances Pinter, London.

Senker, P. and Beesley, M. (1986) The need for skills in the factory of the future. *New Technology, Work and Employment*, Spring.

Starr, G. (1981) *Minimum Wage Fixing*, International Labour Office, Geneva.

Steedman, H. (1987) Vocational training in France and Britain: office work. *National Institute Economic Review*, May.

Steedman, H. (1988) Vocational training in France and Britain: mechanical and electrical craftsmen. *National Institute Economic Review*, Nov.

Steedman, H. and Wagner, K. (1987) A second look at productivity, machinery and skills in Britain and Germany. *National Institute Economic Review*, Nov.

Towers, B. (1987) Managing labour flexibility. *Industrial Relations Journal*, Summer.

Turnbull, P. (1988) The limits to 'Japanisation': Just In Time, labour relations and the UK auto industry. *New Technology, Work and Employment*, Spring.

Valery, N. (1987) The factory of the future. *The Economist*, 30 May.

White, M. and Trevor, M. (1983) *Under Japanese Management*, Policy Studies Institute, London.

White, M. (1986) Working time and employment: a negotiable issue? In *Unemployment and Labour Market Policies*, Ch. 2 (ed. P.E. Hart), Gower, Aldershot

Williams, K. *et al.* (1987) *The Breakdown of Austin Rover*, Berg, Leamington Spa.

Wood, S. (ed.) (1989) *The Transformation of Work*, Hutchinson, London.

Zabalza, A. and Tzannatos, Z. (1985) The effect of Britain's anti-discriminatory legislation on relative pay and employment. *Economic Journal*, Sept.

Financial calculations and business enterprise $\boxed{4}$

It is assumed in the traditional neo-classical economic theory of the firm that the single financial objective or goal of the business is to maximize profitability. Profits are maximized at a production and output level where the maximum difference between revenue (R) and costs of production (C) is obtained. That is where

$$\text{Revenue} - \text{Costs} = \text{Maximum}$$

Implicit in the neo-classical model of the profit maximizing firm are a number of fundamental assumptions. Firstly it is assumed that there is a single owner of the business who also directly controls the day-to-day activities of the firm. Here the 'interests' of the owner and the business are synonymous with the objective of profit maximization. Secondly it is assumed that the owner of the business can act and does act with complete rationality because the owner has perfect knowledge with regard to the price and costs of production and the reactions of competitors.

As we saw in Chapter 1, profit maximization requires firms to set their output where marginal cost is equal to marginal revenue.

$$\text{MC} = \text{MR}$$

You need to re-read the appendix to Chapter 1 on markets for a more detailed explanation of this behavioural rule and how it applies to the theory of perfect competition and monopoly.

In this chapter our purpose is not to reiterate the nature of economic concepts of profit, but rather to examine the forms of financial calculations firms make, in practice, when they are deciding to invest in new technology or when they price a product for sale in the product market. We therefore take as a starting point a summary of the main criticisms of the traditional neo-classical economic model of the profit maximizing firm.

As we have said, the traditional economic model of the firm establishes the rule of profit maximization under environmental conditions of absolute certainty, and organizational conditions where a single owner/controller of the enterprise can be identified. This owner applies marginal cost pricing rules for determining what level of output needs to be produced at any moment in time.

One of the first points of intervention to be made relates to the position of the entrepreneur as being both the owner and controller of the business.

KEY CONCEPT 4.1

OWNERSHIP AND CONTROL

Neo-classical theory abstracts from the organizational complexity of large firms by implicitly assuming that all firms are run by entrepreneurs who combine the functions of owners and managers. Modern corporations (or public limited companies), however, are legal entities which raise capital by issuing shares to shareholders, whose liability for any debts the company may incur is limited to the extent of their shareholding. (For further detail on the limited liability principle, you are referred to our companion volume, *Law in a Business Context*.) While shareholders elect the Board of Directors of the company they typically delegate operational control to professional managers who, although they may have substantial shareholdings, in no sense own the firms which employ them.

Many alternative, 'managerial', theories of the firm, such as those of Baumol (1959) and Marris (1964), focus their attention on divisions within the large firm between managers and shareholders, and on possible conflicts between the objectives of these groups. Many of these theories suggest, on the basis of Berle and Means's study of US corporations (1932), that shareholdings are dispersed among a large number of individuals, and that these individuals have little capacity to control how a corporation is run. Shareholders, these alternative theories suggest, have to delegate not just operational but strategic control to professional managers, who as a result have considerable discretion to pursue their own objectives. Shareholders' interests in maximizing receipts from dividends may lose out to managers' interests in boosting their salaries and ploughing profits back into the business to finance new investment without reference to the capital market.

Many writers feel that the Berle and Means model overstates the significance of the separation of ownership from control in the modern corporation (you are referred to Chapter 3 of our companion volume, *Business in Context*, for a fuller discussion). Two points from this debate are particularly significant for our purposes:

1. Most shares in large UK companies are owned not by individuals but by financial institutions such as insurance and pension funds, which may be more interested in long-term capital gains or in short-term trading profits than in dividend payments. These institutional shareholders have considerable capability to intervene in the corporation's strategic decision-making if their interests require it (Cosh and Hughes, 1987).

2. Corporate managers are constrained in their decision-making not just by the potential intervention of powerful institutional shareholders, but by the wider financial environment in which they operate (Thompson, 1986). As we shall see later on in the chapter, the financial accounting system, developed to safeguard the interests of shareholders, plays an important conditioning role, while, as we shall see in Chapter 6, the lending practices of banks, and the ways capital markets value company shares, also place significant constraints on management discretion.

The separation of ownership and control

The traditional concept of the entrepreneur as both owner and controller of the business abstracts from a number of legal and structural changes that have established, in practice, a separation of ownership and control in business operations generally. Under these changed conditions, control, on a day-to-day basis, is exercised by management on behalf of a dispersed set of shareholders (Key Concept 4.1).

With the advent of limited liability and the need by firms to obtain funds in excess of that provided by the owner of the firm or close family, many firms dispersed part shares of ownership of the firm's capital to shareholders. For example, firms such as ICI are owned by a dispersed set of shareholders who have a right to dividends distributed out of the profits of the organization and in most cases a right to vote at the Annual General Meeting.

Some shareholders can use their influence to alter the composition of the Board of Directors. However, once a system of management is established it is difficult to change in the short run because of the difficulty that small shareholders have in getting to the Annual General Meeting (AGM). Professional managers generally control the day-to-day operational activities of the business concerned.

In addition to the legal framework of limited liability, structural changes, in terms of the size and complexity of business organization under conditions of oligopoly rather than perfect competition, have ensured that a management role is required for the co-ordination of business operations. The organization and control of complex structures would be beyond the capabilities of one individual.

Acknowledgement that there is in practice a separation of ownership and control encouraged the development of a number of alternative theories of the firm. All of these establish that there is no one overriding objective of profit maximization, but a possible range of financial objectives which could lead to less than maximum profits being earned. We look at some of these alternative theories briefly.

Managerial theories

Here it is argued that managers are in control of day-to-day activity of the firm and that managements do not have the same interest in or need for profit maximization that we associate with the single entrepreneur. Managements will have a certain level of discretion and freedom to alter the goals and objectives of the firm they are managing. Managers will wish, it is argued, to pursue those objectives which at least stabilize or improve their own position within the organization over a period of time in either financial or status terms.

W.J. Baumol (1959) argued that management would wish to establish the objective of maximum sales revenue, sacrificing some profit in order to maximize sales and so improve their pay or status within the organization. We can illustrate the implicit trade-off between revenue and profit in Figure 4.1. A profit maximizing owner would set output where the difference between total revenue and total costs is at a maximum (Pm). However management may well aim for a sales maximization position which also maintains sufficient profit for the distribution of dividends to the shareholder (Sm). In order to increase market sales some revenue and hence profit per unit may have to be lost because the price charged to sell extra output falls.

Baumol's theory is a static one which tends to replace one unitary objective (profit maximization) by another (sales maximization). Marris (1964), however, establishes management objectives as those of growth maximization subject to a minimum profit constraint. In this more dynamic model of the firm Marris argues that management seeks a balanced rate of growth in both the output and capital base of the firm. Balanced growth requires that management pays attention to a number of related financial variables which help to secure a long-run career position within the organization. The prime aim is to improve the rate at which the firm is growing over time, but at the same time generating sufficient profits to finance expansion as well as to keep shareholders happy.

Behavioural theories

Some economists (H. Simon, 1955; Cyert and March, 1963) have suggested that in an uncertain environment firms cannot establish the conditions that are necessary for achieving financial maxima but instead management will try to establish satisfactory levels of profitability, sales, dividends and capital growth from one year to the next.

In practice the financial results of the business are the result of the interaction of various interest groups or sub-groups within the organization. An example is where the firm produces financial plans or budgets that specify, in financial terms, the planned trajectory of the firm over the next year or years. These financial plans represent the interaction of a number of sub-groups within the organization such as production engineers, sales personnel, marketing management, accountants, etc., who will all contribute to the shaping of the financial plan and actual financial performance of the business.

Within an uncertain environment, the organization's calculations and decisions about future sales, profits and dividends etc. will be subject to the limits of information and resources available at any particular time. As a result, management cannot have universal and perfect financial rationality as implied by the marginalist rules of neo-classical economics. Rather management's understanding of the future financial position of the firm at certain levels of output is 'bounded' by the imperfect and often incomplete information available to it at particular moments in time (K. Williams *et al.*, 1983).

So far we have established that, in neo-classical economic theory, the unitary financial objective of profit maximization will not operate in practice because the conditions for its operation cannot be established. Fundamentally the separation of ownership (shareholders) from control (management) in large business operations establishes conditions in which complex financial objectives are both set and achieved. It is not possible to

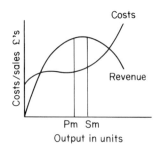

Figure 4.1 A comparison of a profit maximizing and a sales maximizing firm.

establish that all shareholders, or all managers, behave in a way designed to maximize profit. Many shareholders, for example, will be interested in the growth of dividends paid over time rather than establishing whether those dividends are at a maximum level, while, as we have seen, managers may have a vested interest in growth.

Apart from this fundamental point it must also be said that for the profit maximization rule to be established in a technical sense we must be able to identify marginal costs and marginal revenues. That is identification of the costs and revenues that are associated with the production of each and every extra unit of output. In fact, it would be administratively impossible, in terms of the resources and costs involved, to identify marginal cost and marginal revenue, and the practice of identifying marginal costs and revenues is not undertaken by firms. In 1939 surveys carried out by Hall and Hitch established that firms, in practice, apply a markup to average total costs of production to establish the price at which the output of particular products should be sold.

Price = Average variable costs + Average fixed costs + Profit markup. The financial information needed for markup pricing can readily be obtained from the accounting records and information system of the firm. (R. Hall and C. Hitch, 1939).

Most important, for the purpose of this chapter, the previous point emphasizes the importance of the role and principles of accounting in the financial calculations that firms make. Overall the financial calculations of any business enterprise are based upon the principles of accounting. It is accounting convention and accounting methods which determine the following:

- ☐ The presentation of annual report and accounts which detail the financial profit of the firm in the annual profit and loss account and the level of shareholder funds in the balance sheet.
- ☐ The price at which a product should be sold to recover costs and make a contribution to profit.
- ☐ The future profitability of project or strategic investments in new capital equipment.

As we have said, the main feature of the development of the limited liability company was that many people could now invest directly in business operations and take financial rewards in the form of dividends or capital gain. Although some shareholders may be managers as well, the majority of shareholders will not be involved in the day-to-day activities of the business. However, to protect and safeguard the 'financial interest' of the shareholder a system of accounting for the owner of capital has developed. The accounts of limited companies are required by law and are basically prepared for the shareholders in their capacity as owners but with specific provisions to safeguard creditors of the business.

The accounting concept of 'going concern' was established as a means to ensure that the business accounts were constructed on the basis of assuming continuity of operations and preservation of the business capital (shareholders' funds). Financial accounting concepts and conventions have developed as a means for recording, in as consistent a way as possible, the annual profit of the business, whereas cost and management accounting is concerned either to utilize the historical financial accounting records for day-to-day operational control purposes or to calculate strategically the future profitability of a commitment of investor funds to a capital investment project.

In financial terms, profit is the result of accounting calculations and conventions related to such things as the valuation of stocks and the calculation of depreciation expense etc. Accounting profit is therefore not a standard universal measure but subject to how accountants use the conventions at their disposal for the treatment of costs and expenses in the accounts of the business. This concept of profit and its calculation is very different from the concept of profit as specified under conditions of certainty in neo-classical economics (K. Williams *et al.*, 1983 and G. Thompson, 1986).

In traditional economic theory it is argued that resources will be applied most efficiently where those resources are put to use so as to earn the greatest level of profit. Profit is used in economic theory as a means to demonstrate that resources are being efficiently utilized or as a signal to attract resources to where maximum profits can be obtained.

In practice, however, it is accounting conventions which determine the level of profit recorded by the business in the accounts, and where resources such as capital and labour might be most profitably allocated. We will therefore consider in the rest of this chapter how financial accounting calculations affect the allocation of resources in the firm both strategically and operationally. For purposes of simplicity we will take twelve months to represent the operational time period – given that it is the period over which the financial summary profit and loss accounts extend, and the strategic time period to be that greater than one year.

Accounting calculations and decision-making

In any business organization it is accounting practice and convention that determine the nature of a firm's profits (retained profits or net profit pre or post tax). These profits are the result of accounting calculations or double entry records that are summarized and presented in the trading and profit and loss account of the business (for a more detailed review of these practices see the accounting text in this series). Essentially the trading and profit and loss account records the difference between revenue and expenses of the business incurred during the year. The accounting concepts of 'matching' and 'accruals' have been developed to ensure that expenses incurred by the business are matched with revenue earned during the year.

Profit = Revenue (Sales) − Expenses (Purchases, Interest, Depreciation, Rent and Rates, Tax, Dividends etc.)

The calculation of profit is therefore based not on the economic concepts of marginal cost or marginal revenue but on a whole set of accounting rules and conventions that are the stock of accounting literature and professional accounting exams. Profit is therefore something which is subject to the forms of calculations used by accountants when they calculate expenses such as depreciation and tax etc.

Accounting information in the profit and loss account and the balance sheet are also based on what we call historic costs. All accounting information in the annual accounts is based on financial information relating to the previous year's sales earned, or last year's depreciation charge etc. In addition to the calculation of profit in the profit and loss account, the balance sheet shows values for assets etc. that are also based on the historic cost of purchase and are, for example, depreciated on the basis of their original cost. In the mid 1970s a major debate on the relevance of historic cost accounting in times of inflation resulted in recommendations for inflation cost accounting to be introduced. We will not go into any detail here but it must be recognized that in times of inflation the use of historic cost information for decision-making becomes more problematic.

Limited companies have to report their profit and loss position and their balance sheet position each year to Companies House. These financial results are presented in a summary annual report and accounts which are available for public inspection in Companies House and are sent to the shareholders as of right. In the balance sheet of the firm we can obtain a 'snapshot' of the position of the firm at the year end. A typical balance sheet would include the following.

Shareholders' Capital

Shareholders' issued shares,
Retained profits.

Represented by;

Fixed assets

Land and buildings   – accumulated depreciation
Plant and equipment – accumulated depreciation
Motor vehicles etc.   – accumulated depreciation

Plus net current assets

Current assets
Stocks
Debtors
Bank balance
Cash

Minus current liabilities
Creditors
Loans
Overdrafts

From these final annual accounts the student or business manager can undertake a number of calculations or 'ratios' which allow interpretation of the results of the firm. In addition the financial data that form the basis of these accounts can be used to establish future budgets and cost estimates for the purpose of financially controlling the business. In the following sections we shall consider some of the accounting calculations made for product-pricing and investment appraisal.

The accountant's role in pricing decisions

We have already said that firms do not use marginal cost pricing rules but choose instead rules based on average cost plus profit markup. In practice there are a number of accounting methods used to determine the price at which the product(s) should be sold. Historical financial accounting data on sales and costs of manufacture provide the basic input into financial calculations relating to pricing and investment decisions.

It is vital that the firm calculate the 'correct' price because cash inflow and revenue earned by the firm is determined by the product of volume of sales multiplied by unit price.

$$\text{Revenue} = \text{Volume Sales} \times \text{Unit Price}$$

It is vital that the accounting information used to calculate the price is one which will generate a suitable profit margin for the business. In a market where there are a few competitors (oligopoly) it becomes crucial that the firm adopts the 'correct' pricing policy at a particular point in time.

One of the most widely-used accounting price calculations is the cost-plus pricing procedure. In a questionnaire survey of Merseyside businesses, Skinner (1970) found that 70% used this method to determine their prices. In this type of pricing calculation the eventual price will depend on the cost calculations used and the profit markup criteria adopted by the firm. In accounting practice there are a number of methods that can be adopted for the calculation of unit costs; total costs, manufacturing costs etc. The price of the product can therefore be based on a number of different forms of accounting cost calculation rather than on any universal standard criterion like marginal cost. One example of calculating a product's cost is shown below.

```
      Direct materials
    + Direct labour
    + Direct fixed and variable
      overheads
    = Prime or manufacturing costs

    + Indirect fixed and variable
      overheads

    = Total costs per unit.
```

In this case a profit margin judged suitable will have to be calculated and added to the products cost in order to get the selling price. We could, for example, calculate the cost of the above product as the manufacturing cost and ignore one of the main controversial issues in accounting, that of identifying and 'attaching' to each product the indirect overheads such as rent, rates, canteen costs, electricity and administrative costs etc. Here a pool of overheads would still need to be allocated or recovered by the product's price. This could be done by increasing the profit markup as a means of recovering the indirect overhead costs.

It is argued that such cost accounting is necessary because it provides financial information necessary for judging the price at which a product is sold in the market place and as a means to calculate the expected level of market demand for the product. One of the main problems with these accounting calculations based on the expected future unit cost of production is that they do, in fact, make explicit assumptions about the level of future demand in order to arrive at a unit cost calculation.

In fact the pricing calculation is a circular one because it assumes a given sales demand is available from which we can calculate unit cost of production. Using these unit costs for pricing purposes we can now estimate the level of future market demand for the product.

> Unit fixed cost is calculated by dividing total fixed cost by estimated volume. The unit fixed cost is used in the selling price calculation. The selling price will influence sales demand thus affecting management's estimate of future volume. (Drury, 1988)

In order to calculate and assess the sensitivity of future profitability to changes in the price or volume at which the product is sold the management accountant will provide calculations to management based on the cost–volume–profit relation of the product being sold. What, for example, would be the effect of increasing the price of the product when it is expected that volume sales will react adversely to the price change? Or what would happen to profitability where the product's price is reduced by 20% and sales volume increases by 10%?

In economics the graphical relation between cost-volume and profit is considered in Figure 4.2.

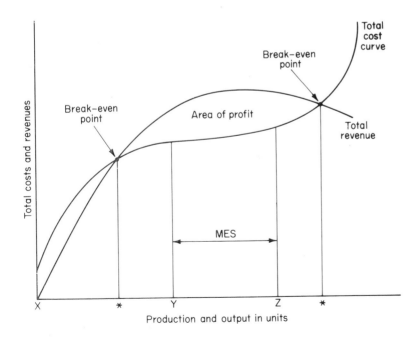

Figure 4.2 Economist's version of break-even chart.

In Figure 4.2 the total revenue curve is shown to increase at a decreasing rate, illustrating that the firm can only sell more output by reducing the price at which that output is sold. In the case of the total cost curve this is shown as at first increasing (X to Y) but at a slower rate as the firm increasingly utilizes the 'lumpy' investment constructed to produce this product, that is, where growth in production increasingly fills the production capacity installed. Over the portion Y to Z the curve is shown to be relatively flat as the firm operates in the minimum efficient scale portion of the plant where unit costs are constant. In this diagram there are two break-even points shown (*) that is where total costs are equivalent to total revenue. Break-even point where

$$\text{Total costs} = \text{Total revenue}$$

The accountant's calculations of the break-even point and the relationship between volume and profit are based on linear curves rather than non-linear economic relations. The total costs curve is made up of the fixed plus variable costs of the product's production, while the revenue curve is constructed by calculating total revenue over a certain volume of sales range.

Consider the example where product A has the following cost and revenue characteristics.

> Fixed costs of production are £120 000.
> Variable costs per unit are £20.
> Sales price per unit £40.
> Plant capacity is 10 000 units.

The break-even chart (Figure 4.3) is constructed below and this illustrates that the break-even point is at an output level of 6000 units. If sales volume is above this level of output then a profit will be earned by the firm, but output levels below 6000 units will incur a loss. The break-even point therefore represents a position in which no profit is made and costs are just covered by revenue earned by the firm.

It is also possible to calculate the break-even point using this formula.

Break-even point (in units) = Fixed Costs (£)/Sales Price per unit − Variable Cost per unit

In this case £120 000/£40 − £20 = 6000 units.

In the above example if the firm were to increase the sales price per unit then the break-even point will fall, whereas if the variable costs increase or fixed costs increase due to say excess material costs (above those planned) and increased construction costs the break-even point will rise.

As a means of illustrating the relationship between volume of future sales and the costs/profit relationship, the accountant's break-even chart is a reasonably useful financial tool. However, there are a number of problems associated with using the technique as a means for management decision-making and the allocation of resources.

Firstly the calculation assumes that the costs curves are linear. When this assumption is relaxed, as in the economist's version of the total cost and revenue curve, then there may well, in fact, be two break-even points and a

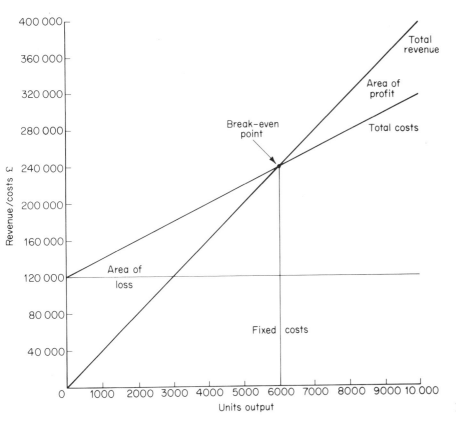

Figure 4.3 Break-even chart.

range of output within which it is possible to obtain a profit contribution beyond which a loss may be incurred.

Secondly the break-even chart relates only to one product and when in practice is necessary to compare the various break-even levels and profit contributions from a range of products produced. Finally there is the implicit assumption that the firm can estimate the future level of product demand with utmost certainty. As we have seen in the chapter on markets, such calculations about the future level of demand for a product are fraught with uncertainty. Miscalculations of demand can be critical, especially when the break-even point can only be achieved after significant growth in demand for product. Obviously the higher is the break-even point for the product being manufactured (i.e. break-even point as a percentage of the theoretical plant capacity) the greater the risk that the plant will not reach a level of volume sales each year that delivers a positive contribution to profit. In the case of highly capital-intensive investments made in industries such as steel or car manufacture, fixed costs of manu-facture are very high indeed and as a result break-even output levels operate at very high levels of plant capacity.

Against this background of uncertainty accountants have developed more sophisticated and complex financial calculations with which to assess the future profitability and hence desirability of an investment strategy or project.

Capital investment decisions needed for the production of new products are made by management on the basis of whether or not future income or net cash inflows (cash outflow − cash inflow) pay back the original capital outlay (including borrowing charges) and make a contribution to profits. As we shall see, mistakes made with small investment projects may not compromise the future viability of the firm but those investments that are strategic in nature (involving a large commitment of company funds) need to be successfully executed or the future financial viability of the organization will be compromised. It is at this stage that we now turn to examine the financial calculations made by management accountants based on the Discounted Cash Flow principle.

Discounted Cash Flow and investment decision-making

Discounted Cash Flow Calculation (DCF)

One of the simplest forms of accounting calculation used by management accountants to decide whether an investment project should be undertaken, is the pay-back financial calculation. This calculation involves assessing the future net cash flows likely to be obtained from an investment. The net cash inflow is calculated as the difference between the future cash inflows and cash outflows. For example, where a firm wishes to evaluate the financial attractiveness of different investment choices it will compare each option in terms of the criterion – how quickly do net cash flows pay back the original investment outlay?

Consider the following simple example in which there are two projects being evaluated, project A costing £2000 and project B costing £4000. Each of these investment projects is expected to have the following net cash flow profiles.

Table 4.1 Costings for projects A and B

		Investment/Outlay £	Net cash inflows £			
Years		0	1	2	3	4
Projects	A	−2000	+1000	+500	+500	+500
	B	−4000	+500	+1000	+1000	+1500

In the above illustration investment project A would incur an investment outlay of £2000 and over four years the net cash flow would account for £2500. In case B an investment outlay of £4000 would reveal net cash flows totalling £4000 by year four. In terms of how quickly each project obtains a net cash flow that 'pays back' the initial investment outlay, project A

This concept provides the basic rationale for the discounting calculation. Where an investment requires the commitment of capital funds in return for an income flow over a number of years, it is assumed that the investor would prefer this income flow to be equivalent to or greater than that which the investor would have obtained from investing the capital fund at the market rate of interest. It is for this reason we argue that the investor would prefer to receive £100 now rather than in one year's time because this £100 could be invested now so as to earn interest on this sum.

Discounting establishes whether the present value of a future income stream is not less than the original capital outlay and that the investor receives an income stream which fully compensates for the interest returns forgone.

KEY CONCEPT 4.2

THE TIME VALUE OF MONEY

would seem the more attractive because the payback would be three years whilst that of project B would be four years.

However, even with such a simple form of accounting criterion such as payback there are a number of problems. Firstly, although on a strict financial payback calculation project A is more attractive than B, it may be the case that project B would deliver other benefits which cannot be considered in purely a strict financial calculation. Project B may be, for example, an important component in an overall set of projects which would eventually contribute strategically to an improvement in the future market position of the firm. Or project B may well contribute to the efficiency of the overall production system, for example reducing the level of stocks held as work-in-progress. But this benefit is not taken into account in the financial calculation of payback.

The decision to invest in particular projects would also need to take into account other factors that may not be easily represented in financial terms but would also need to be considered in the decision-making process.

One major problem associated with the calculation of payback is that it does not take into account what is termed the 'time value of money' (see Key Concept 4.2). It is here that we briefly turn to consider the nature of the Discounted Cash Flow Calculation (DCF). This management accounting investment evaluation technique is dealt with in more detail in the accounting text in this series.

It is argued that the commitment of investment funds by the individual or firm involves an opportunity cost (see Key Concept 4.3). That is, committing investment funds to one particular purpose involves the sacrifice of not being able to place these funds elsewhere. Once a decision is made to invest in a particular project then these funds are essentially locked in to that project. This would particularly be the case when the investment funds are allocated for the purchase of fixed plant and equipment.

What is the sacrifice the firm or investor makes when funds are

KEY CONCEPT 4.3	Because the resources at our disposal are scarce in relation to our wants, we have to make choices. As individuals, we all have to choose how to spend our limited income. Shall I buy a colour television, or save up for a holiday abroad instead? Economists talk of opportunity cost to emphasize the way choosing something involves a cost in terms of the opportunities you have to forgo. Thus if I decide to buy a colour television, its opportunity cost is the holiday abroad I can no longer afford.
OPPORTUNITY COST	For firms, the opportunity cost of using retained profits to finance an investment project is the interest that could be earned by lending them out on the money markets instead. This is not just an abstract possibility – in the late 1970s and early 1980s, for example, net income from cash reserves accounted for more than 10% of GEC's total pre-tax profits.

committed to an investment project? It is clear that at the decision-making stage a firm could place its surplus funds, available for investment purposes, either in a bank where they could gather a compound market rate of interest or in the hands of divisional managers for investment in new physical investment projects. Before the decision to allocate funds to particular purposes is made we are assuming that a choice such as this exists.

It may be that investing surplus funds in the bank or gilt-edged stock would reveal a net cash-flow return to the investor which is greater than that which could be obtained from investments in physical plant and equipment designed to produce a particular product for the market. As such we would argue that the funds would, financially, be better invested in financial rather than physical assets. Managers use the DCF calculation as a means to establish whether or not funds should be used for physical plant and equipment investment or placed in alternative financial assets.

The Discounted Cash Flow (DCF) calculation starts with the presumption that a pound received now is worth more than a pound received in one year's time. This is because the pound received now could be invested at the market rate of interest and therefore be worth more than one pound in a year's time. For example, if we assume that the market rate of interest is 10% and a person or firm has the choice of receiving £100 now or in one year's time. The £100 received now could be invested at 10% and be worth £110 in one year's time.

	Year 0	Year 1
Investment at 10%	100	110

Looking at this problem another way we could say that a person would be indifferent to receiving £100 now or £110 in one year's time (assuming that inflation was zero).

In this simple example it is the principle of compound interest that is used to establish what £1 invested now would be worth in some future time period at given rate of interest. Compound interest calculations are based on the following formula.

$$FVn = Vo \, (1 + i)^n$$

Where FVn = Future value of an investment over n years.
      Vo = Initial investment sum.
      i   = Interest Rate.
      n   = number of years over which investment is to be made.

It is easy to obtain the compound future value of an investment with a given rate of interest from compound interest tables or from simple computer software statistical packages. For example where a person invests £100 over 4 years at a 10% interest rate then the future value of this investment would be £146.40

$$FVn = 100 \, (1 + 0.10)^4$$

or FVn = 100 × 1.464 (from compound tables based on rate of interest and number of years the investment is made for).

In contrast to compounding which establishes the future value of an investment at a particular rate of interest, discounting involves establishing the present value of future net cash flows received. This calculation is used to establish whether future cash flows from an investment project are sufficient to do the following.

☐ Pay back the initial investment outlay.
☐ Recover the interest that could have been earned on the investment funds had they been invested at the market rate of interest.

To calculate the present value of future cash flows we use the formula:

$$PVo = \frac{FVn}{(1 + i)^n.}$$

Where PVo = The present value of future net cash flows

      FVn = The future value of net cash flows in each future year n
      $(1 + i)^n$ = The compound discount factor based on the year in which net cash flow is obtained (n) and market rate of interest (i).

Again it is possible to obtain present value discount factors from statistical tables or from computer software packages.

Once the present value of future net cash flows from an investment project have been calculated they then need to be compared with the initial investment outlay. This final step involves calculating the *net present value* of the investment. To illustrate this financial decision-making tool consider the example below. Here the firm could choose to invest £10 000 of investment funds in a bank at a market rate of interest of 10% or invest in a project which delivered the net cash flow profile over a period of five years as shown in Table 4.2. Note also that in many cases the discount rate of interest will be based on a cost of capital (Key Concept 4.4) calculation which involves taking the weighted average cost of capital invested in the firm by shareholders and creditors.

Table 4.2 Net Present Value calculation

End of Year	Net Cash Flow £		Discount Factor or Present Value Factor	Present Value £
Year 1	2000	*	0.9091	1818.2
Year 2	3000	*	0.8264	2479.2
Year 3	3000	*	0.7513	2253.9
Year 4	3000	*	0.6830	2049.0
Year 5	3000	*	0.6209	1862.7
		Total present value		10 463.0

The present value figure for the end of year one amounts to £1818.2 and it represents the amount that we could invest at the start (year zero) and in one year's time obtain £2000 at 10% cost of capital. Likewise, the figure of £1862.7 in year five represents that amount we could invest now (in year zero) and at 10% compound over five years receive £3000.

However, it is only when we summate the present value column that we see that the total present value of future net cash flows is in excess of the original investment outlay of £10 000. That is the Net Present Value (NPV) of the project is as calculated below.

$$\text{NPV} = \text{Original investment} - \text{The summation of present}$$
$$\text{outlay} \qquad \text{values of future net}$$
$$\text{cash flows}$$

$$\text{NPV} = \int \text{PVo} - \text{Io}$$
$$= £10\ 463 - £10\ 000$$
$$= + £463$$

In this example the present value of future net cash flows from this investment is sufficient for the following.

☐ Cover the interest that would have been received on £10 000 had it been invested in financial assets.
☐ Contribute a positive NPV of £463 i.e. contribute to profit.

KEY CONCEPT 4.4

THE COST OF CAPITAL

The cost of capital is the discount factor used by the firm to establish whether a new investment project will cover the cost of capital that is applied. It usually represents the weighted average cost of capital for the firm as a whole or for a division within the firm.

D. Solomons (1965) defined the cost of capital as 'the expected earnings yield on the current market price of an all equity company or the weighted average cost of capital in a company financed by both debt and equity'.

The cost of capital is therefore an average rate of interest which is paid out to shareholders or holders of debt within the firm. Any investment should therefore make a contribution to income which will cover the cost of funding both the firm's debt and equity.

In the above example we have calculated the net present value (NPV) of a particular project investment. In this case the NPV of the project was found to be positive, demonstrating that a positive contribution to profits would indeed be made. However at any moment in time decision-makers will have a number of possible option choices. As a result it is necessary to compare the relative merits of each investment option open to the business. To do this accountants calculate the NPVs of a number of options and then rank these options in terms of their profitability or NPV.

For example we may have two possible project options to choose from, project A and project B. In the table below we show the net cash flow profiles expected from each project and the initial cash outflow attributable to each project. We also assume that the cost of capital is 10%

Table 4.3 Comparison of Project A and Project B

Outlay year 0	Net cash Inflows year	1	2	3	4	5
Project A (£10 000)		6000	5000	4000		
Project B (£50 000)		10000	10000	20000	20000	20000
Discount factors 10%		0.9091	0.8264	0.7513	0.6830	0.6209
Present values						
Project A		5454.6	4132	3005.2		
Project B		9091.0	8264	15 026.0	13 660	12 418
Net Present Value						
Project A		12 591.8 − 10 000 = +2591.8				
Project B		58 459.0 − 50 000 = +8459				

In terms of a simple ranking of each project using the contribution to profits or level of NPV we would rank the projects as follows:

Project	NPV	Rank
A	+2591.8	2
B	+8459.0	1

However accountants usually construct a ranking that relates NPV to the initial investment outlay in the form of return on capital investment ratio. If we were to do this for the above example we would arrive at the following ranking of the projects.

	Project	NPV/Initial investment outlay.	Rank
2592/10 000 =	A	25.9%	1
8459/50 000 =	B	16.9%	2

In this case although the absolute level of NPV earned favours project B

NET PRESENT VALUE
AND THE CASE OF
BRITISH STEEL

In the BSC's 1972 Strategic Evaluation Exercise (SEE) the BSC financial planners utilized the NPV discounting method as recommended by the government in the White Paper setting up the corporation. In this exercise the BSC evaluated the NPVs of ten different investment options. These all involved the expansion of steel-making capacity to a greater or lesser extent. All the options involved constructing new steel-making plant and equipment. In some options this would require a modest commitment of resources, while in others a very large commitment of financial resources would be needed.

The results of the BSC's calculations of NPV are summarized in the table below and ranked on the basis of the NPV earned by the firm from each different option choice.

Rank	Option	NPV £m
1	6	604*
2	11	567
3	4	541*
4	10	514
5	7	511
6	12	494*
7	8	490
8	9	476
9	5	441
10	2	416

From this list the BSC management eventually chose Options 6,4,12 as the final three. Although Option 6 was the most profitable option in terms of NPV the others in this list of three were ranked 3 and 6 respectively. Finally the option choice made by BSC managers was that of Option 12, ranked 6th in NPV terms.

According to Bryer and Brignall (1983), the BSC management argued that the decision should not be made on financial NPV terms alone but on other considerations. In management's opinion Option 12 should be retained because it was characterized as a 'high capacity: radical plant pattern'. As we have seen from our chapter on technology the economies of scale assumption also played a major part in shaping the final option that BSC management would adopt.

Bryer and Brignall criticize management of the BSC for not adopting the 'correct' option, that is, the one which promised the best NPV per unit of capital investment made.

> ... given the Government's concern with the optimal allocation of resources, it could justifiably be argued that the comparison should have been made using Present Value earned per unit of capital outlay.

In addition Bryer and Brignall criticize the BSC management's use of NPV on a number of other counts. Firstly that they did not carry out a sufficiently wide sensitivity analysis, and that the effect of varying some of the basic assumptions was not examined. It was clear that the BSC's option choice involved a great deal of risk relative to Option 4 because Option 12's NPV profile was negative well into the early 1980s. Option 4 was a more conservative choice, because it obtained a positive NPV contribution much earlier.

Further reading
Bryer and Brignall, *Accounting for British Steel* (Gower, 1983).

we would favour adopting project A using an accounting ranking procedure that relates expected NPV to the initial capital investment outlay.

However if we look at project A we can see that it requires, in comparison to project B, a relatively small capital outlay which promises returns which are reasonably large and more immediate. Whereas project B involves the commitment of a large initial investment outlay in the expectation that net cash flows will improve in the more distant future. It may be, however, that project B involves investing in new plant and equipment etc. which would secure an improved market share for the product being produced. Whereas with project A we may have invested in existing plant and equipment to 'patch up' or 'modify' the existing equipment or product mix. This latter strategy promises more immediate returns but it may compromise the future market viability of the business.

This criticism of the use of NPV for decision-making has been made by Hayes and Abernathy (1980). They argue that the discounted cash flow calculations have a tendency to bias investment option choices. The mathematics of the discounting calculation can be compared to that of a 'reversed telescope' in which distant returns are depreciated more heavily. According to Williams *et al.* (1986), 'Large-scale strategic investment in, for example, new process technology should capture earnings in the long run but these distant and uncertain returns are worth less in terms of present value'.

It is for these reasons that Hayes argues that decisions made using NPV tend to be more conservative. NPV supports a 'patch and mend' mentality which defends existing process plant and technology. This strategy is attractive in NPV terms because it offers short-run returns which are substantial in relation to modest investment outlay. However Hayes points out that preoccupation with the short run may inhibit innovative decision making and the exploitation of new process technology which may well be essential if the firm is to have a sustained long-run market presence.

So on the one hand we have the accountants' use of the NPV calculation and on the other we have the American business school interpretation which privileges a more 'enlightened' use of the NPV model (Hayes and Abernathy, 1980). The former is biased in favour of short-term returns while the latter suggests modifying the use of NPV by taking into account factors other than purely the financial present values.

In the case study on the British Steel Corporation (BSC) opposite we show that the BSC used NPV calculations as a means to evaluate the profitability of ten different investment opportunities open to the firm in 1972. This case study illustrates how the strict use of NPV by accountants leads to one set of conclusions whilst management's 'enlightened' use of NPV can lead to a radically different set of investment choices.

This case study illustrates how malleable the NPV calculation was in the hands of BSC management. It also illustrates that BSC management was not preoccupied with a purely financial rationale for their investment strategy. In fact the BSC management decision might well have been supported by Hayes and Abernathy (1980), in that it was adventurous, and conditioned by other factors such as going for market share and achieving this with an innovative investment strategy.

One of the main problems facing the BSC's investment option choice, namely Option 12, was the nature of its NPV profile over the strategic planning time period. If we return to our previous example in Table 4.1 it is apparent that in the early years of the investment planning period the net present value is negative, that is, investment expenditure minus present value up to and including the year considered. However, over a period of time the net present value improves and becomes a positive value. In this simple example, Option A has an NPV profile which becomes positive between year two and year three in terms of net cash-flow years, while

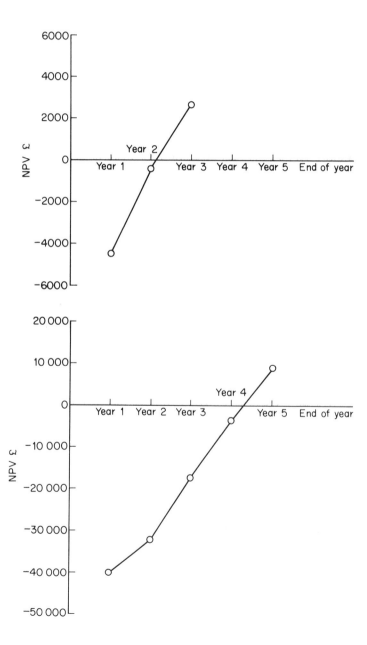

Figure 4.4 NPV profile for Project A.

Figure 4.5 NPV profile for Project B.

project B has an NPV profile which becomes positive in years four to five. The NPV profile for each project is plotted in the graphs on p. 112.

Figures 4.4 and 4.5 illustrate that investment projects often have different NPV profiles and that these are determined by the relationship between the level of investment outlay and the present value of future cash flows earned from the investment project. If the investment project involves a very small fraction of the company's capital assets then any failure to obtain the necessary level of cash inflow will not compromise the profitability of the organization as a whole. However, where the investment project involves the allocation of a very large and substantial level of the firm's capital for strategic purposes, any failure to obtain the necessary net cash flows will have a powerful negative effect on the firm's annual profit and loss account.

In the case of the British Steel Corporation, investment Option 12 involved a substantial strategic commitment of financial resources to an investment plan which did not show a positive contribution to profit until the mid 1980s, fifteen years after the start of the plan. A number of fundamental uncertainties will exist over this period, and these may operate to set the financial net cash inflows off target. In addition any problems associated with the construction of the new steel-making facilities would also have an adverse effect on the realization of positive NPV.

NPV is a purely internal calculation made by the firm to assess the future profitability of a particular investment plan. As such it also tends to ignore the reactions of competitors. Investments made by the firm in new process technology may be 'matched' by competitors doing the same thing with the net result being overcapacity. This has happened in both the European steel and car industries over the last decade. In addition the information revealed from the NPV calculation depends on the discount rate or cost of capital used by the firm. If competitors have access to funds with a lower cost of capital, then their discount rates will also be smaller. The net result is that firms using the NPV calculation can arrive at totally different decisions about similar investment projects.

When a firm has decided to invest strategically it is essential that expected market sales materialize, and that the operational costs of running the investment on a day-to-day basis are budgeted for correctly. It is these two components that determine the annual net cash flow. In addition, construction times and investment costs need to be accurately estimated and executed as planned. With nuclear power reactors, construction costs have been on average above those estimated due to technical problems associated with reactor build. At the Dungeness B Advanced Gas-cooled Reactor (AGR) this involved a construction overrun of approximately 100% or nearly double the original estimate. In such circumstances even where net cash flows are estimated correctly these cannot recover a positive NPV because they have to be set against a much larger than expected investment outlay.

Where the difference between the expected and actual financial variables is adverse and significant, the firm is left in a situation where profit starts to deteriorate. It is at this stage that the operational financial calculations of the annual report and accounts become paramount and take precedence over the strategic.

Strategic and operational financial calculation

Where a firm makes successful strategic financial calculations this will tend also to be revealed in the annual profit and loss account. The firm would see improvements in the profit to sales ratio or profit to capital employed. In this case the relationship between the strategic and operational is a virtuous one financially. For the investment planner it is always important to consider this relationship because in many cases the firm's strategic calculations can operate to frustrate the achievement of an annual profit.

We have examined the nature of strategic financial accounting calculations and in particular the NPV Discounted Cash Flow calculation. In many cases the firm will commit only a small percentage of available financial resources to an investment project. However, cases such as the BSC and Eurotunnel projects have involved, or will involve, a massive commitment of financial resources. With all projects involving a large commitment of financial resources it is vital that the firm establishes a number of fundamental things.

Firstly it is necessary for the firm to establish whether returns from existing investments can cover the cost of the new investment outlay in the early years when the cash flow from the new investment will be negative. Unless the business is a 'greenfield' operation, the existing facilities will have to carry the new investments financially. It is therefore necessary to consider how robust the financial contribution from existing facilities to the new investment will be over a period of time.

Secondly, the firm's calculations concerning future revenue (cash inflow) and future costs (cash outflow) must be made as accurately as possible. Although the NPV calculation can be used to justify the strategic investment opportunity, it is the annual profit and loss account which will financially represent the operational success or failure of the investment. In the case study that follows on the Eurotunnel project, the future financial benefits of the investment are shown in terms of future profit and loss accounts from the year 1993 to 2041.

When a strategic investment project like the Eurotunnel is undertaken, any divergence from the expected financial scenario would have an adverse effect on the business annual report and accounts. If this were to happen the firm would find it very difficult to defend the annual profit level and maintain shareholder interest and confidence.

Where the firm is successful in executing its planned investment strategy then the annual profit and loss account will reveal this fact and confidence in the firm's abilities will usually be maintained. The firm in these circumstances will benefit from a virtuous circle of increased productivity and financial gain.

Failure carries with it a number of operational financial problems which will also have adverse knock-on effects for the firm more generally. When annual profit and loss starts to deteriorate because of strategic miscalculations, the firm will usually try to protect profit by shedding labour and eventually closing down plant and equipment. This connection, between market sales, labour and annual profit, can be made by considering the concept of value added.

In November 1987 the Offer for Sale document for Eurotunnel shares was issued. This document included financial calculations designed to attract funds and demonstrate the future profitability of the tunnel project. In this document a number of calculations were made, some of which we examine here.

Capital costs
It is expected that the tunnel will involve the investment of approximately £5 billion over a six-year period. This capital expenditure consists of money spent on construction costs (60% of the total) and administration and finance charges (40% of the total).

	£million
Construction Costs (July 1987 Prices)	2788
Corporate and other costs	642
Provision for inflation	469
Net financing costs	975
Total capital costs	4874

Profitability
The tunnel is expected to open in 1993 and for the period up to 2041 the Eurotunnel consortium has estimated the profitability each year of its operations. In the table below we have reproduced a sample of these calculations of annual future profit and loss.

Table 4.4 Eurotunnel profit and loss projections

Years	1993	2000	2013	2023	2033	2041
Turnover	488	1254	3236	6184	11 356	17 824
Operating costs	(86)	(235)	(631)	(1207)	(2246)	(3604)
Depreciation	(103)	(171)	(234)	(271)	(328)	(383)
Interest	(229)	(234)	39	173	370	616
Profit after tax	63	374	1476	2986	5605	8880

It is clear that these expected profits figures will crucially depend on a number of very important calculations. Firstly, that the expected construction times and cost schedule can be met and that there are no major problems or delays associated with construction, which would serve to increase the level of capital spend relative to the future earnings that have been projected after 1993. Secondly, that the expected growth rate in passenger traffic is achieved so that revenues earned are not overestimated and finally, that the level of operating costs is kept to a level that was planned. With these calculations of future profitability there are a great many uncertainties. What is certain, however, is that any problems associated with executing the strategy will be reflected in the actual annual profit and loss accounts in future years.

Source: Eurotunnel, 1987.

Labour, profits and value added

Value added represents the addition of value to raw material or semi-finished products to transform inputs into a saleable product. Value added can be calculated in the following way.

Sales Revenue	X
Minus bought-in services and materials	(Y)
Value added (X–Y)	$\underline{Z}$

Some firms, for example Ford UK, present a value added statement in their annual report and accounts. Many firms, however, do not publish a value added statement because this is not a legal requirement. As a result, it is often difficult to make the above calculation because values for purchases etc. are not available in the annual accounts. It is, however, possible to estimate value added because this represents a fund out of which a number of expenses are paid. Value added is distributed to wages and salaries, depreciation, interest charges, dividends, tax and retained profits (B. Cox (1979 p. 30) and E.G. Wood (1978 p. 15)). As a result it is possible to impute a value added figure by adding up the above expenses.

In manufacturing industry, the bulk of the value added fund (65 to 70%) is distributed to labour in the form of wages and salaries (including social costs such as national insurance contributions). In banking and financial services, however, the percentage distribution of value added to labour is much less, at 35 to 40%.

If the value added fund shrinks because of a failure in the market place it is usually labour which has to be shed in manufacturing because labour takes such a large share of the value added fund. It may be possible to let labour's share of value added increase, but this can only be temporary because it is at the cost of capital provision (depreciation and retained profits). With banking and financial services, even though labour's share is relatively much smaller, the firm may still have to make 'normal' provisions for profits/retained funds which necessitate the removal of labour. The connection between the level of value added and employment is a strong one, particularly in the manufacturing sector. Lower profitability is determined by a lower value added fund (which is determined by sales minus bought-in materials etc.), in which labour's share has increased at the expense of profit. In many firms there is a limit to the level at which labour employed can drop without this affecting the operation of plant and equipment. This encourages firms to respond to a decline in market sales by closing plant, so allowing the firm to shed large amounts of labour. This will be particularly the case where these areas of the business are the more technologically backward and use labour-intensive systems.

Operational retreat of this sort is a painful exercise but it is usually the only way a smaller value added fund can be used to support what remains. Retreat may be disorderly (K. Williams *et al.*, 1986) and involve the closure of quite efficient systems or the postponement of half-complete investment projects. However, when a firm makes successful strategic financial calculations, it may well see improvements in the ratios of profit to sales or of profit to capital employed in its annual profit and loss account, creating a virtuous financial relationship between the strategic and the operational.

What this underlines is the need for investment planners to consider the relationship between strategic and operational time frames. Firms in their strategic financial calculations should pay attention to the constraints of their annual profit and loss accounts, and be flexible enough to meet the requirements of the annual financial reporting period.

Further reading

A. Griffiths, and S. Wall, *Applied Economics* (Longman). It is well worth reading chapter 3 on firm objectives and firm behaviour.

P. Donaldson *Economics of the Real World* (Pelican, 1984). Chapters 9 and 10 on perfect competition and aspects of pricing in practice.

C. Drury *Costing, an Introduction* (Van Nostrand Reinhold (UK), 1987). Here we particularly recommend reading Chapters 9 and 11 on cost, volume, profit analysis and capital investment decisions.

B. Ryan *et al. Management Accounts, a Contemporary Approach* (Pitman, 1985). Here have a look at Chapters 6 and 10 on the pricing decision and the distribution of surplus – particularly pp. 246–251.

R. Hayes and W. Abernathy 'Managing our Way to Economic Decline' (*Harvard Business Review*, May/June 1982).

K. Williams *et al.* 'Accounting for the failure of nationalised industries' (*Economy and Society*, May 1986). On the use/misuse of net present value techniques.

C. Drury *Management and Cost Accounting*, 2nd edn (Van Nostrand Reinhold (International) 1988).

Exercises

1. What do your understand by the term separation of ownership and control? What factors have encourage this process to take place?

2. Traditional economic theory places great emphasis on the single objective of profit maximization. How does this objective differ from those that are developed under alternative managerial theories of the firm?

3. Break-even analysis is an accounting tool we can use to understand the relationship between costs, volume and the contribution to profit. How does the accountant's treatment of this relationship differ from that of the economist?

4. From the following accounting information:
   Sales price per unit   £100.00
   Variable cost per unit   £60.00
   Fixed Costs   £1 200 000
   Plant capacity 50 000 units
   You are required to do the following.

1. Calculate the break-even point.
2. Draw the break-even chart.
3. Calculate what happens to the break-even point when
   (a) Variable costs increase by £10.00 per unit, all other factors remaining constant, and
   (b) The sales price per unit falls by £20.00, all other factors remaining constant.

5. A firm has a choice between investing in project X or Y. Project X would involve a cash outlay of £100 000 for updating existing facilities. Project Y would involve the introduction of a new and more flexible manufacturing system. Each project has the following net cash flow profiles.

Project	Outlay (£)	Net cash flows at end of year (£)				
		1	2	3	4	5
X	(100 000)	25 000	30 000	40 000	30 000	20 000
Y	(150 000)	60 000	50 000	40 000	20 000	20 000

Assume for discounting purposes that the cost of capital is 10%.
You are required to do the following.
1. Calculate the NPV for each project.
2. Recommend which project management should undertake.
3. Discuss any other points you might wish to raise other than the strict use of the NPV criterion.

6. What do you understand by the term value added? If a firm suffers from a drop in sales revenue how will this affect the firm's value added and labour's share of value added? How will the firm react to adverse changes in labour's share of value added?

References

Baumol, W.J. (1959) *Business Behavior, Value and Growth*, Macmillan, London.
Berle, A. and Means, G. (1932) *The Modern Corporation and Private Property*, Macmillan, London.
Cosh, A.D. and Hughes, A. (1987) The anatomy of corporate control. *Cambridge Journal of Economics*, Dec.
Cox, B. (1979) *Value Added*, Heinemann, London.
Cyert, R.M. and March J. (1963) *A Behavioral Theory of the Firm*, Prentice Hall, Hemel Hempstead.
Drury, C. (1988) *Management Cost Accounting*, 2nd edn, Van Nostrand Reinhold, Wokingham.
Eurotunnel Offer for sale (1987), Eurotunnel, London.
Hall, R. and Hitch, C. (1939) *Price Theory and Business Behaviour*, Oxford Economic Papers.
Hayes, R. and Abernathy, W. (1980) Managing our way to economic decline. *Harvard Business Review*, July/August.
Marris, R. (1964) *Theory of Managerial Capitalism*, Macmillan, London.
Simon, H. (1955) A behavioral model of rational choice. *Quarterly Journal of Economics*.

Skinner, R.C. (1970) The determination of selling prices. *Journal of Industrial Economics*, July.

Solomons, D. (1965) *Divisional Performance, Measurement and Control*, Richard D. Urwin, USA.

Thompson, G. (1986) *Economic Calculation and Policy Formation*, Routledge, London.

Williams, K. *et al.* (1983) *Why are the British Bad at Manufacturing?* Routledge, London.

Wood, E.G. (1978) *Value Added – the Key to Prosperity*, Business Books, London.

5 Resource management and competitive advantage

Introduction

To prosper, or even just to survive in the longer term, most modern firms need to develop and sustain a distinct competitive advantage for their products in the market. In the previous chapters we have argued that in order to manage resources around competitive advantage firms need to do the following.

☐ Pay adequate attention to detail when making particular enterprise calculations.
☐ Be aware of the interrelationships between their market, production and financial calculations.

In this chapter, we explore in greater detail the requirements for effective resource management, before moving on in the remainder of the book to consider the conditioning effects of the environment within which firms operate.

The economic role of management

Peter Drucker, in his book 'The Practice of Management' (1968), suggests that economists do not view the management of resources as important, because in their theory of perfect competition all that the 'owner' needs to do is adjust factor inputs in a technically and economically efficient way around price changes.

> The economist's 'business man' – the picture that underlies the prevailing economic 'theory of the firm' and the theorem of 'maximisation of profits' – reacts to economic developments. He is still passive, still adaptive . . . Basically this a concept of the 'investor' or 'financier' rather than that of the manager.
>
> (*Drucker, 1968*)

Within the neo-classical theory of the firm, there is no real analysis of what management actually does when it manages resources. We have seen that some economists have put forward alternative 'managerial' theories which take some account of the separation of ownership and control. These theories recognize that within large firms it is managers, not owners, who have day-to-day control of the organization, and that their interests may well differ from those of shareholders. Writers like Baumol and Marris see managers pursuing objectives such as sales maximization or sustained growth, rather than profit maximization, and they go some way towards explaining why firms undertake strategic decisions which are not solely concerned with the unitary calculation of maximum profit.

'Managerial' economic theories are concerned to understand the conditions under which firm objectives and goals are set, and they recognize that different interest groups, both within and outside the organization, have different degrees of control over the setting of objectives. These theories are not concerned with how managements allocate resources to meet their planned objectives – they assume that managers never make mistakes, and always achieve their desired outcomes. In reality, however, the execution of resource management is crucial, and management effectiveness is a critical variable in determining a firm's success or failure. Here we would agree with Drucker's view that management has an active role in organizing the firm's resources to achieve a set of established objectives:

> Managing goes way beyond passive reaction and adaptation. It implies responsibility for attempting to shape the economic environment, for planning, initiating and carrying through changes in that economic environment, for constantly pushing back the limitations of economic circumstances on the enterprise's freedom of action – it is management's specific job to make what is desirable first possible and then actual.
>
> (*Drucker, 1968*)

As we saw in the earlier chapters of this book, a firm's strategic objectives can be affected, either positively or negatively, by the interrelationship between its productive, market, and financial calculations. At the planning stage, for example, management might estimate the benefits of a particular investment in terms of increased market demand or reduced production costs resulting from economies of scale. Such estimates often turn out to be inaccurate, however, because either of two things can happen.

☐ Insufficient attention is given to real production or market limitations that frustrate the anticipated outcome.
☐ The interrelated nature of the productive, market and financial calculations is inadequately comprehended.

In practice, many companies undertake planning calculations which, even on their own terms, fail to take into account important factors which may well operate to frustrate the eventual strategic outcome. Where, for example, a firm calculates the productive benefits from new flexible manufacturing systems in terms of a wider product-mix or a faster response to market demands, it may overestimate the benefits if it cannot fully integrate the new technology with existing processes in its overall system. In addition, the productive benefits may not be realized if the direct labour force have not been adequately re-trained to operate the new system effectively, or if the market does not require a level of product-mix variability to match the potential of the investment.

As we saw in Chapter 4, net present value analysis has become an important strategic financial calculation for many firms in recent years. Management accountants find this analysis a useful tool in improving the efficiency of capital rationing, and helping guide decisions towards those which cover the cost of capital to the enterprise. Because net present value analysis does not focus attention on the real productive and market limitations facing the enterprise, a firm's investment strategy can place a great deal of strain on the operational annual financial accounts. Where this damage to the annual accounts is severe, the firm may have to make adjustments which set a course which diverges from the strategic trajectory originally envisaged. In extreme cases, the firm may become subject to a liquidation order or a takeover bid.

This sort of conflict between strategic and operational time frames was highlighted in the case of British Steel (Case Studies 2.1 and 4.1). The British Steel Corporation's investment strategy in the 1970s promised profits in the long term, in the form of positive net present values, yet the firm was not released from the operational time period of the annual accounts. As the strategy failed, the firm had to take decisions to mitigate the annual reported loss, but these adjustments set it on a course which increasingly diverged from what it had planned.

Strategic planning

Peter Earl (1984) has emphasized that 'In the turbulent environment of modern capitalism, no firm, however large, can survive indefinitely without a sense of where it is trying to go'. Yet one of the problems which all managers face is that they operate in an uncertain environment, with limited information. In such a situation, there is a strong temptation to focus attention on a particular problem to be solved, ignoring other policy issues which might also require their attention. Once strategic calculations are embodied in a formal corporate plan, the enterprise may lock itself into a rigid policy of sticking to the plan at any cost. The plan then becomes an inflexible instrument of resource management and control. Where an enterprise is subject to continually changing internal and external conditions, the calculations made and the strategy followed will be inappropriate for the objectives originally set.

In the case of British Steel, management pursued a long-term strategic vision (of economies of scale), but failed to pay attention to the short-term financial consequences of their investment plans. Elsewhere, as we shall see in Chapter 6, managers may be constrained by financial institutions to focus on short-term financial performance, and fail to undertake the investments which might be necessary to sustain and develop the long-term competitive position of their products. The main lesson is that managers need to be more aware of the links between their strategic vision and the operational organization of production. Day-to-day decisions about resource management should contribute to a strategic outcome, but not compromise operational efficiency.

A great deal of literature from US Business Schools in the post-war period concentrated on the nature of strategic planning. As a result, much work was undertaken on the processes by which a strategic vision and

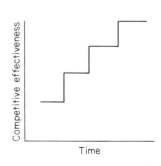

Figure 5.1 Progress through strategic leaps.

overall objectives were established within an organization. More recently, however, there has been a realization, within the US literature, that enterprise calculations designed to achieve a particular goal may, in practice, establish contradictory effects which set the organization on a course which is divergent from the strategic vision initially established.

Robert Hayes (1985) provides a useful framework for conceptualizing these ideas, which is summarized in Figures 5.1 and 5.2. In these diagrams, the vertical axis measures competitive effectiveness (e.g. lower cost, better quality, more features, or faster delivery), while the horizontal axis traces the passage of time. To maintain competitive advantage, firms need to move dynamically from bottom left to top right. They have a choice, Hayes suggests, between *strategic leaps*, in which a few fundamental jumps are made at crucial moments, and *incremental adjustments*, in which the enterprise seeks continually to adjust the relationship between the resources it uses.

Both strategic leaps and incremental adjustments involve strains on the business organization. Strategic leaps, Hayes suggests, can take a number of different forms.

> A product redesign, a large-scale factory modernisation or expansion, a move to another location that promises great improvements in wage rates or labour relations, an acquisition of a supplier of a critical material or component, or adoption of a new manufacturing technology.

In each instance, the firm has to dedicate a high proportion of its resources to the execution of the planned change, and this can bring major benefits if the firm is successful. The risks of committing so many resources are great, however, and the consequences of failure are severe. A major problem with this approach, Hayes argues, is that the logic of strategic leaps inevitably distances planning from implementation. 'A reliance on strategic leaps makes it unnecessary for workers or lower level managers to have a detailed understanding of how their own operations affect – and are affected by – other parts of the organisation' (Hayes, 1985).

With incremental adjustments, rather than putting massive resources into strategic leaps, the firm continually seeks improvements to existing systems. Such a strategy of operational adjustments around a strategic trajectory requires a horizontal development in which the workforce is actively encouraged to take responsibility for what would otherwise be considered 'management' functions. In the Toyota car plants, for example, the Kanban system is used to control the flow of materials through the manufacturing system. These cards are not just assignments of job details but also a form of management accounting in which the workforce actively manages the necessary accounting and production control information on the production line itself. In contrast, a massive investment in new computer software designed to plan and control the flow of materials through a manufacturing system might not involve the workforce in any active sense, and so not bring about improvements in the flow. With such a strategic leap, the objective of the investment, better stock control, may be achieved only partially, because the conditions necessary for improved materials flow have not been established.

The advantage of the incremental approach to strategic development is

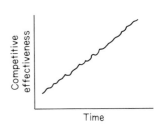

Figure 5.2 Progress through incremental steps.

that it does not place increased strain on resources in the short term. Where a firm is constrained by a need to maintain short-term returns on its investment, incremental adjustments can enable it to manoeuvre around the constraints while at the same time contributing to the strategic objectives it has set itself.

Corporate structure and financial control

In the US and the UK, many large firms over the past 50 years have adopted divisional corporate structures. In parallel with this development firms were encouraged to develop accounting techniques which are designed to enhance central control of strategic and operational financial performance. Firms have, for example, developed strategic financial investment appraisal techniques such as Discounted Cash Flow (DCF), Internal Rate of Return (IRR), and Net Present Value (NPV). Financial measures such as return on investment (related either to fixed assets or to capital employed) have been employed as a means of assessing divisional performance. In addition, budgeting techniques such as standard variance costing have been established to identify activities which have failed to achieve financial targets, and to justify intervention to rectify the variance – the principle of management by exception. The nature and advantages of particular divisional financial control measures are explored in more detail in Solomons (1965), and in the accounting text in this series.

It is possible to devise divisional organizational structures and associated financial measures which allow the divisional manager some discretion over investment resource allocation. Where, in general terms, a divisional manager has direct control over investment resource allocation then the division is called an 'investment centre'. Where, however, investment decisions are made by a central head office, the division would be a 'profit centre' (C. Tomkins, 1973, p. 7). In either case, the emphasis is on dividing responsibilities in a way which best combines central control with delegated initiative in the pursuit of corporate financial objectives.

Following on from these developments in the structure of organizations and the adoption of financial planning and operational control techniques, management education in the US and the UK has strongly emphasized the positive role of financial techniques as instruments of control and management of resources. Recent work by Armstrong (1987) stresses that this represents a distinct change of emphasis in the nature of management education. He argues that the traditional aim of management education was to develop a clearer understanding of the nature of the physical production system, through in–house experience and an education process which was designed to improve physical/practical understanding rather than financial management. The traditional system supplemented practical experience with an understanding of how financial targets could be made to influence the physical variables they were trying to manage – a positive aspect which, Armstrong suggests, is excluded from most current approaches.

Japanese management practices

The recent emphasis in US and UK business schools on the centrality of planning and control through financial variables has tended to shift attention away from the physical organization of productive resources towards indirect financial management. The Japanese, in contrast, have not made the physical the slave of the financial, but rather support strict physical controls over production and product development, with financial measures designed to influence objectives defined in physical terms.

According to Toshiro Hiromoto (Harvard Business Review, Jul/Aug 1988) 'Accounting [in Japan] plays more of an "influencing" role than an "informing" role.' He goes on to argue that 'In general, Japanese management accounting does not stress optimising within existing constraints. Rather it encourages employees to make continual improvements by tightening those constraints.'

Japanese firms are renowned for manufacturing excellence and success in world trade. Clearly this success cannot entirely be explained by the nature of management accounting practices, because the accounting system is but one of a number of conditions which support the effective organization of resources in Japan. Japanese economic success also has much to do with the wider social, economic and institutional framework within which the organization of resources is set.

It has become fashionable in the West to identify Japanese management practices as a key explanation of Japanese economic success, and as an example we should all seek to emulate. It is well known, for example, that Japanese management pursues aggressive marketing policies designed to guarantee that the product is sold at the volume necessary to cover development expenses etc. A recent survey by Doyle (1986) emphasizes that Japanese firms favour focussed marketing and aggressive volume objectives. In this survey 90% of Japanese firms claimed that their aim was 'aggressive growth' and market domination: whereas just 20% of British firms in the Doyle sample had similar aims.

More recent academic literature has emphasized the superiority of Japanese management's attention to physical control and organization of productive resources (Hartley, 1987; Schonberger, 1982). In particular the Toyota Motor Corporation has been praised for its use of Just-In-Time and Kanban materials stock control systems.

New and Myers (1986) and Ingersoll Engineers (1987) have pointed out that eastern best practice on materials management and the control of stock levels presents western management with a significant challenge. They show that materials usually account for 50–60% of total manufacturing costs, and that direct labour takes a much smaller share. This suggests that the attention which Japanese management gives to taking out stocks makes financial sense, and that the western accounting doctrine that stocks are an asset rather than a liability draws attention away from the causes of poor operational control of the production process.

Just-In-Time stock control systems (JIT) and Kanban re-order systems are increasingly seen as opportunities for improving management practices and the management of resources. These concepts are represented as being part of a general philosophy of reducing key aspects, in particular of organizational waste including stocks, labour time, energy inputs, process cycle time, etc. JIT and Kanban are the practices which have been developed by the Toyota Motor Corporation, under conditions where the firm does the following.

☐ Establishes forward linkages to the market place.
☐ Re-organizes internal production methods.
☐ Develops strong backward linkages to suppliers.

The Toyota example thus illustrates a number of distinct management practices which are presented as heralding a new opportunity for the effective management of resources.

In Toyota, production is essentially market-driven through the use of a Kanban card re-order system. This requires that each and every stage in the overall production process produces that output which is just sufficient to satisfy a given demand during a particular period of time. Where, for example, a batch of finished components is despatched, an empty bin is passed back to the previous production stage with an attached Kanban card acting as an instruction to re-order. The object is to minimize levels of finished stocks and of stocks which are held within the production process at any one time (work-in-progress).

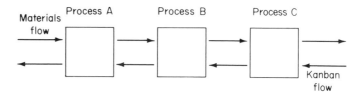

Figure 5.3 Kanban stock control.

Complementary to these methods of organizing flows of materials within the firm and to the market, Toyota production methods utilize a Just-In-Time purchasing system (JIT). Here the firm develops active rather than passive linkages to its suppliers. This mutually supportive relationship is designed to encourage product development and control over the cost of raw material and semi-finished/finished components into the final production process. Value analysis/engineering at the level of the supplier is particularly important when, as we have said, 50–60% of input costs consist of materials purchases and components. Just-In-Time delivery requires that the suppliers deliver in smaller batches just what is required by the production system without an unnecessary build-up of stock.

These aspects of external firm relations involve developing better management practices to minimize external and internal constraints to the effective organization of production. The stock control example we have just discussed exhibits these attributes of management calculation, because effective stock control requires detailed understanding of how external and internal constraints can be removed in order to facilitate effective management of material resources.

Stock is not a homogeneous financial variable as represented in the financial accounts of a company. It has a differentiated composition (raw materials, work-in-progress, finished goods), and is determined by a complex set of internal and external variables. Japanese best practice has sought to tackle the problem of stocks on a number of fronts because companies have realized that high stocks involved the commitment of large financial resources to their management, such as warehousing, transportation, administration, and energy costs, etc. The opportunity cost (Key Concept 4.3) of the resources which have to be tied up in managing stocks is high, and there is enormous scope for putting them to more productive use.

Debate around resource management issues in Britain during the 1950s and 1960s centred around the need for British firms to adopt American financial management practices in order to respond effectively to the American challenge. Attention has now shifted, however, to the challenge of Japanese imports and the 'Japanization' of British industry. It is argued that Japanese superiority in labour productivity, in market sales growth, and in cost and price structures is the result of special management practices and the organization of resources around the objective of competitive advantage.

Optimists argue that the techniques of Japanese management of resources can easily be transferred to the UK. Japanese direct investments such as the Nissan car assembly plant in Sunderland are used to illustrate the successful importation of Japanese work methods and production management. In particular, it is argued that work groups participate in the management process through suggesting how improvements can take place, releasing management from traditional conflict resolution and allowing them to spend more time managing the strategic direction of the firm. Work teams and multi-skilling are also seen as allowing the introduction of flexible work practices which, it is argued, are essential pre-requisites for the effective operation of flexible manufacturing systems and a flexible output mix.

Even if we accept, however, that Japanese firms and management practices offer positive opportunities for success, there is, as yet, not much evidence to suggest that Japanese best management practices have practically affected the management of resources in UK firms. Voss and Robinson, for example, surveyed the adoption of Japanese Just-In-Time management techniques (1987), and found that many UK firms were giving positive consideration to the adoption of certain Japanese management techniques. However, according to Voss and Robinson:

> When we review the findings on actual implementation, the picture is less favourable . . . few companies are actually making a serious attempt to implement JIT, the data suggest that companies are focusing on easy to implement techniques rather than those giving the greatest benefits.

This is illustrated in Table 5.1, which presents a synopsis of some of their major findings. What particularly stands out is the partial approach of most UK firms, and the small number of them who are giving active consideration to a Kanban system of JIT purchasing.

In a more recent report by Ingersoll Engineers (1987), on aspects of material procurement and control which are central to the Just-In-Time

Table 5.1 Ranking of aspects of JIT chosen for implementation by companies that have considered JIT

	Aspects implemented as a percentage of total sample	Aspects planned, implementing or implemented as a percentage of those implementing or planning JIT
Flexible workforce	30.1	80.0
WIP reduction	18.7	67.1
JIT purchasing	15.4	51.4
Work team quality control	11.4	50.0
Kanban	4.1	1.4
Sample size	n=123	n=70 (56.9%)

Source: C. Voss and J. Robinson (1987) *International Journal of Management and Production Control,* **7** (4), pp. 46–51.

approach, UK managements were criticized for their failings. On UK managements' approach to material cost reduction programmes, the report finds that:

> The majority accept the need for a material cost reduction programme but the targets and achievements are too low. In Japan typical targets achieved are 10–15% per year. The fact that the only company to respond with a target and achievement of more than 10% was a Japanese company now operating in the UK bears this out.

The Ingersoll report also notes that active involvement with suppliers is a critical factor in successful JIT management, but that here again UK management practices were not showing any real positive signs of development.

> Only 7% of respondents stated that they always involve their suppliers in cost reduction programmes. Over 20% stated that they have never worked with their suppliers to reduce cost. This really is very disappointing.

From this evidence it is clear that managements are aware of the new techniques, but that there are a number of factors which operate to frustrate their successful implementation, the following in particular.

☐ Management may not be able to implement the changes which are necessary because of a lack of appropriate skills. (The Ingersoll report concludes that: 'Either British industry is simply paying lip service to principles – backed by the occasional desultory attempt to apply them – or there is a genuine gap between strategic thinking and the actual skills required to implement change'.)

☐ The social and economic conditions under which firms operate differ between national economies, and these differences can limit management effectiveness in adopting the new techniques. We need to understand the conditions, both economic and social, against which management practices were introduced and now function. For example, do the economic, social and institutional relations established in Japan help contribute to effective management practices?

With regard to our example of stock control and JIT, it is apparent that in the Japanese manufacturing sector stock reduction (number of weeks that stock is turned over) is not a recent aspect of Japanese manufacturing operations. In fact, according to Williams *et al.* (1988), stock reduction was predominantly achieved in the period 1955 to 1970, when manufacturing output was growing at its fastest rate (Table 5.2). In certain sectors such as car manufacture major gains in stock turnover were achieved in this period of rapid growth, just as new gains in stock turnover are now being achieved in computers and data processing as output expands here also.

Table 5.2 Stock turnover and number of weeks stock is held in Japanese and UK manufacturing sectors

	Japan Turnover	Weeks	UK Turnover	Weeks
1955	5.7	9.2	5.2	10.0
1963	6.6	7.9	5.3	9.8
1970	7.9	6.6	5.1	10.2
1975	6.2	8.4	4.8	10.8
1983	8.3	6.3	4.9	10.6

Source: Williams *et al.* (1988).

Even by 1983, Japanese firms had not managed to make significant improvements to their 1970 performance on stocks, but they were, on average, still 4–5 weeks ahead of average performance in the UK. One of the conditions necessary for the removal of stocks would seem to be a rapid and sustained growth in output, which is itself determined by aggressive marketing and selling activities at home and overseas.

In addition to the general economic conditions necessary to facilitate stock reduction under JIT, work by K. Dohse *et al.* (1985) suggests that Japanese best management practices may not easily be exported because they were developed to function within a social framework that could not readily be replicated in other economies.

Here Dohse *et al.* suggest that there are a number of social/cultural conditions in the Japanese economy which operate to support the successful execution of Japanese management techniques. They argue that those who claim that Japanese management practices are easily transferable fail to appreciate that you would also need to transfer a number of social/cultural conditions in addition.

For example, in Japan a firm's relationship to its suppliers is one which is characterized by a strong dual labour market (Chapter 3). Here large firms pay higher wages than their suppliers, who tend to pay lower wages and make little provision for social benefits. Large firms as a result derive benefits from this dualism in terms of the cost of inputs into their own production processes. Out-sourcing of this type is less pronounced in the UK economy, because wage differentials between the main firm and the supplier are less pronounced (although it should be noted that there are elements of this type of relationship in the case of the food-purchasing policies of supermarket chains, who are able to benefit from low wages in agriculture).

Firms in Japan are more vertically disintegrated than their western counterparts (in terms of the percentage of raw materials etc. that are sourced from outside the firm) yet their relationship with their outside suppliers is much closer than is usual in the West. Small firms in Japan are often economically and legally dependent on the main producer or supplier. This relationship makes it much easier for large firms to have a direct influence over the supplier network.

In the UK, it is possible for a firm to take a direct interest in a supplier by means of a merger or takeover, yet the main motive for this is usually financial (K. Williams *et al.*, 1983). The productive logic of supply linkage, a central feature of the Japanese system, is rarely applied in the UK, and the outcome, as we have seen from the Ingersoll report, is a failure to bring about improvements in the supplier-producer relationship.

Much, as we have said, has been made of the Japanese approach to continuous improvement in every aspect of resource allocation within the organization. The literature on Japanese management and labour practices talks of 'Kaizen' or a step towards improvement. There are parallels here with the work of Hayes in the US, who, as we saw earlier in this chapter, suggests that management should seek continual incremental improvement rather than strategic leaps. Management in Japan, however, requires that labour plays an active role in the resource management process. Toyota, for example, 'places great emphasis on the independent discovery by workers of manpower excesses or unnecessary movements and on the effort to present improvement suggestions for their elimination' (Dohse 1985, p. 128).

In theory this active involvement of the labour force could be obtained by voluntary co-operation between management and labour within the organization – a form of co-operative structure. However, in practice Japanese managements have obtained the necessary changes in work practices by coercive control of the labour process. There, the potential capacity of unions to obstruct the efficient running of the production process was eliminated, giving management an almost unlimited set of prerogatives over labour in the pursuit of their goals.

The latter situation could be replicated in the UK only in a situation where UK unions were reduced to the role of a 'company' union on the Toyota model, in which the collective bargaining function was limited to wage negotiation and employment security rather than aspects related to work organization and working conditions. Even if we were to assume that management, in the context of the UK industrial relations system, could obtain the necessary prerogatives over the use of labour resources, it is doubtful that even these changes would be sufficient to establish the conditions necessary for successful management of resources on the Japanese model. A brief examination of the conditions under which Japanese management of resources takes place suggests that Japanese managements utilize a variety of instruments and policies to achieve their goals. Within this framework the organization of labour is but one factor in a hierarchy of factors for which management have responsibility.

In the case study of Austin Rover by Williams *et al.* (1987), the authors note that even though Sir Michael Edwardes reduced the role of the unions at Austin Rover (now Rover Group), there were other more important problems facing the firm. Some of them were more damaging to the firm's financial position than the labour problem. Increased management control over the labour process at Austin Rover did nothing to improve the firm's deteriorating share of the home market, or make effective use of the investments in inflexible new technology.

There is no doubt that understanding the secret of Japanese economic success requires a consideration of a number of complex issues. The effective management of resources is just one aspect of this greater understanding. However, there are a number of conditions peculiar to the Japanese economy that make the job of managing success far easier than in other economies.

We have talked about the aggressive marketing philosophy of Japanese manufacturers. This approach towards maximization of gross output of the firm is made easier when the domestic economy is to all intents and purposes protected. Protection at home clearly gives manufacturers an advantage when launching a product into overseas markets, while close legal and economic linkages protect the value added chains (Chapter 4) within the domestic economy and go some way towards establishing secure employment opportunities. Financial calculations made by the banks also go some way towards explaining why Japanese management have a greater degree of strategic freedom when deciding to allocate or reorganize capital and labour resources around specific objectives such as market advantage.

At the level of the firm, management's attention to the detailed organization of capital, labour and material resources helps contribute to successful enterprise strategy. The peculiar role of the unions and the position of labour helps establish the conditions needed for a continued incremental improvement in organization efficiency. However, management need also to have a clear and detailed understanding of the production process and the physical limitations that have to be overcome in order to improve the financial performance of the firm. This can be seen from the contrast between the American approach of strict financial control and Japanese management practices which require that significant attention be paid to non-financial factors as well as the financial aspect of control.

> Japanese manufacturing strategy places high premiums on quality and timely delivery in addition to low cost production. Thus companies make extensive use, certainly more than many of their US competitors, of non-financial measures to evaluate factory performance.
>
> *T. Hiromoto, 1988*

The example of the Eurotunnel project illustrates well the point that physical control is an important component affecting the financial results of an investment strategy. In a recent report on the progress of construction it is estimated that the tunnel bore construction is well behind schedule.

> After completing 3.3 kilometres of the 37.5 kilometre service tunnel the contractors have 110 weeks to dig the remaining 34 kilometres, implying a rate of 310 metres a week. Over the past six weeks, however, the UK side has been dug at the rate of only 106 metres a week while on the French side it is just 17 metres.
>
> *Sunday Times, 9th Oct 1988*

The effect of this delay is to increase capital investment costs which then requires the tunnel to generate even greater revenues in the future. This physical problem of the construction rate has already led to the Eurotunnel Consortium increasing its revenue and hence traffic forecasts to cover the costs of increased construction. Obviously any further deterioration in the build rate will add more to capital construction costs and require that the tunnel project generate even more revenue from traffic in the distant future. Given the uncertainty attached to forecasting demand it is clearly important for reasons of value added and profit to obtain and achieve the physical targets set.

Summary

We shall see in Chapter 7 that UK firms operate in a free market economy, and that the removal of non-tariff barriers in the Single European Market after 1992 will make it essential for UK firms to manage their resources more effectively around market advantage. Under these freer market conditions it will be difficult, if not impossible, for a national government to intervene in the interests of particular firms or industrial/commercial sectors. Subsidies and government grants will be looked upon as unfair practices by the European Commission. The freedom of scope for national governments to 'make' the macro-economic climate of a national economy more favourable will be much reduced.

Against this background UK firms are already facing severe problems from foreign competition in the domestic market. Any substantial loss of domestic market share then places severe financial limitations on a firm's ability to maintain export markets and employment levels. Under UK conditions, everything management does needs to be justified financially. Relaxation of the financial conditions at the level of the firm would allow a greater degree of strategic freedom concerning the physical resource planning requirements. However, where a firm suffers from a restricted or contracting market the freedom to alter the management of resources is much constrained. As we have seen with the Eurotunnel project it is often easier for management to alter the financial targets without attention to the real physical limitations which are the root cause of the problem.

In this chapter we have argued that it is vital that resources are managed effectively around competitive market advantage. We have considered the nature of American and Japanese management practices and their relevance for management of the enterprise under UK conditions. In many respects we can learn from the practices of other economies, but we should at the same time understand the particular social, economic and institutional conditions under which these practices have developed. There is no one universal set of 'good' management practices, which can be applied with equal effectiveness across national boundaries.

References

Armstrong, P. (1987) The abandonment of productive intervention in management teaching syllabi – a historical perspective. *Warwick Papers in Industrial relations*, no.15, June.

Dohse, K. *et al.* (1985) From Fordism to Toyotism. *Politics and Society*, **14** (2).

Doyle, P. *et al.* (1986) Japanese marketing strategies in the UK. *Journal of International Business Studies*, Spring.

Drucker, P. (1968) *The Practice of Management*, Pan, London.

Earl, P. (1984) *The Corporate Imagination*, Wheatsheaf Books, Brighton.

Hartley, J. (1987) Fighting the Recession in Manufacturing, IFS, Kempston, Bedford.

Hayes, R. *et al.* (1985) Strategic Planning Forward in Reverse? *Harvard Business Review*, no. 6, Dec.

Hiromoto, T. (1988) Another hidden edge – Japanese management accounting. *Harvard Business Review*, July/Aug.

Ingersoll Engineers (1987) *Procurement, Materials Management and Distribution*, Ingersoll Engineers, Rugby, Nov.

New, C. and Myers, A. (1986) *Managing Manufacturing Operations in the UK 1975 to 1985*, Cranfield Institute of Management, Bedford.

Schonberger, R. (1982) *Japanese manufacturing techniques*, New York Free Press.

Solomons, D. (1965) *Divisional Performance Measurement and Control*, Irwin, Homewood, Illinois.

Tomkins, C. (1973) *Financial Planning in Divisionalised Companies*, Accountancy Age Books, London.

Voss, C. and Robinson, J. (1987) Application of Just-In-Time techniques in the UK. *International Journal of Operations and Production Management*, **7** (4).

Williams, K. *et al.* (1983) *Why are The British Bad at Manufacturing?* Routledge Keegan Paul, London.

Williams, K. *et al.* (1987) *The Breakdown of Austin Rover*, Berg, Leamington Spa.

Williams, K. *et al.* (1988) *Why Take the Stocks Out of Manufacturing?* Mimeo, Aberystwyth University Economics Faculty.

6 The financial environment

Introduction

Most financial calculations take place in a specific organizational context, formed by the separation of ownership from control in the modern corporation. As we saw in Chapter 4, accounting practices, designed to protect shareholder interests, play an important role in conditioning management decision-making. The financial environment of the business will also affect the decision-making process, and we examine in this chapter the influence on the business of external institutions such as banks and capital markets.

We start the chapter by looking briefly at some of the factors which determine the balance between internal and external financing of investment. In a UK company, investment is overwhelmingly financed out of internal funds, and we explore some of the implications of this situation for company performance. We explore the terms and conditions under which external finance is provided to the firm, and how this can influence the behaviour of non-financial companies. We focus chiefly on the UK banking system and stock market, which are the main sources of external finance for UK business. However, we also draw attention to different institutional arrangements for financing business development in other countries.

The organization of business finance

The financial and organizational structure of single-owner firms is comparatively simple. A single person both raises the finance to set up the business (by putting up his or her savings as capital, and perhaps borrowing from relatives and friends or from a bank), and runs the organization.

In the modern UK economy, most production is carried out by large corporations, or limited companies, whose financial and organizational structures, as we saw in Chapter 4, are much more complex. Here the company is a legal entity in its own right. It raises capital by issuing shares, which entitle the shareholder to a dividend (a share in the company's distributed profits). To encourage potential shareholders to put up capital for a venture over which they may have little control, their shares can be bought and sold at any time on the Stock Exchange, and their liability for any debts the company may incur is limited to the extent of their unpaid shareholding. Shareholders can influence who is elected to the Board of Directors of the enterprise, but day-to-day control is delegated to management.

'Going public' is a crucial step in the development of any business organization, because it overcomes the capital constraints which limit the activities of single-owner firms. The costs of administering new share issues are considerable, and most firms do not raise a substantial proportion of their funds for ongoing investments from the stock market. As Table 6.1 shows, capital issues rarely account for more than a tenth of total funds raised by UK firms.

Table 6.1 Sources of capital funds of UK industrial and commercial companies

	1963–67	1968–72	1973–77	1978–82	1983–87
Total funds (£ bn per year)	3.8	6.2	12.4	29.4	49.9
of which					
Undistributed income (%)*	67	52	49	61	69
Bank borrowing (%)	12	19	24	15	15
UK capital issues (%)	12	7	5	4	11
Other (%)	9	21	22	20	4
Total	100	100	100	100	100

* Mainly profits which are retained by the firm and not distributed to shareholders.
Sources: Wilson Committee; *Financial Statistics*.

Most firms borrow from banks to finance their working capital – the short-term funding they need to cover their operating costs or raw material purchases. Bank borrowing can also be an attractive source of finance for longer-term capital investment if the return from that investment exceeds the interest charges. This is, however, risky for the firm, as interest is a fixed cost payable irrespective of whether profits are being made. Where profitability is low and interest rates are high, a firm may find that it cannot afford a loan, or is unable to obtain one because banks doubt its financial security. As we shall see later on in the chapter, banks in the UK are less willing, relative to those in competitor countries, to provide long-term loans for industry. The terms on which funds are provided to firms will affect their decisions regarding their use of such funds. High interest rates coupled with short-term payback conditions may well make firms avoid seeking funds from the banking sector.

The vast majority of company investment in Britain is financed by internally generated funds. These include depreciation provisions, which should be set aside for the eventual replacement of existing capital equipment, but which can in practice be used to finance current investment expenditure. They also include retained profits (profits which are not distributed to shareholders, after allowing for depreciation and stock appreciation). Companies are not obliged to distribute all their profits to shareholders, and while the latter may object if retained profits are boosted at the expense of dividends, finance from retained profits can easily be increased if the total value of profits is rising. However, where

Figure 6.1 Net rate of return[*] on capital employed[†] by UK industrial and commercial companies (excluding North Sea), 1960–87.

[*] Before interest and tax, and excluding stock appreciation and capital consumption at current replacement cost.
[†] Net stock of fixed assets (excluding land) at current replacement cost, plus book value of stock.
Source: British Business, 9th October, 1987 and 22nd April, 1988.

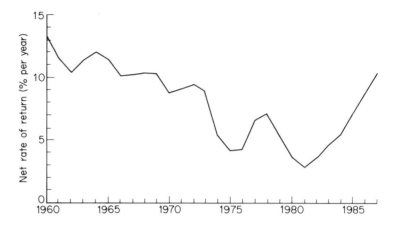

profit rates are declining as they were for most UK firms in the 1960s and 1970s (Figure 6.1), then the capacity to finance new investment from this source is severely constrained.

Internal and external finance

Heavy reliance on internally generated funds has been actively sought by many UK managers for the relative freedom it gives them from external control. It does, however, pose a number of problems, of which the most important is that investment expenditure is heavily dependent on current profit performance. Most seriously, if a company hits bad times, and it relies heavily on internally generated funds, its ability to finance the investment which may be necessary to turn it round is severely curtailed, unless it can obtain extra credit from a bank. A subsidiary problem is the tendency, in an inflationary period, for historic cost accounting conventions to understate the cost of replacing capital equipment and stocks (see our companion volume, *Accounting in a Business Context*, for a more detailed account of inflation accounting). This problem was particularly significant in the inflationary period 1973–76, when published accounts exaggerated the level of retained profits because of stock appreciation and low depreciation provisions. The net result was that firms had not made sufficient provision for the actual cost of replacing capital stock, which was based on inflated, not historic cost, values.

International comparisons of investment finance are difficult to make, because of differences in accounting conventions and in tax legislation. Data such as those in Table 6.2, which are based on net flows of funds over a period of time, avoid most of the possible inconsistencies. The differences which are revealed are dramatic. In Japan and France for example, two fifths of investment spending is financed by borrowing (mainly from banks), whereas, at the other extreme, it is quite common in the UK for all investment expenditure to be internally financed.

There are a number of important consequences which follow from the overwhelming reliance of UK firms on internally generated funds.

Table 6.2 Net sources of funds for investment by non-financial corporations, 1970–85 (Percentage proportion of 1985 capital stock)

	Japan	USA	UK	W. Germany	France
Retentions	65	90	107	73	62
Loans	42	26	5	12	37
Bonds	1	12	−2	−2	1
Shares	4	−3	−4	1	5

Source: Mayer (1988).

Notes: A net source of funds is new issues less acquisitions of the same type of liability, so that funds for the accumulation of financial assets are excluded. A negative figure represents an excess of acquisitions over new issues (the net outflow of share capital from UK companies, for example, reflects the extent of cash expenditure on acquiring shares in other companies).

Columns do not add to 100%, because trade credits and other financial sources are excluded, and because of statistical discrepancies.

The effect of share prices on corporate investment

In neo-classical theory, a firm's share value is assumed to reflect the present discounted value of future distributed profits. A dramatic fall in share values, as occurred in October 1987, would, according to this theory, reflect a decline in confidence in future profits, which would have the effect of discouraging investment. In fact, econometric analysis reveals that the 1987 stock market crash had very little effect on company investment (Bond and Devereux, 1988).

In our view, the finding that investment behaviour is largely independent of movements in share prices is not surprising, for two reasons. First, because the stock market is not a major source of funds for new investment, there is little reason for firms to be influenced in their investment behaviour by movements in share prices (though they may be influenced in their takeover activity). Second, share prices are influenced by the speculative activities of shareholders themselves. As we shall see later in this chapter, Stock Exchange speculation increasingly reflects autonomous expectations of short-term movements in share prices, rather than realistic forecasts of business profits over a long period. The result is an effective de-coupling of the performance of share values from the performance of the real economy, and in particular the profit performance of the firm.

The effect of interest rates on corporate investment

Neo-classical theory suggests that there is an inverse relationship between business investment and the general level of interest rates, on the assumption that the interest rate reflects the cost of financing investment. We would not disagree with the general view that higher interest rates discourage company investment, though we would draw attention to the empirical evidence that this effect is often not significant in practice (Savage, 1978).

Our view of the causal mechanism is, however, different from the neo-classical one. In the UK, retained profits are far more significant than bank loans as a source of finance for investment, and the direct effects of a change in interest rates are likely to be swamped by those of a change in retained earnings. Because firms often rely on bank loans to cover their working capital needs, a rise in interest rates will increase the costs of financing working capital, and this will have a depressing effect on profits. The effect of interest rates on company investment in the UK context is thus more indirect (via the effect on profits) than direct.

The effect of value added on corporate investment

Because the overwhelming majority of the funds used to finance capital investment in the UK are internally generated, it follows that there must be a significant relationship between the amount of investment a firm undertakes and its current financial performance. We have already, in Chapter 4, drawn attention to the value added fund – the difference between a firm's revenues and the costs of its raw materials and bought-in components. In most industries, the most important charge on the value added fund is the cost of hiring labour, and when sales are slack, there is often a tendency for labour's share of value added to rise, squeezing the share of value added which is available to finance new investment. If we regress labour's share of value added against gross fixed capital formation in manufacturing in the following year, we obtain a strong negative correlation ($r = -0.930$ in 1976–85, see Williams *et al.* 1988). This suggests that there is a strong relationship between variations in labour's share of value added and the level of gross fixed capital investment in the UK manufacturing sector.

The main lesson of Mayer's work (1987, 1988) on the sources of investment funds for industrial and commercial companies is that the level of fixed capital formation in the UK is determined by the current individual success of the firm in the market place. This must be the case where the firm's ability to generate sufficient internal funds sets the constraints on the level of physical investment. The peculiarities of the UK financial system are such that it would be possible to float off the real from the financial economy, without any substantial effect on the real economy.

Bank lending

One of the most significant differences between business finance in Britain and in other industrial countries is the traditionally low level of involvement by British banks in medium and long-term loans to industry. Historically, this is related to the earlier development of capital markets (markets for securities such as shares and bonds) in Britain than in most other industrial countries, and the reduced demand for longer-term bank lending that this implied. We shall be exploring the operation of capital markets in the next section. Low bank involvement in longer-term loans to British industry is also related, however, to the lending practices of British banks. To understand these, we need to know something of the structure of the banking system, and especially the different lending practices of retail and wholesale banks.

Retail banks

Retail (or 'High Street') banks offer deposit and loan facilities to personal

Banks make most of their profits from the interest they obtain by lending money to customers, or by investing in securities. Because only a small proportion of deposits will be required at any time in cash form, they can make loans, creating new deposits, up to a multiple of the original cash deposit.

A simple example will illustrate how fractional reserve banking creates deposit money. Suppose there is only one bank (the arithmetic is more complicated with many banks, but the principle is the same), which knows from experience that it needs only 10% of its assets in cash form. If a customer deposits £1000 this will allow the bank to lend out £900 (leaving a cash reserve of £100). The recipient of this loan can buy goods and services to the value of £900, which then returns to the bank as new deposits in the recipients' accounts. The bank can now lend another £810 (90% of the £900). This credit creation process continues until total deposits reach £10 000, of which 10% (the original £1000) is available as a cash reserve. From the original deposit of £1000 the bank has created additional deposits of £9000, as shown in the simplified balance sheet below.

Liabilities		*Assets*	
Initial deposit	£1000	Cash	£1000
Created deposit	£9000	Loans	£9000
Total deposits	£10 000	Total assets	£10 000

In practice, the balance sheet of a commercial bank is more complicated than this. On the liabilities side, deposits are divided into current accounts, deposit accounts, certificates of deposit, and non-sterling deposits. On the assets side, there is a spectrum of assets ranging from those which are high in liquidity (ease of conversion to cash) but low in profitability, to those which are low in liquidity but highly profitable. The precise balance of liquidity and profitability will depend on both the bank's commercial sense, and on government monetary policy as implemented by the central bank, the Bank of England.

The asset structure of a commercial bank
<------------------more liquid
Cash Bills Market loans Long-term marketable securities Advances
more profitable --------------->

KEY CONCEPT 6.1

**FRACTIONAL
RESERVE BANKING**

and business clients, in branches located throughout the country. They perform two main functions.

☐ Money transmission (distributing cash, and allowing deposits to be transferred between accounts by the use of cheques and credit transfer arrangements).
☐ Financial intermediation (bringing together lenders and borrowers).

These two functions are linked by the practice of fractional reserve banking – the creation of new deposits, in the form of loans and overdrafts, so that cash and other liquid assets held by the banks form only a small proportion of their total assets (Key Concept 6.1).

The money transmission activities of retail banks perform an important service for all businesses, and, in addition, retail banks have traditionally provided most of the external finance for small businesses, through overdraft
facilities. Here the bank sets a limit to the amount which the firm can borrow, but actual borrowing (and the interest charged) varies according to day-to-day requirements.

Wholesale banks
The wholesale banks (some of which are specialized subsidiaries of retail banks) are concentrated in the City of London. They are not involved in money transmission, but specialize in buying and selling sterling and foreign currency deposits on the money markets, and in lending large sums both in Britain and overseas.

Within the wholesale banking sector, merchant banks and overseas banks have in recent years become increasingly important providers of external finance to large and medium-sized firms, and they have pioneered the development of longer-term bank loans in Britain. Wholesale bank loans are usually on a fixed term basis, most of them ranging between two and seven years.

Availability of bank lending
There is considerable dispute about why banks in Britain are less prepared than those in other industrial countries to lend money to finance industrial investment. The Wilson Committee Report on the functioning of financial institutions (1980) concluded that, for medium and large firms, low levels of investment in Britain were due more to a lack of profitable investment opportunities than to a lack of adequate funding. Certainly in the late 1970s, when the banks were searching out ways of profitably recycling oil revenues deposited by the oil-exporting countries, there was no shortage of money to lend, and the fact that many of the new loans went to Brazil and Mexico reflected the strong demand by such newly industrializing countries for low-conditionality external finance rather than any perverse desire on the part of the banks to starve British firms of funds.

Critics of the Wilson Committee, however, suggest that supply side factors are important. Carrington and Edwards, for example, point to the shorter periods over which bank loans have to be repaid in Britain than elsewhere, and stress the negative impact this has on firms' ability to earn positive cash flows from their investments (1979, 1981). Poor investment performance in Britain, in their view, depends more on inappropriate conditions under which funds are supplied than on deficiencies in demand.

The issue of whether demand or supply factors are more important in explaining poor investment performance by British firms is clearly complex, yet closer scrutiny of the conditions under which bank finance is supplied certainly suggests that banking practices may have a significant effect on investment behaviour. In overdraft arrangements with companies, for example, it is common for retail banks to set out written agreements giving the bank security on a firm's assets in the event of the company being liquidated or defaulting on the conditions of the loan. The effect of this 'liquidation approach' is for banks to err on the side of 'conservatism' in their lending – they make loans available only if they are sure of getting their money back in the event of liquidation, and they tend to cut back on lending to firms which want to invest for rapid expansion. Such financial 'conservatism' by the banks may well reinforce a reluctance on the part of managers to consider investment projects which produce profits in the longer term.

American wholesale banks in Britain have, in contrast, pioneered a 'going concern' approach to lending. Here, the main focus is on the bank's assessment of a company's ability to repay loans out of future cash flows as a going concern. This requires greater technical expertise on the part of the banks, and formal agreements to provide them with advance warning of any deterioration in the company's financial situation and enable them to take appropriate action to guard against possible default. British banks have, in the 1980s, followed the American example, helping to lessen their traditional obsession with security. As a result, the overall emphasis of British bank lending to industry has belatedly begun to shift away from overdrafts and towards medium-term loans.

Bank/company relations

In countries like Japan and West Germany, banks are directly involved in regular discussions with their business clients about corporate strategy (Hu, 1984; Vittas, 1986; Corbett, 1987), and this has been instrumental in encouraging them to take on some of the risks associated with long-term business finance.

In Britain, however, it has been traditional for banks to adopt arm's-length relationships with their clients. This has been particularly apparent with overdraft arrangements, where, once the bank has been satisfied that repayment would be secured in the event of the firm's liquidation, there is little bank involvement in monitoring company performance. With the recent development of medium-term loans by the wholesale banks, the monitoring of company performance in relation to the terms of loan agreements has become more critical, but such monitoring takes place more at the level of scrutinizing financial ratios than of supervising the production and marketing decisions of the company.

The main exceptions to this occurred in response to the financial difficulties experienced by many firms as a result of the 1979–82 recession. In many cases the banks protected their loans by calling in the receiver. With some larger firms, on the other hand, the banks, encouraged by the Bank of England, took on a more interventionist role, offering to reschedule loan repayments on condition that the company reduced its debts by closing down or selling off some of its operations. As yet, however, banks in Britain have shown little interest in becoming more involved in ongoing strategic decision-making by their clients, and companies have not been willing to provide the information which such an involvement would require. As a result, bank provision of funds for long-term investment remains low.

The determination of interest rates

The interest rate which is charged when a bank lends money reflects a number of factors, including the following.

☐ The term of the loan. Long-term loans will usually bear higher interest rates than short-term loans, reflecting their lower liquidity for the lender, though they may occasionally bear lower rates if short-term rates are unusually high and are expected to fall.

☐ The risk of default. Lenders assess the risk that creditors will default on their loans, and make an allowance for this in the interest rate that they charge, with high risk creditors paying a higher rate than low risk ones.

☐ The general level of interest rates. Interest rates generally rise and fall over time, reflecting changes in the supply and demand of loanable funds, and government monetary policy.

Before the 1970s, interest rates in the UK were determined administratively. The Bank of England set a Bank Rate (subsequently called Minimum Lending Rate) which represented the interest it would charge if commercial banks needed to borrow money from it to maintain their liquid reserves. Most of the interest rates charged by the commercial banks were directly related to this interest rate, so interest rates generally rose or fell with Bank Rate.

In the immediate post-war period (1945–51), Bank Rate was set deliberately low at 2% per year, as part of a government policy to encourage industrial investment and to reduce the cost of the government borrowing which was needed to finance a programme of nationalization. Such a policy could be maintained only in the context of strict controls over the ability of individuals and firms to acquire foreign exchange. Without these controls, savings would have left the country to benefit from higher interest rates abroad, and the supply of domestic loans would have been restricted.

Foreign exchange controls were relaxed in the 1950s, and abolished completely in 1979. Partly as a result of this deregulation, two interrelated developments have occurred – London's emergence as the world centre of the Eurodollar market (Key Concept 6.2), and the determination of interest rates by competitive forces in the international money markets rather than administratively. These developments have created a situation where small shifts in interest rates can cause a rapid movement of funds from one currency to another.

As a result of these changes in financial markets, it is possible for the government to influence either interest rates or exchange rates, but not to control both simultaneously. In this institutional context, the government could not push interest rates below the levels prevailing in international markets, without suffering a shift in funds away from sterling and thus a fall in the rate at which sterling is exchanged against other currencies. (We shall be exploring the issue of exchange rate determination in Chapter 7.)

In the 1980s, the Bank of England abandoned the practice of announcing a Minimum Lending Rate, and allowed short-term interest rates to fluctuate, within an undisclosed band, in response to market forces. The effect of this change should not be exaggerated, for the Bank retained a

KEY CONCEPT 6.2

EUROCURRENCIES

Eurocurrencies are bank deposits and loans in currencies other than that of the country where the transactions take place. They originated in the late 1950s when West and East European holders of dollars opened accounts in Western Europe rather than in the USA, to avoid Federal Reserve Board control over interest rates and capital exports (and, in the case of East European countries, possible political interference). Eurodollars were followed by EuroDeutschmarks and other Euro-currencies, all of which shared the same characteristic of freedom from regulation. It was on the Eurocurrency markets that the oil-exporting countries deposited most of their increased revenues following the oil price rises of 1973–74, and it was these same markets that recycled the money to middle-income countries in Latin America and East Asia later in the decade.

The City of London rapidly became the world centre of Eurocurrency markets, largely as a result of the efforts of the Bank of England to ensure the dismantling of regulatory controls. This encouraged many foreign banks to set up branches in London, competing with each other for dollar deposits. Before long foreign banks began to compete for sterling deposits as well, breaking down traditional agreements and controls on domestic interest rates.

Most Eurocurrency deposits are short-term, and many are passed on to other banks to boost the profits of the lender and to satisfy the short-term liquidity requirements of the borrower. Loans to non-bank borrowers are large in scale and often made on a medium or long-term basis, with variable interest rates to lessen the risks of borrowing short and lending long.

Eurocurrency markets have revolutionized banking practice and the availability of finance throughout the world. They are, however, a source of potential instability, as the international debt crisis illustrates. The developing countries which had borrowed from the Eurocurrency markets at a time of booming export earnings and low interest rates were squeezed in the early 1980s by declining exports and high interest rates. Many debtor countries, notably Mexico and Brazil, were unable to repay their loans on time, and their debts had to be rescheduled. Additional loans to discourage debtor countries from defaulting were accompanied by harsh conditions, and living standards in the debtor countries suffered. The banks, meanwhile, had to write off some of their debts, creating severe pressures on their liquidity. The risks these pressures created affected all major banks (not just those most directly implicated in the debt problem), because of the extent of inter-bank lending and borrowing in the Eurocurrency system.

powerful influence on interest rates, not least through its 'open market operations' (buying and selling short-term paper debt). What was more significant was the willingness of the government to allow greater fluctuation in interest rates over the medium term. This reflected a shift in emphasis away from interest rate stability as a target of government policy, towards allowing interest rate variation as an instrument in achieving other government objectives.

As we shall see in Chapter 9, government policy since 1976 has been strongly influenced by the monetarist idea that the rate of growth of money supply should be controlled. If money supply is growing faster than the target rate, then bank lending, which creates the deposits which form the most significant part of the money supply, has to be restricted. In the absence of direct controls over lending, which the banks have strenuously resisted, this can be achieved only by allowing interest rates to rise. If, as is often the case, demand for credit is interest inelastic, it is possible for interest rates to rise to very high levels without money supply being significantly affected, as in the early 1980s. By the mid 1980s, the government was adopting a more relaxed stance in relation to monetary targets, but it had become increasingly willing to allow interest rates to fluctuate in order to maintain a more stable exchange rate. The main implication of these changes for business is that now, more than ever before, the cost of borrowing depends on changing conditions in the money and foreign exchange markets.

Interest rates as a determinant of investment

The interest rate on a loan is an important representation of the cost of borrowing money to finance investment, but it is also, according to both neo-classical and Keynesian theory, a major determinant of investment activity. This applies to a certain extent even where investment is financed internally, for the interest rate will indicate the opportunity cost (Key Concept 4.3) of the investment in terms of the return which could have been earned by say depositing the money in a bank or building society instead.

At any point in time, there will be a range of investment projects a firm could undertake. Some will have a high expected Internal Rate of Return (Key Concept 6.3), others a low internal rate of return. If firms embark on all investment projects where the expected internal rate of return exceeds the interest rate, then there will be an inverse relationship between the amount of investment and the interest rate. This is illustrated in Figure 6.2, where the investment demand schedule (sometimes called the marginal efficiency of capital schedule) shows how much investment firms would carry out at different interest rates, assuming other influences on investment remained constant. This schedule implies that a rise in interest rates from r_1 to r_2 would result in a fall in investment from I_1 to I_2.

KEY CONCEPT 6.3	The internal rate of return of an investment project is the discount rate for which the Net Present Value of the project (see Chapter 4) would be zero. It thus gives a representation of the project's expected yield over a period of time.
INTERNAL RATE OF RETURN	

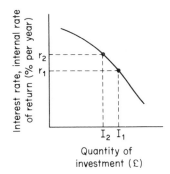

Figure 6.2 Investment demand schedule.

In practice, as we saw in Chapter 4, firms, in making investment decisions, need to consider not just expected long-term returns, but short-term cash flows as well. These will be affected by the period over which the loan has to be repaid, as well as by the interest rate. Indeed econometric evidence suggests that changes in interest rates have had little effect on the amount of fixed investment by UK business (Savage, 1978). There are a number of possible reasons for this.

☐ The effect of changes in interest rates may be swamped by other, more significant, changes, for example in business expectations of future profits (a point which was stressed by Keynes, but ignored by some of his followers), or in capacity utilization (which determines whether or not new investment is needed).

☐ A change in interest rate will in itself alter the monetary values of different items of capital equipment, and thus the expected rates of return on different investment projects, so invalidating the notion of a stable relationship between investment and the interest rate.

☐ As we have seen, only a very small proportion of company investment in the UK is financed by loans.

Capital market finance

As we saw in the previous section, it is often claimed that a major reason for the relatively low involvement of banks in medium and long-term lending to British industry is the highly developed nature of the capital market (or Stock Exchange) in Britain. Yet the data in Table 6.2 suggest that the Stock Exchange makes little net contribution to investment finance in the UK. To understand the role of capital markets in the UK economy, we need to appreciate the two interrelated functions which they perform – to issue new securities, and to trade in second-hand securities.

The new issue market

The new issue market is where companies (and central and local government) seek money from the general public, either directly or via financial intermediaries, against the issue of some form of security. For companies,

KEY CONCEPT 6.4	An ordinary share entitles the holder to a dividend out of the distributed profits of the company. This dividend depends on the current profitability of the company, and on management policy over the proportion of profits which is retained. There is no obligation for the company to pay a dividend, and if shareholders want to dispose of their shares, they have to sell them on the secondary market. Ordinary shares are thus risky assets whose liquidity (ability to be turned into cash) depends on the fortunes of the company.
COMPANY SECURITIES	Preference shares are different from ordinary shares, giving holders the right to a specified dividend which must be paid before dividends on ordinary shares are calculated. They are less risky, but often less profitable for the holder, than ordinary shares.
	Debentures are long-term loans which are repaid at maturity, carrying a fixed rate of interest. They are secured on the assets of the company, so that if the company goes into liquidation, debenture holders have a priority claim to repayment. In the 1960s, when real interest rates were low, debentures were much favoured as a source of external finance for large companies. In the late 1970s and early 1980s, higher and more volatile long-term interest rates made the issue of new debentures unprofitable. In the late 1980s, however, there was a revival in issues by companies of long-term debt, following lower interest rates and the 1987 stock market crash. Much of this debt now consists of Eurobonds, which are securities issued in exchange for Eurocurrencies (Key Concept 6.2).

the main form of security issued nowadays is the ordinary share, though before the 1970s debentures were often more significant (Key Concept 6.4). When a company issues new shares, the costs it incurs (from publishing a prospectus, employing financial institutions to issue and underwrite the shares, and offering the shares at a discount on the existing share price) can be prohibitively expensive for all but the largest firms, and this is an important contributory factor in the preference of most UK firms for financing new investment from internally generated funds. New share issues have become extremely significant in the financing of takeover activity, however, and we shall be exploring this at the end of this section.

The secondary market

Shares are long-term securities which cannot be repaid by the company. The liquidity which savers require if they are to hold long-term assets is provided by the secondary market, where shares can be sold to another party. Since deregulation of the Stock Exchange in 1986 (the so-called 'Big Bang'), share transfers are arranged through dealers who buy and sell securities both on their own behalf and as agents for members of the general public, and set the prices. Share prices rise when purchases exceed sales, and fall when sales exceed purchases.

Shareholders and shareholder behaviour

In the nineteenth and early twentieth centuries, shareholders were, almost exclusively, wealthy individuals. Nowadays, however, the most important shareholders are not individuals but financial institutions such as insurance companies, pension funds, investment and unit trusts. These financial institutions have long dominated the ownership of debentures and preference shares, and the proportion of listed UK ordinary shares that they owned rose continuously from a fifth in the late 1950s to a half in 1980. There has been a revival in direct share ownership by private individuals in the 1980s, stimulated by the government's policy of selling off public sector enterprises such as British Telecom and British Gas. Many of the individuals who were attracted into the stock market by these privatizations sold their shares for a quick profit, however, and within a short space of time the financial institutions became the dominant shareholders in these as in other large companies.

The behaviour of individuals who bought shares in privatized companies suggests that many individual shareholders are motivated more by the prospects of speculative gain than by long-term investment considerations. It might be supposed that financial institutions such as pension and life assurance funds would adopt a less short-term approach, concerned as they are with improving capital values over a long time period. As Table 6.3 shows, however, financial institutions are much less committed than they were to holding company shares in a stable portfolio. This table shows, for example, that pension funds had an average shareholding period of 23 years in the 1960s, but that in the mid 1980s this had fallen by roughly a factor of four to six years, implying a fourfold increase in the turnover of shares.

Table 6.3 Implied average period* for holding shares by financial institutions (years)

	UK and overseas shares			UK	Overseas
	1963–67	1968–71	1973–77	1984–86	1984–86
Insurance companies	23.8	14.9	7.9	6.3	2.7
Pension funds	23.3	9.8	6.1	6.0	2.4
Investment trusts	9.6	6.9	4.6	2.9	2.2
Unit trusts	9.8	3.3	2.2	2.1	1.2
All institutions	15.4	8.5	5.2	5.1	2.1

* Market value of ordinary shareholdings divided by sales activity.
Source: derived from Bain (1987).

Given this change in the behaviour of financial institutions, it is perhaps understandable that 'the majority of transactions (in financial markets) involves a reshuffling, mostly by professional operators, of existing assets' (Goodhart, 1987). Such reshuffling would not be harmful if it resulted in share prices being adjusted in line with informed analysis of changed company prospects. Concern is frequently expressed, however, that share dealings and prices are influenced more by the latest half-year profit figures, and by stock market 'sentiment', than by informed analysis of future yields. As Keynes warned more than half a century ago, professional traders have become largely concerned 'not with making superior long-term forecasts of the probable yield of an investment over its whole life, but with foreseeing changes in the conventional basis of valuation a short time ahead of the general public' (1936). The prime motive for buying shares thus becomes speculative capital gain (from short-term movements in the market price) rather than long-term dividend yield.

Shifting stock market sentiment and speculative activity by traders combine to ensure that periods of rising share prices ('bull' markets) alternate with periods of falling share prices ('bear' markets). When speculation pushes share prices up to levels which are artificially high in relation to asset values or earnings potential, the resulting 'crash' can be severe, as 1929 and October 1987 testify. In this situation, individual share market prices will frequently give a distorted valuation of a company's ability to earn profits in the future.

Short-term attitudes by financial institutions often have negative consequences for business investment. When a firm faces short-term financial difficulties, for example, UK financial institutions will often sell their shares in it, rather than work with it to resolve the difficulties (Bracewell-Milnes, 1987). A low share price will, in turn, reduce the firm's ability to raise new capital, and at the same time possibly increase its vulnerability to the threat of takeover. In this sort of financial environment, a firm may will be forced into making short-term defensive responses. It might be tempted, for example, to cut back on activities such as research and development or training, in an attempt to boost its short-term profits and improve its dividend payout. This would bring short-term relief if it stops shareholders from exchanging their shares to a takeover bidder but it may well damage the firm's long-run competitive advantage. Such defensive short-term preoccupation with maintaining dividend yield may only bring temporary relief where the firm's real productive and market requirements are sacrificed.

Mergers and takeovers

A firm which wishes to grow has the choice of doing so internally, by investing in new fixed assets, or externally, by amalgamating its assets with those of another firm. Amalgamation can take the form of a merger, where the Boards of Directors of each company agree terms, or a takeover, where one firm acquires another by buying more than 50% of the shares of another, despite the opposition of that firm's Board of Directors. In practice, it is often not possible to identify how willing each of the partners are to a merger agreement, so the dividing line between a merger and a takeover is a difficult one to draw, and the terms are often used interchangeably.

Merger activity tends to take place in waves, but over a long time span it can have a significant impact on the structure of asset ownership. In the UK, for example, the share of the largest 100 firms in UK manufacturing net output doubled from 21% in 1949 to 42% in 1976 (Prais, 1976), and most research studies suggest that at least a half of this increased concentration was a result of merger activity.

The valuation ratio is the ratio of the stock market valuation of a firm to its asset value.

$$\text{Valuation ratio} = \frac{\text{number of shares} \times \text{share price}}{\text{book value of assets}}$$

If the stock market values a firm's prospects highly, then its share price, and thus its valuation ratio, will rise. If shareholders are dissatisfied with a firm's financial performance, then they will sell shares, causing the share price, and with it the valuation ratio, to fall.

In Marris's economic theory of managerial capitalism (1964), the valuation ratio plays a crucial role in explaining takeover activity. If one firm values another firm's assets at a higher level than the stock market values the shares, it will be tempted to mount a takeover bid. Management failure to secure satisfactory profits will cause the valuation ratio to fall, making the firm more vulnerable to takeover. In Marris's view, the threat of takeover is an important constraint on management freedom to pursue growth at the expense of profits.

Empirical studies suggest that firms with low valuation ratios are slightly more vulnerable to takeover than firms with high valuation ratios, but that only very large firms are significantly less threatened by takeover than other firms (Singh, 1971 and 1975).

Most economic theories suggest that mergers result from a rational calculation of financial advantage. Neo-classical theory, for example, suggests that firms amalgamate to improve their profitability, either through economies of scale (enabling cost reductions) or through greater market dominance (enabling price increases). Managerial theory gives a different emphasis, suggesting that a firm will bid for another one if it thinks it can run the business more efficiently than its existing management (Gort, 1969). Takeovers, in this view, result from a discrepancy between the value a bidder places on a firm and the value placed on it by its shareholders, as indicated by the valuation ratio (Key Concept 6.5).

Research into the motives and effects of merger behaviour suggests that most mergers in the UK do not involve the precise calculation of financial benefit implied by neo-classical and managerial approaches alike. Newbould, for example, in a classic study of the 1967–68 merger boom (1970), found that mergers were usually rushed affairs, and that managers rarely had the time to analyse alternatives. Few managers were prepared to rationalize the combined assets of the merged firms to the extent that the achievement of economies of scale would imply, and high valuation ratios in 'victim' firms did not deter takeover activity. Most managers involved in mergers were primarily interested in extending or defending the market dominance of their firms, in response to increased uncertainty in their corporate environment. The trigger factor was usually intensified international competition (Case Study 6.1), or mergers by other firms operating in the same market.

The overwhelming conclusion of research on the financial effects of UK mergers is that, in general, profitability declines (Singh, 1971; Utton, 1974;

CASE STUDY 6.1

**GEC AND
BRITISH LEYLAND**

The late 1960s were a period of intense merger activity in the UK. The most prominent mergers were those between Leyland and British Motor Holdings to form British Leyland in the motor vehicle industry, and between GEC, AEI and English Electric to form the enlarged GEC in the electrical engineering industry. The similarities between the two sets of mergers were striking.

1. Both the electrical engineering and motor vehicle industries in the UK had failed to respond adequately to intensified international competition.
2. In each case, a smaller firm (Leyland, GEC) effectively took over a much larger firm (BMH; AEI and English Electric), financing the acquisition by shrewd share exchange deals involving little cash expenditure.
3. Both mergers were actively supported by the government, on the grounds that the superior management teams of the smaller firms would be able to improve the performance of the larger ones, and compete more effectively in international markets.

Despite these similarities, there were significant differences between the two firms in post-merger performance.

The GEC amalgamation, unusually for a UK merger, resulted in dramatic improvements in company profitability. These were achieved largely by plant closures which removed excess capacity, and by the successful introduction of a unified management system based on making each remaining plant a profit centre subject to strict financial controls. The very factors which produced financial success brought about other problems, however. The GEC workforce fell by about 40 000 between 1967 and 1971, largely as a result of the plant closures, but employment continued to decline after 1971 as the company failed to achieve significant increases in output. This, in turn, reflected the inhibiting effect of GEC's stringent financial controls on innovation and new product development.

In British Leyland's case, it was hoped that Leyland's marketing skills could be combined with BMH's production capacity to provide an effective answer to the challenge of foreign competition. In the event, the new management team found it hard to translate the skills of selling buses and trucks to the much more fashion-conscious volume car market, and they underestimated the problems of integrating the different components of the British Leyland empire. Insufficient funds were available to modernize production facilities, and salvation was sought in unattractive new models which failed to generate sufficient sales to even recover their development costs. There was no improvement in the already poor profitability record of volume car production, and by 1975 losses were so great that the firm had to be taken into public ownership to save it from bankruptcy.

Further reading
Cowling *et al.* (1980);
Williams *et al.* (1983);
Earl (1984).

Kuehn, 1975; Meeks, 1977), though new fixed investment increases (Kumar, 1981). In the rare cases where productive efficiency improves after a merger, it is because the superior management of one firm has obtained control over the hitherto poorly-managed resources of another firm (Cowling *et al.*, 1980). In most cases, however, managers are diverted from addressing the fundamental problems their firms face into sorting out the problems of organizational restructuring which mergers create (Sawyer, 1987).

In West Germany and Japan, where financial stakeholders are closely involved with the businesses they lend money to or have shares in, and where institutional arrangements make it difficult for outsiders to 'buy' control over a firm, contested takeover bids are extremely rare (Vittas, 1986). In these countries, the mergers that do occur tend both to be well thought out and to result in improved financial performance (Cable *et al.*, 1980; Ikeda and Doi, 1983).

The greater propensity of UK firms to embark on unsuccessful mergers seems to be closely related to the different financial environment in which they operate (Williams *et al.*, 1983). One of the main factors encouraging UK firms to grow by acquisition rather than by new investment is the ease of obtaining finance for this purpose. As Prais noted in 1976, 'the rise of capital issues made in exchange for acquisitions is one of the remarkable features of the last twenty years.' The result, as Table 6.4 shows, is that, in 'bull' markets, mergers are often financed largely by share issues (unlike new investment, which is financed largely out of retained profits).

Table 6.4 Expenditure on mergers and acquisitions by industrial and commercial companies within the UK, 1980–87

	1980	1981	1982	1983	1984	1985	1986	1987
Total expenditure (£ billion)	1.5	1.1	2.2	2.3	5.5	7.1	14.9	15.4
of which								
Cash (%)	52	68	58	44	54	40	26	32
Ordinary shares (%)	45	30	32	54	34	52	58	62
Preference shares & loan stock (%)	3	3	10	2	12	7	17	5
	100	100	100	100	100	100	100	100

Source: Financial Statistics.

At the same time as the Stock Market was making it easy for companies to buy other companies by printing new share certificates, changes in the financial organization of companies served to weaken their potential to resist hostile takeover bids. In the largest 100 UK manufacturing firms, for example, the Board of Directors typically owns only 0.5% of the shares (Prais, 1976), and the financial institutions which own most of the shares are frequently prepared to sell control to a takeover bidder if the short-term capital gain is sufficiently high. As a result, the threat of takeover is an ever-present one, for all but the very largest companies (Singh, 1975),

encouraging managers in vulnerable firms to focus on short-term defensive
financial calculations rather than on planning for the longer term.

State finance

It is sometimes suggested that the UK financial institutions are at fault, not
in starving industry of funds, but in providing funds and failing to use the
potential influence this gives them to stimulate and guide industrial
development. Fine and Harris, for example (1985), argue that by
responding too readily to company demands for 'easy' credit, UK
commercial banks have blocked the need for state intervention, which
might have guided industrial development along more co-ordinated lines.

Certainly the UK government, unlike those elsewhere in Europe and in
Japan, has only been minimally involved in the active promotion of
industrial investment, despite Keynes's suggestions (1936) that the state
should take greater responsibility for organizing investment to avoid the
harmful effects of speculation. As we shall see in Chapter 9, there has been
little consistency over time. In the 1960s, for example, the emphasis was on
investment grants for regions of high unemployment and funding industrial
reorganization. In the 1970s, an increasing proportion of state funds were
allocated to bailing out 'lame ducks' like British Leyland and to 'prestige'
projects like Concorde. In the 1980s, state funding of private industry has
been cut, and is focussed on selective support for individual profitable
enterprises, particularly to promote new technology.

Finance for small business

More than half a century ago, a government report identified a so-called
'Macmillan Gap' in financial provision for companies that were too small
to raise capital on the Stock Exchange (Macmillan Committee, 1931).
Soon after the war, the Industrial and Commercial Finance Corporation
(now part of 3i, and financed by retail banks) was set up to help fill that
gap. The ICFC has played a valuable, if small, role in providing start-up
capital and medium-term loans for small businesses. The Stock Exchange,
however, continued to ignore smaller companies, and small firms remained
dependent for most of their external finance on short-term loans from
retail banks, with all the disadvantages we identified earlier in this chapter.

The Wilson Committee, concluding in 1980 that supply of finance was
not a constraint on investment, made a significant exception of smaller
firms. Since its report was published, a number of measures have been
taken to improve the financial situation of small firms. The most important
of these are the following.

☐ The establishment of an Unlisted Securities Market, enabling small and
medium-sized firms to obtain share capital on the Stock Market at a
much lower cost than would be incurred with a full listing.
☐ The introduction, on an experimental basis, of a Loan Guarantee
Scheme, with the government guaranteeing 70% of bank loans to small
firms.

☐ The introduction of a Business Expansion Scheme under which investors in unquoted companies are offered income tax relief.

☐ The development by retail banks of medium-term loans, at fixed interest rates, for small businesses.

Conclusion

Managerially-controlled corporations in the UK finance a high proportion of their investment from retained earnings. The institutions which provide external finance are, however, extremely influential in conditioning their economic behaviour. Financial institutions are less directly involved with their business clients in the UK than in many other industrial countries, and this may also contribute to poor UK business performance. In the UK, the banks and the capital markets allocate funds to companies mainly on the basis of short-term financial criteria, and there is little opportunity for external scrutiny and guidance of firms' long-term development plans. As a result, firms are encouraged to pursue short-term gains rather than to embark on investments whose returns are long-term, and to grow by acquiring the assets of other firms rather than by developing new products, processes and markets.

Further reading

The Economics of the Financial System, by A.D. Bain (Martin Robertson, 1981) gives a comprehensive account of the UK financial system, which, for more recent developments, should be supplemented by the Money and Finance section of *Prest and Coppock's the UK Economy*, edited by M.J. Artis (Weidenfeld and Nicolson, new edition every two to three years). A more critical approach will be found in *The City of Capital* by Jerry Coakley and Laurence Harris (Basil Blackwell, 1983).

S.J. Prais's *The Evolution of Giant Firms in Britain* (Cambridge University Press, 1976, 2nd impression 1981) highlights the role of financial factors in the growth of large firms, while the Autumn 1987 issue of *The British Review of Economic Issues* contains two interesting articles on mergers, by Malcolm Sawyer (*Mergers: a case of market failure*) and Keith Cowling (*Merger policy, industrial strategy and democracy*).

For a good analytical treatment of recent debates in monetary theory you should refer to *Money matters*, by Sheila Dow and Peter Earl (Martin Robertson, 1982).

Exercises

1. Using data presented in recent issues of *Financial Statistics*, outline the main changes which have taken place over the past five years in the sources of capital funds of UK commercial and industrial companies. How would you explain these changes?

2. In what ways might the adoption by banks of a liquidation approach to business loans affect the investment behaviour of firms?

3. Why do long-term loans usually bear higher interest rates than short-term loans?
   In what circumstances might the reverse be the case?

4. In what ways have the development of Eurocurrency markets affected interest rates?

5. What have been the main changes in the structure of share ownership in the UK in recent years, and how have these affected business?

6. Why do so few UK mergers result in improved business performance?

7. Periods of intense merger activity are often associated with 'bull' markets on the stock exchange.
   What reasons can you suggest for this association?

8. What economic arguments can you see for and against greater government involvement in the allocation of investment funds to private firms?

References

Bain, A. (1987) Economic commentary, *Midland Bank Review*, Summer.

Bond, S. and Devereux, M. (1988) Financial volatility, the stock market crash and corporate investment, *Fiscal Studies*, April.

Bracewell-Milnes, B. (1987) *Are Equity Markets Short-sighted?* Institute of Directors, London.

Cable, J.R. *et al.* (1980) The Federal Republic of Germany 1962–74. In *The Determinants and Effects of Mergers* (ed. D.C. Mueller), Oelgeschlager Gunn and Hain, Cambridge, Mass.

Carrington, J.C. and Edwards, G.T. (1979) *Financing Industrial Investment*, Macmillan, London.

Carrington, J.C. and Edwards, G.T. (1981) *Reversing Economic Decline*, Macmillan, London.

Corbett, J. (1987) International perspectives on financing: evidence from Japan. *Oxford Review of Economic Policy*, Winter.

Cowling, K. *et al.* (1980) *Mergers and Economic Performance*, Cambridge University Press, Cambridge.

Earl, P. (1984) *The Corporate Imagination*, Wheatsheaf, Brighton.

Fine, B. and Harris, L. (1985) *The Peculiarities of the British Economy*, Lawrence and Wishart, London.

Goodhart, C.A.E. (1987) The economics of 'Big Bang'. *Midland Bank Review*, Summer.

Gort, M. (1969) An economic disturbance theory of mergers. *Quarterly Journal of Economics*, Nov.

Hu, Yao-Su (1984) *Industrial Banking and Special Credit Institutions*, Policy Studies Institute, London.

Ikeda, K. and Doi, N. (1983) The performance of merging firms in Japanese manufacturing industry 1964–75. *Journal of Industrial Economics*, March.

Kuehn, D.A. (1975) *Takeovers and the Theory of the Firm*, Macmillan, London.

Kumar, M. (1981) Do mergers reduce corporate investment? *Cambridge Journal of Economics*, March.

Macmillan Committee (1931) *Report of the Committee on Finance and Industry*, HMSO, London.

Mayer, C. (1987) Financial systems and corporate investment. *Oxford Review of Economic Policy*, Winter.

Mayer, C. (1988) New issues in corporate finance. *European Economic Review*, June.

Meeks, G. (1977) *Disappointing Marriage: a study of the gains from merger*, Cambridge University Press, Cambridge.

Newbould, G. (1970) *Managers and Merger Activity*, Guthstead, Liverpool.

Prais, S.J. (1976) (2nd impression 1981) *The Evolution of Giant Firms in Britain*, Cambridge University Press, Cambridge.

Savage, D. (1978) The channels of monetary influence: a survey of the empirical evidence. *National Institute Economic Review*, Feb.

Sawyer, M. (1987) Mergers: a case of market failure? *British Review of Economic Issues*, Autumn.

Singh, A. (1971) *Takeovers*, Cambridge University Press, Cambridge.

Singh, A. (1975) Takeovers, economic natural selection, and the theory of the firm. *Economic Journal*, Sept.

Utton, M.A. (1974) On measuring the effects of industrial mergers. *Scottish Journal of Political Economy*.

Vittas, D. (1986) Banks' relations with industry: an international survey. *National Westminster Bank Quarterly Review*, Feb.

Wilson Committee (1980) *Report on the Functioning of Financial Systems*, HMSO, London.

Williams, K. *et al.* (1983) *Why are the British Bad at Manufacturing?* Routledge, London.

Williams, K. *et al.* (1988) *Do Labour Costs Matter?* Mimeo, University of Aberystwyth Economics Department.

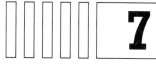

7 The international environment

Introduction

Modern business operates in an increasingly international context. Flows of trade between different industrial economies are becoming more and more intricate, as businesses feel the need to expand their export markets if they are to benefit from product differentiation without losing the cost advantages of large scale production. Greater sophistication in telecommunications and computerized information systems is making it possible for transnational firms to reorganize their production and marketing systems on a continent-wide or even global basis. Similar developments have made financial markets international, with financial centres competing with each other to lend money or issue securities to customers who are free to choose where in the world they make their transactions.

We start this chapter with overviews of the main changes in international trading patterns and investment flows. We then examine the balance of payments accounts, exchange rate determination, and the role of the International Monetary Fund in supervising the international monetary system. Analysis of the UK's trading situation focusses on the enormous shifts which have taken place in the composition of UK's current account in recent years, and particularly on the significance of the deterioration in the manufacturing trade balance. Analysis of UK capital flows draws attention to the increased vulnerability of the UK balance of payments to changes in remittances of profits from overseas investment. Finally, we end the chapter with a discussion of the creation of a 'single market' within the European Community in 1992, and the implications for British business.

International trade

Continued industrial growth requires increased inputs of raw materials and expanding markets. Early on in the development of an economy, this leads to an expansion of foreign trade, and businesses which succeed in foreign markets often increase their competitive advantage as they experience increasing unit cost advantages from the resulting growth in sales. In the early nineteenth century, Britain developed a virtual world monopoly in mass-produced manufacturing goods, and this was made possible by a pattern of trade where she produced a surplus of manufactured goods in exchange for primary products (food and raw materials) from abroad.

Ricardo's theory of comparative advantage states that it is differences between countries in the relative production costs of commodities which determine patterns of specialization and trade, not absolute cost differences. Suppose, to take Ricardo's example, Portugal can produce a unit of wine with 80 hours of labour, and a unit of cloth in 90 hours, while England can produce the wine in 120 hours and the cloth in 100. Portugal has, on these figures, an absolute advantage in both wine and cloth, but Britain could not import both on a long-term basis, for she would have nothing to offer in exchange. Profitable trade can take place on the basis of the different relative costs, however. Because in Portugal one unit of wine exchanges for 8/9 unit of cloth, while in England it exchanges for 12/10 units of cloth, Portugal has a comparative advantage in wine, and England in cloth. If Portugal produces two units of wine and England two units of cloth, then the same total output in the two countries can be produced in thirty less hours. Provided a mutually acceptable basis for exchanging Portuguese wine for English cloth can be found, both countries will benefit from specialization and trade.

KEY CONCEPT 7.1

COMPARATIVE ADVANTAGE

Labour hours involved in production

	Before specialization			After specialization		
	Wine	Cloth	Total	Wine	Cloth	Total
Portugal	80	90	170	160	–	160
England	120	100	220	–	200	200
			390			360

Ricardo identified differences in technology as the main source of production cost differences. In the twentieth century, two Swedish neo-classical economists, Heckscher and Ohlin, modified Ricardo's theory by suggesting that different factor endowments, rather than different technologies, were the main source of comparative advantage. If, they suggested, all countries have equal access to technology, then countries where labour is relatively abundant (and therefore cheap) would be encouraged by free trade to specialize in labour-intensive goods, while countries which are well-endowed with capital would specialize in capital-intensive goods. The analysis of the sources of comparative advantage is different in each case, but the policy conclusion is the same – prosperity will increase if barriers to trade, which prevent full specialization on the basis of comparative advantage, are removed.

David Ricardo, an early nineteenth century English political economist, attempted a justification for this trading pattern with his theory that world output would be maximized if each country specialized in producing the goods in which it had a comparative advantage (Key Concept 7.1). On the basis of this theory, he argued that a regime of free trade would maximize the gains from trade. What Ricardo's theory left out, however, was any indication of how the gains from trade might be distributed. As it happened, development of manufacturing industry brought about dynamic gains from improved efficiency of resource use and new product development, gains which were ignored by the static comparative advantage approach.

Productivity gains in the industrial countries eventually took the form of increased wages. In the primary producing countries, however, the benefits of productivity increases in the export sector were transferred abroad in the form of reduced prices, and the terms of trade (the rate of exchange between exported and imported goods) moved in favour of the industrial countries. There was more than a hint of self-interest, then, in the free trade policies which were espoused by the British government in the mid-nineteenth century.

In the late nineteenth century politicians in countries like Germany and Japan realized that if they adhered to the rules of the free trade game, they could never build up their own industries and the benefit from the increased incomes these would provide. They decided instead to develop their own industries behind protective barriers, forgoing the short-term advantages of free trade in order to develop more powerful advantages in the long term. In Japan's case, a distinctive policy of consciously channelling resources into areas of greatest potential long-term advantage has continued to the present day. Meanwhile, most of the economies that continued to specialize in primary products remained poor, both initially as colonies of the industrial countries and subsequently as independent nations. The main exceptions, the oil exporters, became rich not so much through free trade but because in the 1970s they took collective action, through the Organization of Petroleum Exporting Countries (OPEC), to raise revenues by restricting oil supply to the world market.

After the second world war, there was an enormous expansion of international trade, most of which took the form of two-way trade in manufactured goods between industrial market economies. As we saw in Chapter 1, markets for many consumer goods have become more sophisticated, with non-price factors becoming ever-more significant as determinants of demand as disposable incomes increased. Some consumers have turned to imports to satisfy their particular requirements, and domestic firms have had to differentiate their product range in order to limit losses in their market share to importers. As domestic product markets have fragmented, many firms have been encouraged to seek out new export markets, in order to increase their returns on new product development.

Expanding two-way flows of imports and exports between industrial countries have been accompanied, and encouraged, by reciprocal reductions in tariffs (negotiated through GATT, the General Agreement on Tariffs and Trade), and by the creation of regional free trade areas (especially the European Community, or EC). As Table 7.1 shows, three quarters of all manufacturing exports from industrial market economies now go to other industrial market economies.

Growth in manufacturing exports from most industrial market economies has slowed since 1973. This period has, however, seen big increases in manufacturing exports from some developing countries, most notably Singapore, Hong Kong, Taiwan, South Korea, Brazil, and Mexico. As we

Table 7.1 Destination of manufactured exports from industrial market economies (Percentage of total)

	1965	1986
Other industrial market economies	67	74
Developing economies	30	22
High income oil exporters	1	3
USSR etc.	2	2
	100	100

Source: World Bank (1988).
Notes: The classifications used are those of the World Bank. 'USSR etc' is a group of nine centrally planned economies for which the World Bank has inadequate data.

saw in Chapter 3, much of the manufacturing growth in these Newly Industrializing Countries has involved labour intensive processes such as clothing manufacture and electronics assembly, and comparative advantage in labour costs is obviously a relevant factor here. It is worth noting, however, that South Korea and Brazil are now competing successfully against industrial economies not just with these sorts of products, but with more capital intensive products such as steel, ships, cars, and aircraft. As Ajit Singh has stressed (1983), 'many Newly Industrialising Countries are at a level of industrial development similar to, if not higher than, Japan 25 years ago.'

Recession in industrial market economies in the mid-1970s encouraged a partial return to protectionism (mostly in the form of non-tariff barriers such as subsidies for domestic producers or informal import quotas) as the governments of those countries sought to keep down domestic job losses. Much of this 'new protectionism' was aimed specifically at developing countries. Despite this, and thanks largely to the success of the Newly Industrializing Countries, the developing economies as a whole now export more manufactured goods than primary products, and they account for almost a sixth of world manufacturing exports, as Table 7.2 shows.

Table 7.2 Share of manufactured exports* by country group (percentage of total)

	1965	1986
Industrial market economies	91.4	84.0
Developing economies	8.5	15.6
High income oil exporters	0.1	0.3
	100.0	100.0

* Excluding those from USSR etc.
Source: World Bank (1988).

In understanding recent changes in manufacturing trade, it is often more useful to focus on the changing organizational, technological and market environments of modern manufacturing than on the comparative costs of classical theory. In particular, we have observed two things.

☐ Where product markets are differentiated and fixed costs of production are high, firms need buoyant export markets both to compensate for lost market shares at home and to maintain a level of output which reduces average fixed costs to a minimum.
☐ Where product life cycles are short, firms need increased exports to maximize the returns from sales of existing products which are needed to finance new product development.

As we saw earlier in the book, some Japanese firms have recently begun to utilize the opportunities of flexible manufacturing systems to increase their penetration of export markets by creating products which are more clearly differentiated from those of their competitors, and tailored to meet local demands. In this situation, the gains from trade for the consumer come not so much from lower prices but from greater product variety.

International capital movements

The classical model of international trade implicitly assumes that factors of production are mobile within, but immobile across, national boundaries. In reality international movements of labour and, especially, of capital have played significant roles in the development of market economies. We have explored some of the implications of international labour migration in Chapter 3, and concentrate here on international movements in capital. These take three main forms.

☐ Portfolio investment
☐ Direct investment
☐ Bank lending and borrowing

Portfolio investment

Portfolio investment is investment in securities issued by foreign governments or companies. Historically, this type of international investment became significant in the late nineteenth century, when British rentiers often invested more abroad (usually in government or government-guaranteed stocks) than they did at home. Its popularity declined after the 1930s, when a number of Latin American governments defaulted on their debts, but has revived again in recent years. Most portfolio investment nowadays takes the form of active trading by financial institutions in the shares of foreign companies and in the gilt-edged securities of foreign governments, and this has been encouraged by more relaxed government attitudes to foreign exchange control. Many investors have seen an international spread of securities as a way of diversifying their risks and avoiding too close a dependence on the financial performance of one particular national economy. Even so the events of October 1987 demonstrated the domino effect brought about by capital markets that have become so interlinked that a crash in one national market will affect all the others.

Direct foreign investment

Direct foreign investment involves an investor in one country purchasing and acquiring a controlling interest in assets in another country, or adding to (or deducting from) such a controlling interest. It can be financed by a transfer of cash, by an exchange of shares, or from profits made by local subsidiaries which are not remitted back to head office. Direct investment is used largely for the establishment or expansion of branch plants overseas by transnational corporations, or the acquisition of overseas companies.

There are many reasons why a firm might wish to establish production facilities overseas. Dunning (1979) suggests that a firm will be interested in international production when three conditions are satisfied.

- ☐ The firm has *ownership advantages* over competitors, such as privileged access to technologies or supplies.
- ☐ There are *internalization advantages* which encourage the firm to exploit these ownership advantages by direct investment rather than by licensing arrangements. The firm may prefer to have direct control over a technology it has developed, for example, to protect returns on its research and development investment.
- ☐ There are *locational advantages* of producing in another country, rather than exporting to it from its domestic base, resulting from lower production or distribution costs, for example, or from the possibility of getting round trade barriers.

Direct foreign investment has grown rapidly since the war, helped by technological innovations in communications which made it much easier for an international head office to control foreign branches at a distance. Transnational operations have grown particularly rapidly in technologically advanced manufacturing industries, in high volume consumer goods industries, and in business services like banking. As Table 7.3 shows, most direct foreign investment originates in industrial market economies, though the predominant role of US firms has been eroded in recent years by competition from Japan in particular.

Table 7.3 Origin of direct foreign investment by world's largest 483 companies (percentage share of flows)

	1962	1982
USA	68	49
UK	8	8
Other EEC	16	20
Japan	4	12
Other industrial market economies	4	6
Developing economies	–	5
	100	100

Source: Dunning and Pearce (1985).

Industrial market economies are the main destination, as well as the main source, of direct foreign investment, as Table 7.4 shows. There has in recent years, however, been an increase of direct foreign investment in developing economies, particularly Newly Industrializing Countries like Singapore, Hong Kong, Brazil and Mexico.

Table 7.4 Destination of direct foreign investment (percentage share of flows)

	1965–69	1980–83
Industrial market economies	79	63
Developing economies	18	27
Other and unreported	3	10
	100	100

Source: World Bank (1985).

The relationship between direct foreign investment and international trade is an intricate one. There is intense international rivalry between large firms in sectors like electronics and cars, and often if a firm is to survive in the face of increased competition from imports in its home market, it has to develop markets overseas. In some cases, firms will prefer to produce at home, and export to a new market. In other cases (where trade barriers or transport costs are significant, for example) they will prefer to allow a local firm to produce their products under licence, or to set up their own production facilities locally. In the latter case, direct foreign investment will usually be accompanied by exports of capital equipment and components – almost a third of all exports from UK firms go to 'related concerns' abroad, for example.

International trade between different branches of the same firm is one of the sources of competitive advantage which transnational corporations have over national firms. Transnational corporations can, for example, do both the following.

☐ Manipulate transfer prices to minimize their tax burden (Key Concept 7.2).
☐ Re-organize their production globally so as to minimize production costs (Case Study 3.2).

Transnational corporations can also develop a competitive financial advantage by exploiting differences in national economic conditions – by obtaining finance where interest rates are low, by lending cash reserves where interest rates are high, by altering the timing of profit remittances from subsidiaries to head office, or even by actively speculating in foreign exchange.

Bank lending and borrowing

As we saw in Chapter 6, banking activities have become more international in scope in recent years, and flows of borrowing and lending across national boundaries have become much more frequent. Some of this

A transfer price is the administered price used in a company's management accounting system to represent the value of goods and services which are transferred from one division of the firm to another. Transfer prices can be market-based (reflecting the market price of comparable external goods and services), cost-based (reflecting actual internal costs), or negotiated (between the divisions and company headquarters). These methods can produce quite different results, and for transnational corporations there may be considerable scope to set transfer prices artificially low or high so as to reduce taxes and duties payable to national governments.

Consider a car manufacturer which exports engines from its branch in Mexico, to be assembled with other components in the United States into a car which sells mainly in the United States. If there are duties payable on the import of engines from Mexico to the United States, then the cost of duties to the firm will be minimized by setting the transfer price low. If tax on profits is higher in the United States than in Mexico, however, then the burden of profits tax will be reduced by setting the transfer price high, which will exaggerate the proportion of global profits which can be shown to accrue in Mexico. The transfer price which is most advantageous to the company will depend on the levels of duty and tax levied in each country. In many countries such manipulation of transfer prices is illegal, but the law is often difficult to enforce, for governments cannot easily determine what an undistorted transfer price would be.

KEY CONCEPT 7.2

TRANSFER PRICES

borrowing and lending is extremely short-term – London banks will lend deposits overnight to New York and Tokyo, for example, and receive them back (with interest) the following morning. Some, however, is much longer-term, for example the recycling of OPEC oil surpluses to Newly Industrializing Countries via the London Eurocurrency markets in the late 1970s.

Loans set up under the Eurocurrency system are often extremely intricate, with deposits passing from bank to bank before they reach the ultimate borrower. As a result, the precise extent of bank lending and borrowing across national boundaries is often difficult to measure, and international banking activities are difficult for national monetary authorities to control. Many observers fear that this situation is particularly vulnerable to financial crisis, as difficulties experienced by any participant bank (as a result of default by a major debtor, for example) will be transmitted rapidly through the Eurobanking system as a whole.

Exchange rates and the balance of payments

Foreign trade necessarily involves the exchange of one currency for another. If, for example, a British engineering firm purchases a new lathe from a West German firm, its pounds have to be exchanged into

Deutschmarks. If, on the other hand a West German family come to Edinburgh for a holiday, they will have to change Deutschmarks into pounds. Foreign exchange markets exists to establish rates of exchange between different currencies which equate purchases and sales of each currency. Suppose, for example, the current exchange rate between pounds and Deutschmarks is £1 = DM3. If, at this exchange rate, purchases of Deutschmarks exceed sales, and sales of pounds exceed purchases, then the exchange value of the pound in relation to the Deutschmark will fall to a level where purchases again equal sales, at, say, £1 = DM2.98.

The balance of payments

A country's balance of payments is an accounting record of all transactions, in a given period, between its residents and residents of other countries. A summary of the UK balance of payments for 1985–87 is shown in Table 7.5.

Table 7.5 UK balance of payments summary, (£ billion)

	1985	1986	1987
Visible trade (balance)	−2.35	− 8.72	−10.16
Invisibles (balance)	+5.68	+ 8.54	+ 7.47
Current balance	+3.34	− 0.18	− 2.69
Net financial transactions	−8.93	−14.40	− 2.32
Balancing item	+5.59	+14.57	+ 5.00

Source: Economic Trends.

The visible trade balance (sometimes called the balance of trade) shows exports less imports of commodities (food, fuel and other raw materials, manufactured goods), while the invisibles balance brings together exports less imports of services (financial services, transport, travel, etc.), profits, interest and dividends on foreign investments, and transfers (such as payments to European Community institutions). The current account balance is the sum of the visibles balance and the invisibles balance. A negative figure, as in 1987, indicates a current account deficit, with expenditure on imports exceeding earnings from exports.

When there is a surplus or deficit on current account, this must be balanced by an equal and opposite deficit or surplus on net financial transactions. This item covers international capital flows such as direct and portfolio investment, bank transactions, currency speculation, and government transactions (including the use of official reserves to influence exchange rates by purchasing and selling currencies). In practice, though the published current balance and balance on net financial transactions should add up to zero, they rarely do. This is because of incomplete statistical coverage, particularly relating to short-term capital flows in response to interest rate or exchange rate changes. To compensate, the statisticians include a balancing item, which in 1986 was, as you can see, unusually large.

Changes in exchange rates

Before 1972, monetary authorities in the industrial market economies announced fixed rates at which their currencies exchanged against the dollar. From 1967 to 1971, for example, the exchange rate of sterling was £1 = $2.40. The Bank of England used its gold and foreign exchange reserves to balance supply and demand at this exchange rate. In the event of a rise in UK imports of US goods, increasing demand for dollars, the Bank of England would use its dollar reserves to buy sterling, so restoring the 'par' exchange value. In the event of a continued drain of reserves to support the exchange rate, the authorities had to take action to reduce the current account deficit (for example, by restraining demand, and therefore demand for imports), to increase inflows of private capital (for example, by raising interest rates), or to decrease outflows of private capital (for example, by controlling access to foreign exchange). Only in exceptional circumstances (as in 1967, when sterling was devalued from £1 = $2.80 to £1 = $2.40) was action taken to change the exchange rate itself.

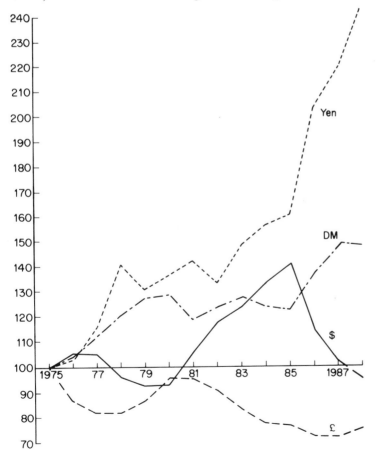

Figure 7.1 Effective exchange rates 1975–88 (annual averages, 1975 = 100). *Source: Bank of England Quarterly Bulletin.* *Note:* Effective exchange rates measure changes in the value of a currency against a basket of other currencies, weighted according to their importance in the country's trade.

KEY CONCEPT 7.3 **PURCHASING POWER PARITY**	If trading partners experience different rates of inflation, nominal exchange rates would have to change for real exchange rates to be maintained at a constant level. Thus if, over a period of ten years, the price of goods in the UK rose by 100%, but the price of goods in West Germany remained unchanged, to maintain the same rate of exchange between UK goods and West German goods, the exchange rate of the £ against the D-mark would have to halve. Purchasing Power Parity theory suggests that exchange rates change to maintain the purchasing power of each currency, so that in periods where inflation is rising faster in the UK than in other countries, the exchange rate of the £ will fall, and vice versa. In the long term, exchange rates do tend to move in the direction that Purchasing Power Parity theory suggests (though not necessarily to the extent that the theory would predict). Over shorter time periods, however, other influences predominate, and the activities of foreign exchange speculators are often the most significant determinant of changes in exchange rates.

The fixed exchange rate system broke down in the early 1970s, following the inability of the US authorities to satisfy foreign demands for dollars in the wake of the Vietnam war. Since 1972, exchange rates have been determined primarily by market forces. Despite frequent attempts by monetary authorities to inject some stability into a turbulent situation, by using reserves, or manipulating interest rates, to moderate changes in exchange values, the changes in exchange rates over this period have been dramatic, as Figure 7.1 indicates. While some movements in exchange rates are needed, to maintain purchasing power parity for example (Key Concept 7.3), the evidence suggests that there is a large speculative element in foreign exchange markets which intensifies any change in prices. If, for example, speculators expect the pound to depreciate against the dollar, they will use pounds to purchase dollars, forcing the exchange rate of the pound lower than their initial expectation.

The role of the International Monetary Fund

The International Monetary Fund (IMF) is an international institution, founded at the end of the second world war, which attempts to harmonize the exchange rate and balance of payments policies of member governments. Each government has a quota of Special Drawing Rights (international money created by the IMF), which can be used for balance of payments settlement. Governments can in addition borrow up to 25% of their quotas in foreign currencies from the IMF to finance balance of payments deficits. Further borrowing from the IMF is possible, but only on condition that the government adopts economic policies which meet the IMF's approval. The conditionality clauses of IMF programmes are highly controversial, with critics claiming that the IMF gives too much emphasis to short-term monetary adjustments (such as cuts in public expenditure), and gives insufficient attention to long-term structural factors which give rise to deficits (such as dependence on uncertain revenues from primary product exports).

The IMF has also been involved in attempts to find solutions to the international debt crisis. This crisis arose because developing economies which had borrowed heavily in the 1970s to finance ambitious development programmes were squeezed in the early 1980s by rising interest rates and declining export markets (Key Concept 6.2). Some Latin American governments were unable to repay their debts on time, and such was the scale of the debt that their creditors (commercial banks in the USA and Western Europe) faced the prospect of severe liquidity problems, and in some cases bank failure. The IMF stepped in to persuade the creditors to reschedule their debts, in return for which it negotiated tough austerity programmes with the debtor countries. The IMF's policies have been heavily criticized for placing most of the burden of adjustment on the debtor countries, even where the problem has been caused by factors outside their control (Griffiths-Jones, 1987; George, 1988). In some cases, debtor countries have found the IMF conditions too onerous, and have unilaterally limited their debt repayments. The threat of a major default, and consequent bank failure, has receded, but it remains real.

The effects of a change in exchange rates on business

Business is affected by a change in exchange rates in a number of different ways. If the exchange rate of sterling against other currencies rises, for example, this raises the prices of UK products in export markets, and makes it harder for UK firms to maintain export sales. If the exchange rate falls, on the other hand, UK firms may gain an immediate price advantage in export markets, but the price of imported raw materials and components will rise. Labour costs may also rise if rises in the cost of living, brought about by higher import prices, filter through into higher pay demands.

Changes in exchange rates also influence where transnational corporations raise and deploy funds, and the extent to which they repatriate profits from branches to head offices. If UK-based transnationals expect the exchange rate of sterling to fall, they will shift funds out of the UK (by reducing the repatriation of profits from overseas branches, for example), thus adding to speculative pressure against the pound.

It was partly to ease the deleterious effects of instability in the foreign exchange markets on business planning, and on the capital and invisibles accounts of the balance of payments, that monetary authorities in the mid-1980s made tentative moves towards restricting exchange rate movements to a target range, thus taking a step back towards a more managed exchange rate system. As with fixed exchange rates, the monetary authorities can use official reserves to influence exchange rates, or foreign currency borrowing to counter speculative movements of capital. In most countries nowadays, official reserves account for only a small proportion of total external assets, and the authorities have had to rely more and more on changing short-term interest rates to gain greater control over the exchange rate.

Changes in the interest rate can have knock-on effects not only on the exchange rate but also on monetary growth, and on business finance. As a result the authorities are often faced with a dilemma. What may seem an appropriate interest rate from the point of view of exchange rate policy may be inappropriate in terms of counter-inflation policy. In 1988, for example, the UK authorities are allowing interest rates to rise, as part of their policy of keeping down the expansion of domestic consumer credit and hence inflation. This will push up the costs to firms of bank borrowing, and at the same time will attract foreign funds into the UK, raising the foreign exchange value of sterling. Many UK firms will find profit margins squeezed between higher borrowing charges and reduced export earnings. As a result unemployment could start to rise again as firms attempt to cut costs.

However, it is important not to exaggerate the effects of changes in exchange rates on business fortunes. Japanese exporters to the USA, for example, suffered an enormous loss in price competitiveness as a result of the dramatic appreciation of the yen in relation to the dollar after 1985 (Figure 7.1). Yet Japan continued to run a large trade surplus with the USA in this period. What this reflects, of course, is the enormous significance of non-price factors in many product markets. Where a business has a competitive edge over its rivals in terms of quality, delivery, reliability, and after-sales service it may be able to sustain considerable increases in its relative prices before it experiences significant loss of sales. In addition we must note that the Japanese economy is essentially closed and when the yen appreciates it would also be possible to cross subsidize exports with domestic sales revenue.

UK trade performance

For most of the period since the Industrial Revolution, the UK has relied heavily on imports of food and raw materials, and has used foreign exchange earned from manufacturing exports to pay for them. This pattern of specialization reached its zenith around 1950, when 10% of the Gross Domestic Product (GDP – Key Concept 7.4) of the UK went into net

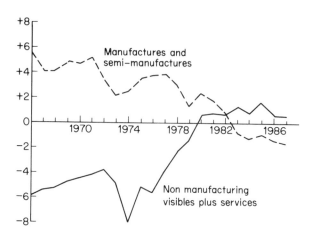

Figure 7.2 UK trade balances as a percentage of GDP, 1966–87

Gross Domestic Product (GDP) is an indicator of the national income of a country. It is the monetary value of the output of all marketed goods and services in an economy in a given period (usually one year). GDP can be measured in any of three different ways – by adding incomes from employment, value added, or final expenditure on domestic goods and services.

Gross National Product (GNP) is another commonly-used indicator of national income. It includes net property income from abroad as well as GDP.

There are important limitations to the use of GDP and GNP calculations as indicators of aggregate economic activity. These stem from (a) excluding non-marketed activities, such as housework and child-care within the family, or, in low-income developing economies, subsistence farming and (b) including consumption of stocks of finite natural resources (which reduces future production potential) (see Chapter 8).

KEY CONCEPT 7.4

GROSS DOMESTIC PRODUCT

manufacturing exports, to help pay for an even bigger net deficit in non-manufacturing trade. Since then, as Figure 7.2 indicates, the structure of the UK's trade has been transformed almost beyond recognitiion. As trade in manufactured goods between industrial countries intensified, there was a dramatic increase in manufacturing imports into the UK, so that by the early 1980s a third of all domestic demand for manufactures in the UK was met by imports. Growth in manufacturing exports failed to keep pace with this increase in imports, however, and in net terms manufacturing surpluses, expressed as a per cent of GDP, declined fairly steadily through the 1950s, 1960s, and 1970s. By the early 1980s, for the first time in centuries, the UK was importing more manufactured goods than she exported, and by the late 1980s the manufacturing deficit had reached crisis proportions.

There have been equally dramatic changes in non-manufacturing trade. The UK has become more self-sufficient in food, as a result of government subsidies and increased use of chemical inputs, though she continues to be a net importer. Dependence on imported raw materials has also declined, as a result of changes in industrial demand and the development of synthetic substitutes. UK trade in fuels has, however, been transformed by the combined impact of North Sea oil (increasing fuel supplies) and recession and energy conservation (reducing fuel demand). Whereas in 1976 net imports of oil into the UK reached almost £4bn, by 1980 the UK was a net exporter of oil, and in 1985 net export earnings from oil peaked at more than £8bn. The service sector, too, saw a significant increase in net exports in the period from the late 1960s to the mid 1980s, reflecting the rapid development of the City of London's role as the leading world centre of the Eurocurrency markets, and the associated influx of foreign banks. Taking non-manufacturing trade as a whole (including services, which are classified with property income and other 'invisibles' in the balance of payments accounts), the UK, which was a substantial net importer in the 1950s, became a net exporter in the early 1980s. By the late 1980s, however, deficits on manufacturing trade had become too great to be

CASE STUDY 7.1

**UK TRADE IN
MOTOR VEHICLES**

Up to the early 1960s, UK motor vehicle manufacturers supplied the vast majority of the UK domestic market, and earned in addition substantial export revenues. Since the mid 1960s, however, importers have achieved dramatic increases in their shares of the UK market, while UK manufacturers have failed to maintain their position in export markets. These trends – of increasing import penetration and falling export sales ratios – are illustrated graphically for the period since 1976 in the figure below.

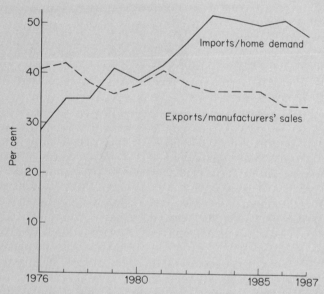

Figure 7.3 Import penetration and export/sales ratios for motor vehicles and parts, 1976–87

Source: Annual Abstract of Statistics

There are four main elements in this changing picture

1. The failure of British Leyland/Austin Rover (the main UK car producer until the 1970s) to develop new models which were sufficiently attractive to customers, and its strategic miscalculation to retreat from European markets.
2. The integration by Ford and General Motors (Vauxhall-Opel) of their European operations, and the concentration of much of their new investment on plants in West Germany and Spain.
3. The decisions of both Ford and GM to enter the small car market (traditionally dominated in the UK by British Leyland/Austin Rover) with new models, many of which are assembled in Spain.
4. The further fragmentation of UK car markets by imports from producers based elsewhere in Europe or in Japan.

Further reading
Dicken (1986), Chapter 9;
Williams *et al.* (1987), Chapter 4.

The net result of these and other processes has been the transformation of the UK from being a substantial net exporter of motor vehicles in the 1960s to being a substantial net importer in the 1980s.

compensated by surpluses on non-manufacturing trade, even including services.

In Table 7.6 below we can examine the compositional changes in the balance of payments since 1979. From this we can make a number of points about the nature of change in the UK's balance of payments. In 1979 the UK was a net importer of oil but, as we have said, by 1985 the UK exported £8101 million more oil than it imported as North Sea Oil came fully on stream. In addition to the growth in the oil surplus up to this point in time the contribution from invisibles, mainly services, also increased from £2902 million to £5683 million. In total, then, the contribution to the balance of payments from oil and invisibles added up to £13 784 million. In contrast, however, we can see that there has been a substantial deterioration in the UK's non-oil balance of trade. This includes categories such as food, drink, mining and manufacturing activities generally. This trade balance has deteriorated by roughly £8 billion over the period 1979 to 1985 from minus £2660 million to minus £10 446 million. Overall up to 1985 the contribution from oil and invisible earnings served to keep the overall current balance in surplus, that is, + £3338 million. However more recent figures suggest that the underlying trade deficit trend increase in the non-oil sector of the economy has not been compensated for by invisible earnings and oil. After a collapse in both the price and production of oil, the UK oil surplus stood in 1988 at roughly 30% of its 1985 level – a loss of almost £6 billion. The surplus on invisibles was only £½ billion greater in 1988 than in 1985 – not sufficient to offset the deterioration in oil, let alone the £18 billion overall loss in oil and non-oil trade. By 1988 these trends had combined to push the current account into a staggering £14 billion deficit (equivalent to about 3% of GDP).

Table 7.6 The UK current account 1979 to 1988 £m

	Current balance A+B	Visible balances Total A	Oil	Non-oil	Invisibles total B
1979	−496	−3398	−738	−2660	+2902
1980	+3122	+1353	+308	+1045	+1769
1981	+6936	+3350	+3105	+245	+3586
1982	+4685	+2218	+4639	−2421	+2467
1983	+3831	−1076	+6972	−8048	+4907
1984	+2022	−4580	+6932	−11 512	+6602
1985	+3338	−2345	+8101	−10 446	+5683
1986	−175	−8716	+4056	−12 772	+8541
1987	−2687	−10 162	+4184	−14 346	+7475
1988	−14 270	−20 335	+2344	−22 679	+6065*

* Provisional figures.
Source: Economic Trends and *British Business Magazine.*

Looked at in these terms, it might seem that, because of the improved performance of non-manufacturing trade, the UK's new-found deficit in manufacturing is no cause for concern – that, as Bob Rowthorn has put it (1986), 'Britain is no longer a massive net exporter of manufactures because she no longer needs to be'. There are, however, five reasons why we need to be concerned about the compositional shift from manufacturing to oil and services-related trade.

☐ *Jobs.* Changes in the structure of industry rarely result in a smooth transfer of labour from one sector to another. In fact, as we saw in Chapter 3, most of the new UK service sector demand for labour has gone to female part-timers, while many of the male full-timers displaced from manufacturing have joined the ranks of the unemployed. In addition, the changing structure of UK trade has brought about a significant net loss (in value terms) of full-time equivalent jobs. This is because the share of value added distributed to labour is much higher in manufacturing than in financial services or oil. As a result, the deterioration in manufacturing net output/value added has resulted in heavy job losses in manufacturing (particularly over the period 1979–82), while the net output/value added gains in oil and financial services have generated far fewer new jobs.

☐ *The level of aggregate demand.* Aggregate (total) demand in macro-economic terms is determined by the addition of consumption, investment and government expenditure and, in an open economy, the difference between imports and exports. Where the difference between exports minus imports is positive (a positive balance of trade) the economy will benefit from a positive boost to aggregate demand, say through tax cuts or more government expenditure. However where the economy suffers from a deteriorating balance of trade this will serve to dampen the dynamic multiplier effects of increased government expenditure or tax cuts on the domestic economy. In addition any reflationary expansionary policy may well serve to exacerbate the balance of trade deficit where domestic consumers have a higher propensity to import relative to our overseas customers (these issues are explored further in Chapter 9).

☐ *Competitiveness.* It is argued that recent trade surpluses in oil and financial services have boosted the exchange value of sterling above what it would otherwise have been, and as such this has increased the relative price of UK manufactures on world markets. This argument suggests that as the exchange rate falls this will automatically price manufactured exports back into the world market. There is considerable evidence to suggest, however, that UK manufacturing performance is deteriorating more because of a failure to provide the sort of products that consumers want, especially in non-price terms. Here, improved export performance would require not only price adjustments, but action to deal with a number of real production and distribution problems which might not easily be resolved in the short term.

☐ *Sustainability.* North Sea oil (and gas) has been a windfall gain to the UK economy but the supply of oil from the North Sea is finite. In fact physical production reached its peak in 1985 and is expected to fall by 5% per annum (House of Lords Select Committee, 1984). In addition revenues have been further hit by the subsequent slump in the world market price of oil. As fields approach exhaustion in the 1990s, surpluses from oil will disappear, and, if consumption patterns do not alter, the UK will again become a substantial net importer of oil. The possibilities of a growth in net exports of services that will compensate for the loss of manufacturing and oil is limited because of the quality and extent of those earnings. After the October crash the level of invisible earnings each month fell from an average of £700 million in the first half of 1987 to a level of £470 million in the first half of 1988. These income flows are vulnerable to fluctuations in the exchange rate and world economic growth rates. For example profits and dividends remitted back to the UK have to be converted to sterling by the exchange rate. If the exchange rate is £1 = $1.50 then $100 of dividends is equivalent to £66.7 but if the exchange rate rises to say £1 = $1.80 then the remitted value of $100 in sterling is £55.50.

It is therefore crucial that UK manufacturing industry start earning positive surpluses again if we are to pay for our imports. However the UK's ability to do this has been considerably weakened by the losses in technological infrastructure, skilled labour, and marketing channels overseas which took place in the period of oil surplus. UK manufacturing firms will, in addition, be struggling to cope with intensified competition from firms based elsewhere in the EC as a result of the creation of a single European market in 1992.

☐ *Stability*. The big increases in the surpluses of the financial services sector which have been achieved in recent years are a direct result of the lack of regulation of this sector. In the UK this has encouraged a high proportion of the world's Eurocurrency borrowing and lending to be located in the City of London. As we saw in Chapter 6, Eurocurrency markets generate a lot of instability, over which monetary authorities have little control. In terms of the balance of payments, the Euro-currency markets encourage speculative movements of funds between currencies, which affect not only exchange rates (and thus the relative prices of exports and imports), but also movements of capital across national boundaries, and corresponding shifts on the invisibles account in profits, interest, and dividends. If unregulated Eurocurrency markets are maintained, the only response a UK government could make to counter a speculative flight of capital from sterling would be to allow interest rates to rise to unprecedently high levels, which would in itself be destabilizing. The cost of a high level of dependence on the foreign exchange earnings of the City of London is thus a high level of in-stability in the UK balance of payments, and in the economy generally.

International capital movements and the UK economy

Thanks to the dominant role of the City of London in the economy and to the legacy of colonialism, the UK has a long history of involvement in the export of capital and in international finance. In analysing this involvement, it is important to distinguish between different types of international capital transaction, and between stocks and flows (Key Concept 7.5).

Flows of portfolio investment by UK residents in shares and bonds overseas have increased dramatically since the abolition of foreign exchange controls in 1979, as have the overseas transactions of UK banks. By the end of 1987, the stock of foreign portfolio assets (shares and bonds)

KEY CONCEPT 7.5 **STOCKS AND FLOWS**	A stock is an amount of something at a point in time, whereas a flow occurs during a period of time. Thus wealth is a stock, while income is a flow. Investment can be measured both as a stock or as a flow, and so it is particularly important not to confuse the two meanings. Each year, for example, there is a flow of direct investment by UK firms overseas, which in 1987 was valued at £15.3bn. At any point in time, however, there will be a much greater stock of direct investment by UK firms overseas, which has built up over the years – at the end of 1987, this stock was valued at £91bn. To complicate things further, a stock of investment at any point in time yields a flow of income in subsequent years – in 1987, the net earnings from direct investment by UK firms overseas came to £10.6bn.

held by UK residents was £118bn, as against foreign portfolio holdings in the UK of £52bn, while the overseas assets of UK banks (excluding portfolio and direct investment) totalled £425 bn, compared with total overseas liabilities of £474bn (UK Balance of Payments pink book).

Transnational firms play an unusually important role in the UK economy, which has expanded in significance throughout the period since the second world war. The UK is both a major source and a major recipient of direct foreign investment, which nowadays is financed mainly out of profits of subsidiaries which are not repatriated to company head offices. Flows of outward direct investment (overseas investment by firms based in the UK) regularly exceed those of inward direct investment (investment in the UK by firms based overseas). At the end of 1987, the total accumulated stock of external assets built up from UK direct investment overseas was valued at £91bn, as against a £53bn valuation of overseas companies' assets in the UK. As Table 7.7 indicates, the USA predominates both as the major source of foreign direct investment in the UK and as the major destination of UK direct foreign investment abroad.

Table 7.7 Stock of UK outward and inward direct investment*, by destination and origin, end 1984

Area	Outward investment destination	Inward investment origin
Total	£75.7bn	£38.5bn
of which (%)		
USA	35	51
EC	21	30
Other developed countries	26	13
Rest of world	18	5
	100	100

* Excluding property investment.
Source: British Business, 22 May 1987.

There are important differences in structural composition between UK direct investment abroad and foreign net investment in the UK. Almost three quarters of the direct foreign investment stock of UK companies is in non-manufacturing industries, and much of the manufacturing investment is in low-technology sectors like food, drink and tobacco. Investment by foreign firms in UK non-manufacturing industries has risen with the development of North Sea Oil and Eurocurrency markets, but manufacturing still accounts for more than two fifths of the direct investment stock of foreign firms in the UK, and much of this is in high-technology sectors like engineering products and pharmaceuticals.

Looking at capital flows in overall terms, the period since the abolition of foreign exchange controls has been characterized as one in which considerable net outflows of capital from the UK have taken place. This is in contrast to the mid-1970s when inflows exceeded outflows. Net outflows of capital from the UK build up the UK's stock of external assets less liabilities, which usually generates a stream of net inflows of interest, profits and dividends. These flows of property income from abroad form part of the invisibles balance on the current account in the balance of payments. In 1980, there was, unusually, a net outflow of interest, profits and dividends from the UK, but since then net inflows have been substantial, reaching £5.5 bn per year in 1987.

Not all of the inflows of profits, interest and dividends which are shown in the balance of payments accounts represent a gain for the UK economy. Most of the net profits earned by UK firms from foreign direct investment do not physically return to the UK, but are reinvested abroad. These unremitted profits, which came to £7.1bn in 1987, are included both as invisible earnings in the UK's balance of payments (even though they never enter the country) and as new outward direct investment. Similarly, the unremitted profits made by overseas firms in the UK (£2.9bn in 1987) are included in the UK balance of payments both as a debit on the invisibles balance and as new inward direct investment.

It is clear from the scale of these figures that transnational corporations, whether based in the UK or elsewhere, have considerable scope to bring about massive shifts in the UK balance of payments and in the exchange value of sterling, merely by altering the proportion of profits which they remit from subsidiaries to head office. This could occur for a variety of reasons, including a change in market conditions, tax rates, interest rates, relative inflation rates, expected exchange rates, or government policy. Even minor shifts in portfolio investment, or in short-term bank deposits, could have a similar destabilizing effect.

The European market and 1992

By 1992 the UK will form part of a unified European internal market. Unifying this market of 320 million presupposes that Member States will agree to abolish trade barriers of all kinds through a harmonization of rules, approximation of legislation and tax structures, strengthening of monetary co-operation and any other measures that will encourage European firms to work together.

It is argued that a free market within Europe will bring benefits to individual market economies within Europe generally. These benefits will be the result of welding together twelve individual market economies with a total population greater than that of North America. In addition an expanding European market which is unified should bring greater mutual benefits to individual economies that participate in the market. Finally, within a free European market, it is suggested, resources such as labour and capital should be mobile enough to move to those areas of greatest economic advantage.

Underpinning this view of a European market lies the economic model of a perfectly competitive market. In this economic model of the market a number of very strict conditions need to be met: all products are homogeneous, there is perfect information and knowledge, there are many buyers and sellers and finally, in the long run, there are no barriers to entry into the market and resources are perfectly mobile (see Appendix, Chapter 1). Although these conditions cannot be established in practice, it is apparent that the terminology and objectives of unification are directed towards establishing an approximation to this economic model.

Contradicting this vision of a liberal free market in post 1992 Europe is the proposal that market expansion within a European oligopolistic structure will offer opportunities for firms to develop economies of scale and lower unit costs of production. According to the European Commission (1988), substantial restructuring through merger and take-over activity will be needed in order to achieve these scale economies. We have, however, seen that economies of scale are often difficult to obtain in practice (Chapter 2) and that the logic of mergers and take-overs is often financial rather than productive (Chapter 6).

In order to execute the objective of a unified internal European market it is argued that a number of preconditions need to be established. We will consider each of these briefly and in turn.

The removal of physical barriers

Under present regulations customs and excise duties and quantitive restrictions related to intra-community trade have been abolished. However it is now proposed to remove internal frontier controls except where there is a need to control such things as drugs traffic and terrorism. One of the main functions of customs checks is to ensure that indirect tax (Value Added Tax) and excise duties are complied with and paid. As we shall see below it will therefore be necessary to establish unified taxation rates.

It is clear that when differential physical and fiscal measures (quotas and tariffs) have been removed, the need to comply with the formalities of authorization from internal frontiers will be much reduced.

The removal of technical barriers

Removing physical controls over the movement of trade cannot in itself create a genuine common market. It is also proposed that technical barriers to trade will be removed. By 1992 a particular national economy will not be able to frustrate imports from another member state on the sole argument that the imported product has been manufactured to technical specifications which do not match those used by the importing country. In addition the importing country cannot submit the product to extra nationally-prescribed tests. In order to achieve technical unification of markets the control of technical specification/standards will be passed into the control of European agencies such as the *Comité Européen de la Normalisation* (CEN).

In addition public procurement which involves domestic national government expenditure on public services, roads, housing, defence, etc., is usually marked by a tendency to keep contracts within the confines of the national economy. Here the Commission will try to ensure a greater liberalization of public procurement activities, which usually cover a sizeable part of individual national gross domestic product of the member European Community nations.

Finally the Commission considers that it is essential to remove obstacles that still exist in the free movement of labour and capital within the European Community (EC). It is argued that in areas such as services (banking, insurance and general marketed services) liberalization should also be extended. That is, there is a need to open up cross-border markets in banking and insurance. The liberalization of financial services would, in itself, also require the free movement of capital funds across member states.

The free movement of capital and the development of cross-border services are seen as complementary developments to the free movement of goods in order that trading firms and individuals have access to efficient financial services.

The removal of fiscal barriers

Fiscal measures figure as one of the main obstructions to freer trade within Europe. Goods which pass across frontiers are subject to a variety of customs excise duties and indirect taxes. In itself this creates the need for sophisticated customs procedures which may slow down the movement of goods. In addition it is argued that taxes such as Value Added Tax (VAT) on merchandise distort trade flows and price signals. At present national economies in Europe have a variety of different VAT rates as we can see in Table 7.8.

Table 7.8 Rates of VAT in member states (March 1985)

	Percentage
Belgium	17.0
Denmark	22.0
Germany	14.0
France	18.6
Ireland	23.0
Italy	18.0
Luxembourg	12.0
Netherlands	19.0
UK	15.0

The variation in rates from top to bottom is as much as 11% and an average rate of VAT would represent a considerable adjustment on the part of Ireland and Luxembourg. Leaving this aside, the normalization of VAT rates would allow customs to simplify their calculations by applying the same rate of VAT on purchases and sales across borders.

Although these adjustments to the framework of trading relations between member nations of the EC are presented as being of benefit to member nations and an opportunity to national firms, it must be stressed that these benefits can only be positively realized where firms have the resources and abilities to take advantage of the opportunity offered by a free European market. For the UK economy this is particularly important to stress when a large percentage of our trade is now with the EC, and trade with EC countries now accounts for all the UK's manufacturing trade deficit (Table 7.9). Case Study 7.2 illustrates the problems facing UK manufacturers of cellular radio-phones. We can see that although the necessary preconditions for a freer market in cellular phones are now being positively established, there are large relative differences in firm/industry capability to win market advantage from these changes. At the level of the firm, changes in the regulations concerning trade within Europe may be a necessary condition for an improvement in sales but not a sufficient condition, when increased sales and output depend crucially upon the actions taken by the firm itself.

It is argued that the changes made to the operation of the European market will be beneficial to member states both collectively and individually. In order for this to be the case individual national economies must have, in

CASE STUDY 7.2	A European market for radio-phone networks, using common standards is due to be ready by 1991. Joint ventures are now being established and advances in new technology could produce a phone system that fits conveniently into a person's pocket and is cheap to mass produce.
CELLULAR PHONE NETWORKS AND 1992	Colin Davis, Managing Director of Cellnet, points out that there have been truly spectacular achievements with fifteen operators coming together and 14 countries agreeing to a common standard specification for a service that will be available to 350 million people.

Orbitel, the UK manufacturer of cellular radio-phones, is a joint venture with Plessey and Racal and it has collaborative deals with Ericsson in Sweden and Matra in France, and is bidding to supply three continental cellular operations, whereas a consortium led by Alcatel in France with Motorola from the US and NEC from Japan, is the frontrunner, and is bidding to supply all continental markets. It is expected that the total EC market for such systems would reach £800 million by 1999.

The problems facing Orbitel are related not to establishing the EC market framework of a standard reference design but to the limited physical and financial resources the firm can commit, relative to its competitors, so that it can establish itself in these markets.

Source: Peter Lange, 'Hitech and Lowly Ambition' *The Guardian* July 11th 1988.

Table 7.9 UK trade balance in manufacturing, by geographical area, 1983–87 (£m)

Area	1983	1984	1985	1986	1987
EC (12)	−8072	−8843	−9544	−10837	−11085
Rest of W. Europe	−1516	−1947	−1945	− 2707	− 2796
USA	− 950	−1213	− 312	+ 1124	+ 927
Japan	−2654	−2913	−3206	− 3918	− 4165
Rest of world	+8343	+8608	+9201	+ 8093	+ 7125
Total	−4849	−6308	−5806	− 8245	− 9994

Note: In this table, exports are measured 'free on board' (f.o.b.), while imports include in addition carriage, insurance, and freight (c.i.f.).
Source: DTI

aggregate, firms that are capable of taking market advantage from these opportunities. We have argued in Chapter 5 that, at the level of the firm, this involves making sensible balanced enterprise calculations which achieve competitive market advantage. If we represent successful market advantage in terms of the balance of trade in manufactures with the EC, then the UK is going to be well behind the start when the 1992 gun goes off.

Conclusion

In an open economy, foreign trade is a crucial determinant of domestic economic activity. Where, as in Japan and West Germany, a country's firms are successful in foreign markets, export earnings can significantly boost domestic output and employment. Where, on the other hand, a country's firms are less successful internationally, domestic output and jobs are threatened, and the government may take measures which intensify the decline in order to restore balance of payments 'equilibrium'.

UK manufacturing firms have suffered an enormous decline in international competitiveness in recent years. The effects of this decline on the current account of the balance of payments were masked, up to the mid-1980s, by growth in exports of oil and financial services. We have already experienced a number of problems associated with this shift in the composition of UK trade, particularly in respect of unemployment. It is quite possible that the negative consequences of UK manufacturing decline will intensify in the 1990s, as North Sea oil runs out, and as the UK becomes fully integrated into the European internal market.

Further reading

The standard textbook on international trade and the international monetary system is *International Economics*, by L. Alan Winters (George Allen and Unwin, 3rd ed., 1985). For a more critical approach, emphasizing the significance of different perspectives on the international economy, see *The Fragmented World* by Chris Edwards (Methuen, 1985).

Peter Dicken's *Global Shift* (Harper and Row, 1986) is a mine of useful information on the global production systems which have been developed by transnational firms in recent years, while for detailed information on the changing structure of UK trade *De-industrialization and Foreign Trade*, by R.E. Rowthorn and J.R. Wells (Cambridge University Press, 1987), is invaluable.

Exercises

1. Using current issues of the *Bank of England Quarterly Bulletin*, the *Balance of Payments* pink book and the *National Income* blue book, and *Economic Trends*, update Figures 7.1 and 7.2 and Table 7.6. How would you explain the trends revealed?

2. Assess the arguments for and against the view that there is nothing wrong with a deficit on manufacturing trade so long as it corresponds to surpluses on non-manufacturing trade.

3. Discuss the main changes in the role of the IMF since it was founded. How would you evaluate its handling of the Third World debt crisis?

4. Assess the effects on the UK balance of payments of the abolition of exchange controls.

5. Choose a transnational corporation, and assess why it has evolved its particular global distribution of production.

6. In many markets, non-price factors have become more significant than price as determinants of consumer demand.
   What are the implications for
   (a) Firms seeking to expand export sales?
   (b) Government trade and exchange rate policy?

7. Choose a UK industry, and assess the likely effects of the creation of a European internal market in 1992 on
   (a) Company profits in that industry.
   (b) UK employment in that industry.
   (c) The balance of imports and exports for that industry.

References

Dickens, P. (1986) *Global Shift*, Harper and Row, London.
Dunning, J.H. (1979) Explaining changing patterns of international production. *Oxford Bulletin of Economics and Statistics*, Nov.
Dunning, J.H. and Pearce, R.D. (1985) *The World's Largest Multinational Enterprises*, Gower, Aldershot.
European Commission (1988) *Research on the Cost of Non-Europe*, vols 1–3, HMSO, London.
George, S. (1988) *A Fate Worse than Debt*, Penguin, Harmondsworth.

Griffiths-Jones, S. (1987) Learning to live with crisis. *The Banker*, Sept.

Rowthorn, B. (1986) De-industrialisation in Britain. In *The Geography of De-industrialisation* (eds R. Martin and B. Rowthorn), Macmillan, London.

Singh, A. (1983) A third world view. In *Money Talks* (eds A. Horrox and G. McCredie), Thames/Methuen; also in *The Guardian*, 18 February.

Williams, K. *et al.* (1987) *The Breakdown of Austin Rover*, Berg, Leamington Spa.

World Bank (1985) *World Development Report*, Oxford University Press, Oxford.

World Bank (1988) *World Development Report*, Oxford University Press, Oxford.

8 The natural environment

Introduction

One aspect of the environmental context of business which is often neglected is the natural environment. This neglect is unfortunate, because services which are made available to us by nature, such as raw materials (including air and water) and waste disposal facilities, are essential to economic activity, and to life itself. Because these services are provided 'free of charge', business calculations have not paid much attention to them, focussing as they do on the flows of production and consumption which result from the transformation of raw materials, not on how these flows affect stocks of natural resources. Stocks and flows are, however, interconnected, and business calculations which divert attention away from problems of resource depletion and pollution can stimulate forms of economic activity which degrade and ultimately destroy the natural systems on which they depend. Case Study 8.1 illustrates this in relation to the problems which arise from intensified consumption of fossil fuels.

Since Rachel Carson's classic denunciation of the destructive effects of the toxic chemicals used by the agricultural industry for pest control (Carson, 1962), public awareness of the dangers of environmental degradation has been increasing, and few people now doubt the need for some form of environmental controls. There is considerable dispute, however, over how much control is needed, and over what form it should take. We explore in this chapter two specifically economic contributions to this debate, that of neo-classical theory, and that of 'steady state economics', before going on to examine environmental controls in practice, and how business responds to them.

The neo-classical approach to the natural environment

Neo-classical theory suggests that market forces can be relied upon to solve problems of resource depletion, but that market prices need to be modified to take account of the harmful effects of pollution.

Resource depletion

Neo-classical economists suggest that market forces guarantee an optimal rate of depletion of natural resources (Beckerman, 1974; Kay and Mirrlees, 1975). Resource conservation, their argument runs, is a form of investment, in that costs (in the form of forgone consumption) are incurred in the present to obtain benefits (in the form of extended consumption for future generations) in the future. This investment needs to be evaluated according to the same rules, and using the same discount rate, as any other investment. As a result of the procedure whereby future costs and benefits are discounted back to present values (Chapter 4), there is no point in worrying about the rate at which a resource is depleted until shortly before its known reserves are exhausted. At this point, its price will increase, and this will simultaneously have four effects.

☐ Stimulate new exploration, and the discovery of new reserves.
☐ Stimulate technological advances which increase the recoverability of existing reserves.
☐ Stimulate an increase in the efficiency of resource use.
☐ Encourage producers to substitute abundant resources for the scarce resource (the substitution effect – see Key Concept 3.1).
☐ Reduce real incomes and thus consumption (the income effect).

Elegant though this 'solution' is theoretically, it is extremely doubtful whether the price mechanism could be relied upon in practice to solve all the problems of exhaustion of a key non-renewable resource. Total stocks of most minerals in the earth's crust are still large in relation to current rates of use, and a high proportion of the minerals which are consumed in the production process could, in principle, be recycled. The technological and financial constraints on recovering low concentrations of minerals are considerable, however, and there is no guarantee that these constraints could be overcome. Substitution of abundant for scarce resources would avoid the problem, but such substitution is not always technologically feasible, and we cannot assume that abundant substitutes for scarce resources will always exist. In a situation where a number of key resources faced exhaustion simultaneously, price changes would result in generalized inflation, not substitution.

An additional complication is that when firms discount future costs and revenues at a high rate, they may delay embarking on the necessary technological research until it is too late. As Hans Aage has emphasized, widespread increases in rates of resource recovery and recycling would require abundant, non-polluting sources of energy, and these we do not have. As a result

> Prices . . . cannot be expected to fulfil automatically the functions allotted to them in neoclassical analysis, and they cannot be relied upon in themselves to ensure continuous sufficiency of resources. Proposals for economizing on resources are not inconsequential, their main justification being to gain time in the race between depletion and technical advance.
>
> *Aage, 1984*

Pollution

Since Pigou's *Economics of Welfare* (1920), neo-classical economists have recognized pollution as an 'externality' (Key Concept 8.1) – a cost imposed by the polluter on others, for which no compensation is paid. The

KEY CONCEPT 8.1

EXTERNALITIES

Externalities are positive or negative effects which transactions have for people who are not parties to the transaction. When a firm pollutes a river, it creates external costs for people downstream who want to use the river for drinking water, and now need to install an extra purification plant. Similarly, if you smoke a cigarette in a public place, you create external nuisance and health costs for other individuals who have to breathe in the smoke. When, on the other hand, a new underground railway is opened, it creates external benefits for road users, who experience reduced congestion as a result of some road users transferring to rail.

Externalities represent a misallocation of resources, because producers of negative externalities will not have to pay the external costs, while bestowers of external benefits will not receive revenue for them. Generally speaking, an unregulated market results in too much production of goods and services which create harmful externalities, and insufficient production of goods and services which create beneficial externalities.

solution to this problem most favoured by neo-classical economists is to internalize the externality by imposing a tax on polluters, equal to the damage caused to other parties. This, it is suggested, would cause polluters to cut back on the pollutants they produce (by restricting output, and/or introducing pollution control equipment), and a social 'optimum' would be reached where the marginal social cost of production was equal to the marginal social benefit (in terms of consumers' willingness to pay) of the output.

This is illustrated diagrammatically in Figure 8.1. The horizontal line MPC(1) represents the marginal private cost of a production process to a firm, while MSC represents the marginal social cost, including the external cost of the pollution associated with the process. If D is the consumer demand curve, representing the marginal benefits of the product to consumers, then the competitive market equilibrium is at price P_1 and output Q_1. This is inefficient, however, because there is an excess of social costs over social benefits, represented by the shaded area in the diagram.

Now suppose the government imposes a tax, which adds T to the cost of the product. The marginal private cost schedule of the firm moves up from MPC(1) to MPC(2), and there is a new equilibrium at price P_2 and output Q_2. This is socially efficient because now the marginal social costs are equal to the marginal benefits. Note that the price to consumers is higher, and the output lower, than in the original situation. The extent of the price rise and of the reduction in output both depend on the slope of the demand curve – the higher the price elasticity of demand, the smaller the proportion of the tax which is paid by consumers in higher prices, and the greater the reduction in output. If the firm introduces pollution control equipment, because its cost is less than that of the tax, the effects on price and output will be correspondingly less. In terms of the diagram, the MPC schedule will move up by less than T, the MSC schedule will move close to

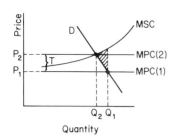

Figure 8.1 The effect of a pollution tax.

Before the Industrial Revolution, much of the energy we consumed came from renewable sources – woodburning, wind and water power. Relying in this way on natural flows meant that low levels of economic activity could be sustained, but that there were constraints on growth. In pre-industrial Europe, as in low-income Third World countries today, if people cut wood faster than the rate at which new trees could regrow, the end result was a fuelwood crisis.

The Industrial Revolution required massive additional inputs of energy, which have been met largely by intensified use of fossil fuels – first coal, then oil and natural gas. Fossil fuels are formed from the remains of marine and plant life, but the process takes millions of years, so that from a human perspective they can be regarded as fixed in supply. Such has been the rate at which these stocks have been run down, that world oil production has probably passed its peak. World coal supplies are much less scarce than those of oil, but intensified use of coal as a fuel would pose severe problems for the atmosphere.

All fossil fuels produce air pollution, but the problems are particularly acute with coal. Three major problems are involved.

1. *Sulphur dioxide (SO$_2$)*. When fossil fuels are burnt, they emit fumes containing large quantities of smoke and SO$_2$. Concentrations of sulphurous smoke cause bronchial problems, and the London 'smog' of December 1952 killed about 4000 people. Since then, smoke control zones have been created in urban areas, and tall power station chimneys disperse their SO$_2$ emissions over a wide area, lessening the incidence of 'smog'. These emissions, however, contribute to acid rain, which in recent years has caused lakes to be poisoned and trees to die throughout large areas of the world. It was only after intense international pressure that the UK government agreed in 1986 to authorize the Central Electricity Generating Board to install Flue Gas Desulphurization equipment to reduce SO$_2$ emissions from some of its power station chimneys.

2. *Benzoalphapyrenes*. It has long been known that Victorian chimney sweeps suffered high rates of cancer because of their exposure to soot and coal tar. This was due to the presence of benzoalphapyrenes, carcinogenic hydrocarbons which are probably also responsible for the clusters of cancers which have been discovered among people living in the vicinity of coal fired plants. Coal conversion (the addition of hydrogen to coal to produce a liquid fuel) has been found in the USA to be particularly carcinogenic.

3. *Carbon dioxide (CO$_2$)*. Emissions of CO$_2$ from burning fossil fuels accumulate in the atmosphere, preventing heat from the earth escaping into space, and causing the earth's surface to warm up. This so-called 'greenhouse effect', if unchecked, would bring about climatic changes which would jeopardize agricultural systems in many parts of the world. Eventually, it could start melting the polar ice caps, with disastrous effects on sea levels and life in coastal regions.

CASE STUDY 8.1

FOSSIL FUELS

Further reading
Schumacher (1985);
Pearce (1986, 1987).

the new MPC schedule, and the new equilibrium price will be somewhere between P_1 and P_2, with output somewhere between Q_1 and Q_2.

The practical problems of devising an appropriate pollution tax are immense. When Pigou discussed externalities, he used as an example the emission of smoke from factory chimneys, and identified social costs such as extra laundry expenses, which were readily quantifiable. Recent experience points, however, to atmospheric pollution having an environmental impact which is both more extensive and less amenable to precise costing than Pigou's illustrations would suggest. Changes such as the acidification of lakes and forests, or the build up of carbon dioxide in the atmosphere (Case Study 8.1) have profound and often irreversible effects, but scientists are seldom able to make an exact estimate of the amount of damage caused by a particular amount of a particular pollutant. Precise identification of marginal social costs is, therefore, rarely possible.

Steady state economics

The origins of Steady State Economics can be traced back to the chapter 'Of the Stationary State' which John Stuart Mill wrote, with Harriet Taylor, for his *Principles of Political Economy* in 1848. Mill and Taylor agreed with the classical political economists that the end point of industrial progress was a state where growth in population and capital would cease. Far from being dismayed by this prospect, however, they felt that a stationary state would be an improvement on existing conditions of industrial growth.

> I am not charmed [Mill wrote] with the ideal of life held out by those who think that the normal state of human beings is that of struggling to get on; that the trampling, crushing, elbowing, and treading on each others' heels, which form the existing type of social life, are the most desirable lot of human kind, or anything but the disagreeable symptoms of one of the phases of industrial progress.

He went on to suggest that

> It is only in the backward countries of the world that increased production is still an important object: in those more advanced, what is economically needed is a better distribution, of which one indispensable means is restraint on population', and that 'a stationary condition of capital and population implies no stationary state of human improvement.'

Mill, 1965

A leading contemporary advocate of a stationary economy is Herman Daly. In his book *Steady-state Economics* (1977), Daly emphasizes that economic growth involves both benefits (in the form of satisfactions from the consumption of products) and costs (in the form of depletion and pollution of natural resources). While growth is desirable when its marginal benefits exceed its marginal costs, environmental costs increase as growth proceeds, until at some point the marginal costs of growth outweigh the marginal benefits. We do not have the information to determine 'optimum' stocks of population and products, where marginal benefits equal marginal costs, but we do know that industrial growth over the past two centuries has been based on running down 'geological capital' – non-renewable stocks of minerals and fossil fuels. This type of growth cannot be sustained in the long term, making the pursuit of ever-increasing levels of consumption an impossible dream. The policy implications, Daly suggests, are clear. Instead of making economic growth the principal objective of economic activity, we need to do two things.

☐ To limit our use of natural resources to the minimum which is necessary to secure constant stocks of population and products.
☐ To limit national and global inequalities in income and wealth, so as to secure a sufficient standard of living for everyone.

To minimize environmental degradation, Daly argues that it is more effective to control resource depletion than to tax pollution. This is because depletion is easier to monitor and control, and because depletion controls would in themselves limit aggregate pollution. Governments, he suggests, should set quotas determining the amount of each resource which can be depleted each year, which they then auction to the highest bidders, using the revenues so gained to fund income redistribution. Once the political authorities have placed physical limits on resource throughput, the price mechanism can be relied upon to ensure that the scarce resources are used with maximum efficiency.

Daly's work is a stimulating antidote to those economists who skate over environmental problems, but there are important limitations to his analysis. Some environmentally-concerned economists, for example, would favour a more pragmatic approach, focussing attention on those forms of pollution that cause the most environmental damage, and exploring patterns of growth which could be sustained ecologically. At a practical level, too, few would share Daly's optimism about the feasibility, within the current international political environment, of limiting and auctioning resource-depletion rights.

Types of environmental control

In attempting to ensure that firms take more account of the environmental consequences of their activities, authorities can choose between charging firms for the environmental damage they cause and regulating firms to ensure they conform to environmental standards. Different though the approaches of Pigou and Daly are, they share a conviction that price incentives would ensure the optimum use of natural resources.

Theoretical issues and practical problems

From the standpoint of economic theory, charges have a significant advantage over administrative controls in that they provide continuing incentives for firms to search out new and more economic methods of reducing pollution and/or conserving resources, rather than just meet what the regulations require. Exclusive reliance on price incentives would be

CASE STUDY 8.2

**CAR EXHAUST
EMISSION CONTROL**

Internal combustion engines pass a number of pollutants through their exhaust systems and into the atmosphere. These include nitrogen oxides (which combine with sulphur dioxide in the atmosphere to produce acid rain), lead (which can cause brain damage, particularly in young children), and benzene hydrocarbons (which are carcinogenic). Increased car usage and the development of high-compression engines which need leaded petrol have interacted in the post-war period to intensify environmental destruction and ill health.

Petrochemical smogs, triggered by nitrogen oxide emissions, became a pervasive feature of city life in the US and Japan, and early in the 1970s both countries introduced legislation to control car exhausts. The new laws required all new cars to be fitted with catalytic converters (add-on devices which clean the exhaust after it leaves the engine), and required filling stations to provide the unleaded petrol which catalysts need. These measures have done much to reduce atmospheric pollution in the US and Japan, though pollution from factories remains a severe problem. They have also had the effect of restraining car imports, as the modifications needed to make European cars conform to the new standards add significantly to their dollar and yen prices.

The EC country affected most acutely by atmospheric pollution is West Germany, where in the early 1980s a third of all trees were damaged by acid rain. Not surprisingly, environmental consciousness has been higher here than elsewhere in Europe, producing significant electoral gains for the Greens, a political party which places environmental protection high on its agenda. The West German government has responded to these pressures by pushing for stricter EC controls over car exhausts. West German car firms, initially resistant to environmentalism, now welcome the rewards which investment in pollution control measures will bring them, not least through improving their competitiveness in the lucrative North American market.

Environmental awareness in Britain is less well developed – perhaps because most of the acid rain produced there is blown across the North Sea. The Rover Group, the main domestic car producer, is committed to lean burn technology, which burns more fuel inside the engine to lower fuel consumption. The lean burn approach is cheaper than using catalysts, but it produces more modest reductions in exhaust emissions. The UK government, eager to protect Rover's position in the domestic market against competitors who are more experienced in catalyst technology, has fought within the EC to oppose any exhaust controls which could not be met by lean burn methods.

Under EC legislation, leaded petrol is already being phased out. The EC has also also negotiated a compromise agreement for non-lead emissions, to come into effect for all new cars by the mid-1990s. The proposed European controls are more lenient than those in the US, but are stricter for large cars (with an engine capacity of two litres or more) than for the medium and small cars which account for most UK car sales. Present indications are that the EC standards for small and medium-sized cars could be met by lean burn engines, and the UK government has stated that it would not implement EC standards for large cars if, as seems likely, these required catalysts to be fitted.

Further reading
Day and Hodgson (1985);
ENDS report no.146 (March 1987);
Baker (1988).

effective if governments could be relied upon to provide an accurate and fair balance of total costs and benefits, and if market prices, adjusted to include environmental costs, could be relied upon to guarantee that resources are used with maximum efficiency. Practical experience suggests, however, that each of these assumptions is questionable.

As we have already seen, there is often considerable scientific disagreement both about available reserves of natural resources and about the extent of environmental damage cause by particular pollutants. This makes consensus on the valuation of costs and benefits difficult to achieve. Even where the scientific evidence is incontrovertible, there may be political conflict, based on different vested interests, over the degree to which environmental controls are accepted as appropriate, Governments may, for example, refrain from introducing effective controls if they fear these will adversely affect company profitability or jobs, even where the environmental costs of not introducing controls are considerable. (Imagine, for example, a situation where a government was confronted with a highly polluting chemical plant, owned by a transnational corporation, in an area of high unemployment. It might well be tempted to take a lenient attitude to the pollution, if it feared the firm would close the plant and re-locate in another country.) The undervaluation of environmental costs is particularly common where a high proportion of the costs are borne in countries other than where the pollution originated. Much of the acid rain which is created by British power stations and car exhausts, for example, is blown across the North Sea to Scandinavia and Northern Germany, lessening the incentive for the UK government to impose stringent controls (Case Study 8.2).

Even if the practical problems of modifying prices to reflect environmental costs could be resolved, how firms responded to the changed price signals would remain problematic. The firm's organizational structure, and the institutional context in which it operates, are both significant here. If, for example, branch managers have to obtain head office clearance to finance the installation of major pollution control devices, they may prefer instead to pay higher charges and 'hide' them within current cost budgets. Similar outcomes may result when small firms are unwilling to seek external funds to finance the necessary capital expenditure. The end result in each case is that firms would incur higher charges than a strict cost comparison would suggest, but that they would continue to cause excessive pollution.

Implementation

In practice, no government has relied exclusively on price incentives to solve environmental problems. Many governments have introduced effluent charges to limit the pollution of inland water supplies, but for controlling atmospheric pollution most rely on regulation. In Britain, the most serious emissions of air pollutants are regulated by government inspectors, who, for more than a century, have required industrial plants to be equipped with the 'best practicable means' of preventing the discharge of 'noxious and offensive gases'. The 'best practicable means' is determined on a case-by-case basis, taking into account factors such as the state of technical knowledge, the financial cost to the firm of installing control devices, and local environmental conditions. Standards determined in this way are known only to the control agency and the regulated firm, and although legal sanctions can be used in the event of infringement, the inspectors prefer not to prosecute, relying instead on co-operation and persuasion.

Supporters of the British approach to regulation claim that its flexibility ensures that the right balance between economic and ecological considerations is struck (see, for example, Atkins and Lowe, 1977). Critics, however, claim that inspectors give undue weight in their deliberations to the negative implications of controls for firms' balance sheets, and not enough to positive impacts on environmental quality (see, for example, Frankel, 1974). Certainly there is evidence in Britain that many infringements of consent standards remain undiscovered, that standards are slow to change in response to new evidence of environmental damage, and that when new standards are introduced they apply to new but not to existing plants, slowing down the impact of improved abatement technologies.

Outside Britain, environmental regulation often takes the form of single uniform standards which are determined by a political bargaining process which is open to public scrutiny. Critics of this approach argue that uniform standards ignore the situation-specific nature of many environmental problems, and that the process by which they are determined is unduly influenced by political 'fashion'. Supporters claim, however, that the relative 'openness' of the standards approach ensures consistency, and avoids suspicions that firms may have 'bribed' inspectors into setting lenient standards. In practice, uniform standards are often more lenient than would be required to ensure adequate environmental protection, but there is evidence that countries such as the USA which adopt a standards approach are quicker to respond to new concerns, like the destruction of the atmosphere's ozone layer by chlorofluorocarbons, than countries like Britain which rely more on a consensus approach.

Traditionally, environmental protection has taken different forms in different countries, and different types of pollution have been regulated according to different criteria, even within the same country. Recently, however, governments have come under pressure to adopt a more consistent approach. In Britain, air pollution, water pollution, radioactivity, and the disposal of wastes on land have been controlled by different authorities. One result of this has been that some firms have been able to get out of a need to clean up their waste by choosing as their medium of waste disposal the one which is least effectively controlled. It was partly in response to this that a unified Inspectorate of Pollution was set up in 1987, and encouraged to explore with operators the 'best practicable environmental option' for disposing their wastes. Within the EC, too, member governments are being urged to adopt uniform standards in relation to certain emissions. This reflects concern about phenomena such as acid rain which do not respect national boundaries, and a desire to ensure that countries do not gain an unfair trading advantage over their competitors by adopting lenient control standards. Recently, in addition, some business organizations have demanded consistency in environmental standards to encourage exports of clean technologies.

Project appraisal

If account is to be taken of the environmental consequences of business decisions, it is not sufficient to influence current business activities. There has, in addition, to be some way of incorporating environmental concerns into the evaluation of investment projects which have an effect in the future.

KEY CONCEPT 8.2

COST BENEFIT ANALYSIS

Cost benefit analysis is a form of project appraisal which enumerates and evaluates all relevant costs and benefits – i.e. including externalities as well as private costs and revenues. As far as is possible a monetary value is attached to each cost and benefit – thus if a new underground railway line reduces travel times for road users, saved working time could be valued in terms of average gross hourly earnings, and increased leisure time in relation to net earnings. All costs and benefits are dated, and costs and benefits accruing in the future are discounted back to present values (or values at the start of the project) by use of an appropriate discount rate. The basic decision rule is that a project should go ahead only if total (discounted) benefits exceed total (discounted) costs, though the actual decision will depend on other factors as well (for example, political feasibility or financial constraints).

There are three elements of cost benefit analysis which pose particular problems for decision-makers.

1. *The monetary valuation of non-market exchanges and the treatment of risk and uncertainty.* There is necessarily a large subjective element in assigning a money value to, for example, travel time, noise, or loss of life. In addition, many outcomes of projects are difficult to predict accurately. Cost benefit analysts need to be aware of these issues, and show how sensitive their results are to alternative evaluations, rather than just present single point estimates of values.

2. *Distribution effects.* Most cost benefit studies merely compare aggregate benefits and costs, and ignore how these benefits and costs are distributed between different sections of the population. For many projects, however, distribution issues may be crucial. A project may, for example, have positive net discounted benefits, but worsen the position of people who are already disadvantaged. It would be preferable if analysts gave some indication of the incidence of costs and benefits, as well as the aggregate picture.

3. *Choice of discount rate.* In Britain, government agencies using cost benefit analysis have to use a 'test discount rate', set at the average rate of return on private sector investment. This has the virtue of ensuring some consistency between private and public sector projects, but it means that benefits or costs occurring far in the future are given low weighting. For certain projects, long-term environmental impacts may be irreversible, reducing the options for future generations. If we place a positive value on the welfare of those generations, then this implies that a lower discount rate should be considered.

Further reading
Pearce (1983);
Colvin (1985);
Levacic (1987), Chapter 10.

Cost benefit analysis

In accounting for the environmental consequences of projects, economists tend to favour some form of cost benefit analysis (see Key Concept 8.2). Essentially this is an extension of the principles of Discounted Cash Flow analysis, which we explored in Chapter 4, to cover externalities as well as private costs and benefits. Cost benefit analysis originated with the evaluation of water resource projects in the USA in the 1930s and 1950s. The outputs of these projects (irrigation, flood control, etc.) could readily be quantified in terms of money, and cost benefit analysis was a useful way of taking into account benefits which were not reflected in the revenues of the water authorities. As we saw earlier, however, many of the most significant environmental effects of business activity cannot readily be quantified, and attempts by economists to place precise money values on them have often been rejected by decision-makers.

CASE STUDY 8.3

COSTING NUCLEAR POWER

Many electricity suppliers, worried about depletion of fossil fuels, have embarked on a policy of meeting increases in demand from nuclear fission reactors. Compared with coal-fired power stations, nuclear plants have low operating costs, but high initial construction costs, and high decommissioning costs at the end of their useful life. Environmentally, nuclear power poses special dangers. Uranium mines and nuclear plants emit low-level radiation on a regular basis, while at the end of the nuclear fuel cycle radioactive wastes have to be stored securely for hundreds of thousands of years. In addition, there are the risks of high-level accidental discharge (as at Chernobyl in 1986), and of encouraging the proliferation of nuclear weapons.

The Central Electricity Generating Board (CEGB), in calculating the costs of new plant, estimates for the expected lifetime of the plant capital charges (excluding research costs borne by the Atomic Energy Authority), fuel costs, and other operating costs (including, for a nuclear plant, reprocessing costs and those decommissioning costs incurred soon after the end of its life). These costs are discounted to present values at the government's test discount rate (currently 5%), and compared with any savings which the new plant would bring to overall system costs (by allowing older, less efficient plant to be retired early, for example). This produces a 'net effective cost', expressed in £ per kW per year.

Critics of the CEGB's costings claim that they are systematically biased to present nuclear power in a favourable light. In particular, many observers consider that CEGB figures underestimate the actual construction costs of nuclear plant, overestimate likely future coal costs, and fail to include the costs of actually dismantling the reactor (which are considerable, but which need not be incurred until several decades after it is shut down).

Health and environmental risks do not feature directly in the CEGB's cost analysis, but are covered by the safety standards it works to. Critics claim that these standards are not sufficiently stringent for nuclear plant, citing the following examples.

Continued over page

Continued from previous page

1. The policy of setting radiation standards 'as low as reasonably achievable', where recent findings on the health hazards of low-level radiation would suggest a more stringent absolute safety requirement.
2. The policy of the Nuclear Installations Inspectorate to recommend improvements only when they cost less than £150 000 per expected life saved. (This contrasts with survey results based on people's willingness to pay for improvements in safety while travelling, which imply a value of around £2 million per life saved.)
3. The lack of allowance for human error in the CEGB's low assessment of the risks of nuclear accidents, despite the significant role this factor has played in most major nuclear accidents.

In the light of these deficiencies, some economists have suggested that the advantages and disadvantages of nuclear power could be adequately assessed only by a full cost benefit analysis. Because of the significance of uncertain, long-term effects, however, assumptions about risks and the appropriate discount rate would be critical. As one cost benefit analyst has noted, if an accident involving nuclear waste takes place in 500 years time, at a cost of £10 billion in today's prices, and this is discounted at 5%, the present value of the accident works out at only 26 pence (Pearce, 1983).

An additional complication occurs in countries, such as the USA, where nuclear power generation is privately funded. As we saw in Chapter 6, private capital markets often take a short-term view of investment opportunities. Where initial costs are high, and the investment is perceived to be risky, as is the case with nuclear power generation, potential shareholders will require an above-average return on their capital, which will have the effect of pushing up the cost of electricity generated by nuclear power. This has been an important issue in the controversy surrounding the UK government's 1988 proposals to privatize the electricity supply industry.

Further reading
Jeffery (1987);
Marin (1988);
Pearce (1988);
Yarrow (1988);
Burton and Haslam (1989).

Perhaps the most serious problems in applying cost benefit analysis to environmental problems relate to the assessment of risk and to intergenerational equity. When we interfere with natural ecology, there is often a risk of severe environmental damage. The threshold between 'acceptable' and 'unacceptable' risk is almost impossible to define, and the costs are often paid by generations as yet unborn, whose interests are literally 'discounted' by the technique. These issues are particularly prominent in attempts to cost the environmental impact of nuclear power (Case Study 8.3), but they feature wherever a project results in an irreversible change to the environment. If sustainability is a priority economic objective, as a 1987 United Nations report suggests it should be (World Commission on Environment and Development, 1987), then analysts will need to be prepared to use much lower discount rates than they have hitherto (Pearce, 1977; Myers, 1977).

Environmental impact assessment

An alternative to cost benefit analysis which emerged in the USA in the early 1970s is environmental impact assessment. Any proposed major federal action in the USA which affects the quality of the environment has by law to be accompanied by a statement detailing its impact on different aspects of the environment, and possible alternative courses of action. A number of techniques of environmental impact assessment have been used, but most require agencies to identify all the actions that are part of a project, and to evaluate the magnitude and importance of their impact on a checklist of environmental variables (e.g. water quality, soil erosion, endangered species).

Most environmental impact assessments are less ambitious than cost benefit analyses, in that they do not seek to reduce all environmental impacts to a common measure. They do, however, place an obligation on authorities to search out all the relevant environmental effects of a proposal. While there is little evidence that the priorities of federal agencies in the USA have been changed as a result of the need to prepare impact statements, environmentalists have welcomed the explicit recognition of environmental impacts which the statements provide, and the opportunities they provide them to make a more informed case for protection.

This side of the Atlantic, some businesses have adopted environmental impact assessment on an ad hoc basis. BP, for example, used the technique to help determine the best route for a pipeline to carry oil from the Wytch Farm field in Dorset to deep water facilities in Southampton Water. In many cases, users of the technique have found that full consideration of environmental issues before the start of a project can benefit them by avoiding lengthy planning delays or by reducing the costs of pollution control. Since July 1988, EC law has required member governments to ensure that the environmental impact of most major developments (public or private) is adequately assessed, and that alternatives are evaluated.

Business responses

Confronted with demands that they behave in an environmentally responsible manner, business managers can often experience environmental controls solely as a threat to be resisted. In a short-term sense, contempt for the natural environment is often highly profitable, and there is much in the market and financial environments of modern business which encourages it to ignore the longer-term consequences of environmental degradation.

There are signs, however, that this situation may be beginning to change. Carlota Perez (1983, 1985) has observed that each upswing in a 'long wave' of economic development (Key Concept 8.3) is characterized by a particular technological style. The post-war upswing in the world economy, she suggests, centred around mass production technologies based on the widespread availability of cheap oil, while the next will centre around flexible technologies, of the sort we examined in Chapter 2, based

Long waves, sometimes called Kondratiev cycles after the Russian economist of that name who investigated them in the 1920s, are cycles of economic development lasting about half a century. From aggregate output statistics, it is possible to identify in most capitalist economies periods of rapid growth, starting in the 1840s, 1890s, and 1940s, which were followed by periods of slower growth, around the 1880s, 1920s, and 1980s.

Long wave theorists differ in their interpretations of the cycles, but most see boom periods as dominated by production systems organized to encourage the rapid diffusion of particular clusters of technological innovations. These were based on low-cost steam transport in the mid-nineteenth century, low-cost steel and electric power around the turn of the century, and low-cost oil in the period after the second world war. Boom periods are followed by periods of crisis in which profits fall as a result of rising input costs and/or market saturation. New technological innovations emerge in the depression phase, but they have a delayed impact on profits and output because they need massive institutional changes, including new materials, new capital equipment, new management styles, new skills, and new financial arrangements.

One prominent long wave theorist, Carlota Perez, focusses attention on the need, in a period of depression, to initiate social and institutional changes which facilitate the diffusion of new technological advances. In the present context, she suggests, this means finding an appropriate framework for encouraging flexible technologies, based on low-cost electronics, which provide product diversity.

KEY CONCEPT 8.3

LONG WAVES

Further reading
Perez (1983, 1985);
Freeman (1985).

---

on low-cost electronics. The most successful businesses in the post-war period were those which opened up new markets by designing products based on cheap energy to meet unmet consumer demands. The implication is that the most successful firms in the 1990s will be those which diversify away from energy-intensive products into information-intensive products like telecommunications equipment and computer software, or into related materials like optical fibres and fine ceramics. Such developments would not be motivated by a desire to protect the natural environment, but they might result in a pattern of output which is more environmentally sustainable than that which we experienced in the post-war boom.

Popular opposition to environmental degradation is also growing. In this changed political situation, firms are beginning to discover that failure to meet raised environmental standards can result in lost markets, while new market opportunities can be created by responding positively to environmental challenges. West German car manufacturers like Daimler-Benz have argued, for example, that the EC should adopt standards for exhaust emissions as stringent as those in the US. This, they suggested, would meet the demands of environmental pressure groups, appeal to more environmentally conscious customers, and enable European car firms to compete more effectively in the US market (Case Study 8.2).

The opportunities which environmental controls can present for business take three main forms – gains from better resource management; gains from product redesign; and gains from expanded markets for clean technologies.

☐ *Better resource management.* When there is a significant increase in the price of a natural resource, or when pollution control standards rise, businesses have to re-examine the ways they use natural resources, and this can often result in significant improvements in the efficiency of resource use. An early example of this is provided by the alkali (sodium carbonate) works of nineteenth century Britain, which used a process which released huge quantities of hydrochloric acid into the atmosphere. Such were the destructive effects of this pollution, particularly for agriculture, that as early as 1863 an Alkali Act was passed, requiring manufacturers to condense 95% of their emissions. What the manufacturers then discovered was that the hydrochloric acid which they had been disposing as a noxious pollutant could be used to make bleach – a product whose commercial potential was even greater than alkali itself! More recently, many businesses have been forced by the oil price rises of the 1970s to re-assess their fuel requirements, and have found considerable scope for reducing resource use through energy conservation and heat recovery systems. Increased raw material prices, too, have encouraged producers to recycle a higher proportion of waste products.

☐ *Product re-design.* Significant gains can be made by businesses who redesign their products to meet the raised environmental concerns of consumers. In 1983, for example, the Kenyan Renewable Energy Development Project designed a clay-lined stove which could be made by local workers using local materials, and which burned a third less charcoal than traditional stoves made from scrap metal. This increased fuel efficiency brought running costs down to such an extent that the purchase cost of the new stoves could be recovered in two months, and total sales of the new stoves reached 180 000 within two years (Harrison, 1987; Opole, 1988). In developed countries, micro-electronic control devices are being introduced which can have equally dramatic effects on the fuel-efficiency, and thus running costs, of cars and central heating systems. New houses, too, are being designed to reduce energy consumption by incorporating low-conductivity insulation and utilizing passive solar heat.

Consumers are not just interested in resource-saving when it reduces their bills, and some businesses have discovered that there are considerable profits to be made from appealing to the environmental awareness of their customers. Perhaps the most dramatic example of this in Britain is The Body Shop, a cosmetics retailer which grew in its first decade from one small shop in Brighton to 230 shops (two thirds of them overseas), doubling its turnover each year. Financially, The Body Shop is one of the most successful businesses in Britain, but from the start it emphasized environmental values, concentrating on vegetable products, tested without cruelty to animals and sold in refillable containers.

☐ *Expanded markets for clean technologies.* In an era when popular demands for a better environment are being translated into tougher emission standards, there are big market opportunities for businesses which can provide cleaner products and processes – businesses like Johnson Matthey Chemicals (who make catalytic converters for car exhausts), Davy McKee (who make flue gas desulphurization equipment for reducing sulphur dioxide emissions from power stations), Bio-Technica (who have developed a method of using microbes to biodegrade toxic chemicals on contaminated land), and Vertical Axis Wind Turbines (who have pioneered wind generators with inclined blades to control the power output). British firms such as these have, however, found that their capacity to compete effectively in export markets has been hampered by a lack of domestic demand for their products. Firms based in countries where pollution controls are tight, on the other hand, have been encouraged to develop more advanced techniques, placing them at a competitive advantage in export markets.

Summary

In an unregulated market, there is little incentive for firms to consider the negative impact of their activities on the natural environment, and the resulting pattern of development is often not ecologically sustainable. One suggestion which is frequently made by economists is that governments should make firms consider their environmental impact by modifying prices so that they reflect externalities as well as private costs and benefits. This solution is not always practical, however, and political demands for better environmental quality have usually resulted in a framework of controls within which business has to operate.

Environmental controls are often resisted by firms which adopt a short-term approach. Recent experience suggests, however, that some firms which have a longer time horizon can come to perceive environmental controls more as an opportunity than as a threat, and that countries which operate lax controls may suffer in terms of trade as well as environmentally.

Further reading

Judith Rees's *Natural Resources: Allocation, Economics and Policy* (Methuen, 1985) provides a comprehensive textbook coverage, which is usefully supplemented by *Sustainable Environmental Management*, edited by Kerry Turner (Belhaven Press, 1988).

The Living Economy, edited by Paul Ekins (Routledge, 1986) is a stimulating, if uneven, collection of writings which attempt to rethink established economic premises from an ecological standpoint. John Elkington's *The Green Capitalists* (Victor Gollancz, 1987) is a sympathetic account of business responses to environmental challenges, though it tends to overstate the constructiveness of those responses. *ENDS*, the monthly report from Environmental Data Services, is an invaluable monitor of those environmental issues which are most relevant to business.

Exercises

1. If governments were to auction resource depletion rights, as Daly suggests, what would be the effects on
   (a) Resource prices?
   (b) Resource conservation and recycling?
   (c) Consumer prices?
   (d) The pattern of aggregate output of goods and services?

2. Assess the advantages and disadvantages of taxes and emission standards as methods of controlling pollution.

3. Why do you think some European car manufacturers are arguing that lenient emission control standards in the EC are hampering their efforts to expand export sales in the USA and Japan?

4. You represent a Central American government which has been approached by a US-based firm for permission to chop down some of your tropical rainforest in order to ranch cattle. You know that the prospects for earning dollars from exporting beef to hamburger chains are good, but you are worried about the effects on forest dwellers, and about possible climatic changes which will reduce water supplies for local agriculture.
   How might economic analysis help in coming to a decision as to whether or not to grant permission?

5. Only two thirds of owners of central heating systems have space temperature controls, even though installing a suitable device can often pay for itself in reduced fuel bills within a couple of years.
   (a) Why do you think this might be the case?
   (b) What alternatives might a government concerned to improve energy conservation consider to remedy this situation?

References

Aage, H. (1984) Economic arguments on the sufficiency of natural resources. *Cambridge Journal of Economics*, March.

Atkins, M.H. and Lowe, J.F. (1977) *Pollution Control Costs in Industry*, Pergamon, Oxford.

Baker, A. (1987) Emissions and their influence on air quality. *Automotive Engineer*, Dec. 1987/Jan. 1988.

Beckerman, W. (1974) *In Defence of Economic Growth*, Jonathan Cape, London.

Burton, W.R. and Haslam, C. (1989) *Power, Pollution and Politics*, Croom Helm, London.

Carson, R. (1962) *Silent Spring*, Houghton Mifflin, Boston, Mass.

Colvin, P. (1985) *The Economic Ideal in British Government*, Manchester University Press, Manchester.

Daly, H. (1977) *Steady-State Economics*, W.H. Freeman, Oxford.

Day, J. and Hodgson, D. (1985) Pollution Control: the cases of acid rain and lead in petrol. *Economics*, Autumn.

Frankel, M. (1974) The Alkali inspectorate. *Social Audit*, Spring.

Freeman, C. (1985) The economics of innovation. *IEE Proceedings*, July.

Harrison, P. (1987) *The Greening of Africa*, Paladin, London (also extracted in *New Scientist*, 28 May, 1987).

Jeffery, J.W. (1987) The Sizewell Report: a foregone conclusion. *Ecologist*, **17** (2).

Kay, J. and Mirrlees, J. (1975) The desirability of natural resource depletion. In *The Economics of Natural Resource Depletion* (eds D.W. Pearce and J. Rose), Macmillan, London.

Levacic, R. (1987) *Economic Policy Making*, Wheatsheaf Books, Brighton.

Marin, A. (1988) The cost of avoiding death: nuclear power, regulation and spending on safety. *Royal Bank of Scotland Review*, March.

Mill, J.S. (1965) *Collected Works*, vol. 3, University of Toronto Press, Toronto.

Myers, N. (1977) Discounting and depletion. *Futures*, Dec.

Opole, M. (1988) The introduction of the Kenyan jiko stove. In *Sustainable Industrial Development* (ed. M. Carr), Intermediate Technology Publications, London.

Pearce, D. (1977) Accounting for the future. *Futures*, Oct.

Pearce, D. (1983) *Cost Benefit Analysis*, 2nd edn, Macmillan, London.

Pearce, D. (1988) The social appraisal of nuclear power. *Economic Review*, March.

Pearce, F. (1986) How to stop the greenhouse effect. *New Scientist*, **18**, Sept.

Pearce, F. (1987) Acid rain. *New Scientist*, **5**, Nov.

Perez, C. (1983) Structural change and assimilation of new technologies in the new economic and social systems. *Futures*, Oct.

Perez, C. (1985) Microelectronics, long waves and world structural change. *World Development*, **13**.

Pigou, A.C. (1920) *Economics of Welfare*, Macmillan, London.

Schumacher, D. (1985) *Energy: Crisis or Opportunity*, Macmillan, London.

World Commission on Environment and Development (1987) *Our Common Future* (the Brundtland report), Oxford University Press, Oxford.

Yarrow, G. (1988) The price of nuclear power. *Economic Policy*, April.

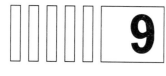

9 Government economic policies

Introduction

One of the most important agents in the environmental context of business is the state, and in this final chapter we look at the influence of government economic policies on business. We start with macro-economic policies, which attempt to influence the overall levels of output, employment, and inflation in the economy. The main focus here is on the shifts which have occurred over the years from Keynesian policies, emphasizing demand management to bring about full employment, to monetarist policies, emphasizing monetary controls to achieve price stability. The chapter ends with a look at micro-economic policies, contrasting the *ad hoc* approaches which have been adopted in the UK with the more strategic approaches developed in countries like France and Japan.

Keynesian theory

Before Keynes, neo-classical economists assumed that market forces would guarantee the full employment of all resources, including labour. They argued that if there were more people looking for jobs than there were jobs available, wages would fall, raising profits and encouraging employers to take on more labour. In the long run, wage flexibility would have the effect of eliminating involuntary unemployment. Within this perspective, if unemployment persisted, it could only be as a result of the actions of trade unions in resisting wage cuts.

In his *General Theory of Employment, Interest and Money*, written at the end of the great slump (1936), Keynes rejected the neo-classical assumption that market forces would ensure full employment (Key Concept 9.1). He was mindful of the political infeasibility of massive wage cuts at a time of mass unemployment, but he pointed out that even if wages did fall, full employment could not be guaranteed. Prices, for example, might fall in line with money wages, leaving real wages at their previous level. In this case, there would be no reason for employers to take on more labour.

In addition, even if real wages did fall, employment would rise only if the positive effects for firms on labour costs outweighed the negative effects on product demand. An inverse relationship between wages and jobs might apply at the level of individual firms, as illustrated in Figure 3.1. Such a relationship would depend on product demand being unaffected by a

Full employment is a concept which is often referred to, but seldom defined. Beveridge's (1944) description comes close to what most economists understand by the term: 'Full employment means that unemployment is reduced to short intervals of standing by, with the certainty that very soon one will be wanted in one's old job again or will be wanted in a new job that is within one's powers.' In other words, full employment does not mean zero unemployment, but allows for some measure of 'acceptable' unemployment, e.g. frictional unemployment while switching jobs.

Beveridge suggested that full employment would exist when the number of unfilled vacancies exceeded the numbers registering as unemployed (thus ignoring problems due to job vacancies being in a different region or requiring different skills). He thought that full employment would correspond to an unemployment rate of 3% (an estimate which Keynes felt to be too low). In fact, the average UK unemployment rate for the two decades after the war was below 2%, and in the more prosperous regions like the South East and West Midlands the unemployment rate was seldom above 1%.

Deficiencies in the compilation of official statistics make it difficult to define full employment with any precision. The unemployment figures, for example, have since 1982 counted only those unemployed people who claim benefit at an Unemployment Benefit Office. The unemployment count thus excludes the voluntarily unemployed and temporarily stopped. It also excludes significant numbers of people who are unemployed but are not entitled to benefit, either because they have not paid the requisite contributions, or because the government has changed the entitlement rules. The official job vacancy figures, too, give only a partial picture, as vacancies notified by employers to Job Centres or Careers Offices are thought to represent less than half of total vacancies.

change in wages – a legitimate assumption at the micro-economic level, where employees of a firm account for only a minute proportion of demand for its products. At the macro-economic level, however (the level of the economy as a whole), a fall in wages would result in a decline in consumption expenditure, and thus a decline in aggregate demand (Key Concept 9.2) for output and labour. Wage cuts, which might create jobs at the micro level, could destroy them at the macro level.

In place of the neo-classical emphasis on self-clearing markets, Keynes argued that output, and thus jobs, were determined by the level of effective demand (Key Concept 9.2). The main components of effective demand behaved independently of each other, and there was no reason to suppose that they would interact in such a way as to guarantee full employment. To understand what, in Keynes's theory, determines the level of employment, we need to examine the two main components of effective demand, consumption expenditure by households and investment expenditure by firms.

KEY CONCEPT 9.2

AGGREGATE AND EFFECTIVE DEMAND

Aggregate demand (sometimes called aggregate expenditure) is a schedule which shows how the volume of expenditure in an economy varies with the level of income. Effective demand is a point on this schedule which represents the actual value at a particular time of the sales which firms anticipate.

There are four components of aggregate demand – consumption expenditure on domestic products by households (C), investment expenditure by firms (I), government expenditure (G), and net exports, or exports minus imports (X–M). In the diagrams below, we assume that I, G, and X are autonomous (i.e. they are determined independently of current domestic income), but that C and M increase as domestic income increases.

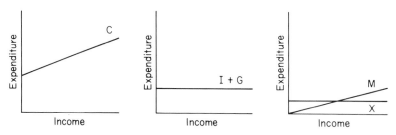

Figure 9.1 Components of aggregate demand.

A simplified aggregate demand schedule, made up from these components, is shown in Figure 9.2. Adding I and G to C shifts the aggregate demand schedule upwards, while adding net exports changes its slope as well. Expenditure on imports increases with domestic income, so the slope of the open economy aggregate demand schedule (AD) is flatter than that of the domestic consumption schedule (C).

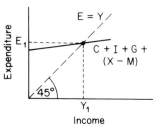

Figure 9.2 A simplified aggregate demand schedule.

The 45° line E=Y shows the amount of expenditure which is needed to sustain a given level of income, so the point where AD intersects this line, at an effective demand of E_1, represents an 'equilibrium' national income of Y_1. As Keynes emphasized, there is no guarantee that this 'equilibrium' will be sufficient to guarantee full employment.

Consumption expenditure

For most of the General Theory, Keynes assumed a closed economy, ignoring the distinction between consumption of domestic products and expenditure on imports. He suggested that current income is the main determinant of consumption, and postulated a 'fundamental psychological law' that as incomes rise, consumption rises, but by less than the rise in income. Post-war experience in the UK, at least up to the early 1980s, confirmed that the average propensity to consume (Key Concept 9.3) tended to decline as incomes rose over time. Algebraically, the consumption function can be represented as an equation of the form

$$C = a + bY_D$$

In this equation, C is consumption expenditure and Y_D personal disposable income (personal incomes less income taxes and social security

Average propensity to consume (apc) is total consumption expenditure divided by total personal disposable income (C/Y_D). As incomes rose in the post-war period, apc fell, from around 0.99 in 1948 to around 0.86 in 1980. There are, however, indications of a reversal in this trend in the 1980s, fuelled by an expansion of consumer credit.

Marginal propensity to consume (mpc) is the proportion of a change in income which is consumed ($\Delta C/\Delta Y_D$). Its value has, before the early 1980s, been fairly stable over long periods of time, averaging around 0.87 when measured in current prices. When measured in constant prices (revaluing the expenditure and income figures by an index of consumer prices, to remove the effects of inflation – as described in Key Concept 9.5), the average value of mpc has been around 0.79.

On a year-by-year basis, there have been considerable fluctuations in the value of mpc, as the figures below illustrate. Values of mpc were generally much higher in the mid 1980s than they had been previously.

Table 9.1 Average and marginal propensities to consume, selected years

Current prices (£ billion)

Year	C	Y_D	ΔC	ΔY_D	apc(C/Y)	mpc($\Delta C/\Delta Y_D$)
1954	12.21	12.65	0.70	0.62	0.97	1.13
1960	17.11	18.48	0.82	1.33	0.93	0.62
1968	27.71	30.13	1.98	1.87	0.92	1.06
1972	40.49	44.84	4.67	6.01	0.90	0.78
1980	137.47	160.33	19.11	24.28	0.86	0.79
1983	183.84	205.58	15.68	14.15	0.89	1.11
1987	257.11	272.32	20.58	16.94	0.94	1.21

Constant prices (£ billion at 1980 prices)

Year	C	Y_D	ΔC	ΔY_D	apc(C/Y)	mpc($\Delta C/\Delta Y_D$)
1954	73.61	76.23	2.92	2.39	0.97	1.22
1960	87.62	94.59	3.25	5.85	0.93	0.56
1968	107.44	116.82	2.91	2.01	0.92	1.45
1972	121.50	134.56	7.01	10.44	0.90	0.67
1980	137.47	160.33	−0.02	2.30	0.86	−0.01
1983	144.46	161.54	5.65	3.52	0.89	1.61
1987	171.03	181.15	8.46	5.62	0.94	1.51

Source: Economic Trends
Note: Personal income in the UK national income accounts includes the incomes of unincorporated businesses, charities, and life assurance and pension funds, as well as those of households. Since 1970, the Central Statistical Office has also published figures for the household sector alone. These suggest that apc for households exceeded 1.0 in 1986–87.

contributions). The parameter a represents autonomous consumption demand (demand unrelated to current income), and its positive value reflects the fact the many individuals will respond to a decline in income by financing consumption from savings or borrowing. The parameter b represents the marginal propensity to consume (Key Concept 9.3).

The marginal propensity to consume tends in practice to be positive and less than one, but on a year-by-year basis it is far less stable in value than Keynes had assumed. In attempting to explain observed fluctuations in marginal propensity to consume, some economists in the 1950s suggested that people attempt to even out fluctuations in their consumption by relating this not to their current income but to their average income in the long run (the permanent income hypothesis). This has the effect of raising marginal propensity to consume when people suffer an unexpected drop in income, and reducing it when people receive an unexpected increase.

More recent experience suggests that other factors may also be significant. Cuthbertson, for example, notes that in times of high inflation, such as 1974–75 and 1979–80, the real value of liquid assets has fallen. At these times, he suggests, individuals try to maintain the value of their liquid assets by increasing their savings from current income, and thus reducing their propensity to consume (Cuthbertson, 1982). The expansion of consumer credit in the 1980s, however, appears to have had the effect of boosting consumption at the expense of saving.

Investment expenditure

As we saw in Chapter 6, Keynes followed neo-classical economists in positing an inverse relationship between investment spending by firms and interest rates. Unlike the neo-classicals, however, Keynes was acutely aware of the unstable nature of this relationship. The rates of return businesses expect from their investments are based on their expectations of an uncertain future. These expectations fluctuate, Keynes argued, in response to shifts in the 'animal spirits' of entrepreneurs, which affect their confidence in the future. Investment expenditure by firms thus varies with current interest rates and with future expected demand, but not with current income.

The subjective element which Keynes identified in business predictions has profound consequences for the level of economic activity. Business confidence may remain stable over long periods, but then be shaken by a surprise event such as a collapse in share values brought about by speculative activity. If a decline in confidence depresses investment spending, this will depress aggregate demand and thus output (and profit) levels in the future. Swings in business confidence can thus be self fulfilling – a decline in business expectations of future profits resulting in a drop in effective demand and thus an actual decline in future profits.

The circular flow of income

The impact of a change in effective demand on the level of economic activity can be illustrated by a simple model of the macro-economy which focusses on the circular flows of income between firms and households (Figure 9.3).

Imagine a closed economy (where there is no foreign trade) with no government expenditure and no taxes. Households receive incomes from firms (wages and salaries, profits, and rents) in return for the factor services they provide (labour, capital, and land). Some of this income is saved, but most is passed back to firms in the form of consumption

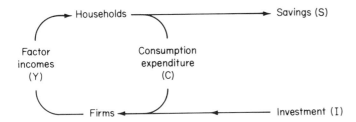

Figure 9.3 The circular flow of income in a closed economy with no government.

expenditure, in return for products. Household savings represent a leakage from the circular flow of income, as they reduce the consumption expenditure which is passed on to firms, and thus the amount of income which can be passed back to households. Firms' receipts are, however, boosted by the investment expenditure of other firms, which constitute an injection into the circular flow.

Before Keynes, neo-classical economists assumed that interest rates would fluctuate to equate savings with investment expenditure, so that income flows could be maintained at a level which corresponded to full employment. Keynes rejected the idea that interest rate changes could be relied upon to perform this market-clearing function, for three main reasons.

KEY CONCEPT 9.4

THE MULTIPLIER

Any change in expenditure has a direct effect on income and employment. It also has secondary effects, resulting from the changes in consumption expenditure induced by the change in income. Different multipliers can be calculated for different purposes – the one which is most commonly used in practice is the ratio of total change in national income to the change in expenditure which brought it about.

The size of the multiplier is limited by the extent of leakages from the circular flow of income. For most of his General Theory, Keynes ignored leakages other than savings. In reality, however, part of any increase in expenditure will go on undistributed profits, income and expenditure taxes, and spending on imports, all of which represent significant additional leakages from the circular flow.

If we want to estimate the effect of an increase in expenditure on income and thus jobs within a domestic economy, the key variable is the marginal propensity to purchase new domestic output – the proportion of an increase in expenditure which results in increase in consumption expenditure on domestic products. If there is an initial increase in domestic expenditure of £100 million, and the marginal propensity to purchase new domestic output is 0.25, then the 1st round increase in income is £100 million. Of this £100 million, £25 million (25%) is passed back to domestic firms as increased consumption expenditure. The process continues in successive rounds, as shown below, until a total increase in income of £133.3 million is achieved. The multiplier in this case is 1.33.

Continued over page

Continued from previous page

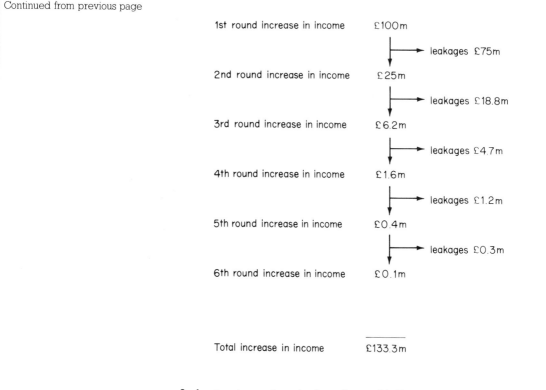

1st round increase in income	£100m	
		leakages £75m
2nd round increase in income	£25m	
		leakages £18.8m
3rd round increase in income	£6.2m	
		leakages £4.7m
4th round increase in income	£1.6m	
		leakages £1.2m
5th round increase in income	£0.4m	
		leakages £0.3m
6th round increase in income	£0.1m	
Total increase in income	£133.3m	

A short cut way to calculate the multiplier is to use the formula:

$$\frac{1}{1 - \text{marginal propensity to purchase new domestic output}}$$

Multiplier calculations have to assume stability in the marginal propensities to consume and import. They ignore changing stock levels, and give no indication of the time lags between an injection of expenditure and the ultimate increase in income. They can, therefore, only roughly predict the effect of a change in expenditure on national income.

☐ Speculative activity in financial markets was an important independent influence on short-run interest rates.
☐ The general level of interest rates had little influence on the savings decisions of households, which were chiefly income determined.
☐ Firms' investment decisions were influenced as much by subjectively based predictions of future returns as by current interest rates.

In Keynes's theory, changes in effective demand have a multiplied impact on income, and thus on output and jobs (Key Concept 9.4). In this analysis, it is changes in income, not changes in interest rates, which bring about equilibrium between savings and investment. Suppose an economy is at full employment with a national income (Y) of £1 million, and that the consumption function takes the form C = £100 000 + 0.75Y. Consumption expenditure is £850 000 per year, and savings £150 000. Investment spending (I) then has to be kept at £150 000 per year to maintain national income at the full employment level.

If businesses become pessimistic about future returns, and investment spending falls to £100 000 per year, then firms' receipts will fall by £50 000, and household incomes will fall initially by the same amount. This is not the end of the matter, however, for any reduction in income will induce further reductions in consumption and savings. National income will in fact continue to contract until it reaches a new equilibrium level at £800 000, where savings are again equal to investment at £100 000 per year. Note that in this example a fall in investment spending of £50 000 brings about an eventual fall in national income of £200 000, suggesting a multiplier of four (£200 000 ÷ £50 000).

To make the simplified model of Figure 9.3 more appropriate to the real world, we have to allow for the effects of foreign trade and government, as in Figure 9.4. Receipts from exports and government expenditure count as injections into the circular flow, while expenditures on imports and tax payments constitute leakages.

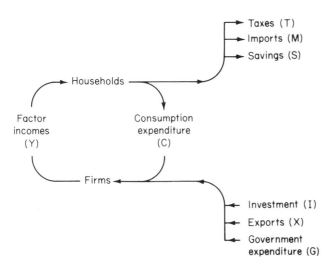

Figure 9.4 The circular flow of income in an open economy with a government.

The additional leakages which result from taking account of the government and foreign trade sectors have the effect of reducing the size of the multiplier. As we have seen in Chapters 1 and 7, many UK manufacturing firms have failed in recent years to provide the range of product characteristics that modern consumers demand, and one result of this has been an increased propensity of UK consumers to buy imported goods. This has played a significant role in reducing the size of the domestic multiplier in the UK, to current levels which are typically below 1.5.

Keynesian policies and their effect on business activity

Keynes's chief aim in the General Theory was to develop a theoretical understanding of why market forces do not guarantee full employment. He did, however, draw clear policy implications from his analysis. His main political conclusion was that if capitalism was to be preserved, governments should make the achievement of full employment a priority policy objective. The most effective instruments of achieving this objective, Keynes argued, would be low interest rates and government controls over investment, to ensure a stable level of investment spending which would be sufficient, together with consumption spending, to guarantee full employment (Keynes, 1936, 1943).

Post-war UK governments followed Keynes in giving priority to the achievement of full employment. They rejected, however, Keynes's suggestions that they should assume greater control over investment spending, preferring instead to use fiscal policy (the relationship between government spending and tax revenues) to influence the level of effective demand.

Consider the circular flow diagram in Figure 9.4. If there is a shortfall in private sector investment spending, so that the economy is working at less than full employment, the government can increase its spending or reduce its taxes. This has the result of boosting effective demand, and returning the economy closer to the full employment level. Initially, as government spending exceeds tax revenues, the government will have to borrow to finance its deficit, but eventually incomes and consumption expenditure will rise, increasing tax revenues again.

The effect of an increase in government expenditure on effective demand and therefore on national income can be analysed with the help of a device we introduced in Key Concept 9.2, the income-expenditure diagram. Figure 9.5, which is based on this diagram, shows an Aggregate Demand schedule AD_1, with an effective demand of E_1 resulting in a national income of Y_1. An increase in government expenditure by ΔG shifts the Aggregate Demand Schedule up from AD_1 to AD_2, which, after the multiplier effect has worked through the economy, increases effective demand from E_1 to E_2 and national income from Y_1 to Y_2.

For two decades after the war, the UK economy, in common with other industrial economies, experienced an economic boom of unprecedented duration. During this period, real GDP grew by about 2.5% per year, and the number of registered unemployed hardly ever exceeded 2% of the labour force. This long boom coincided with the adoption by government of 'Keynesian' demand management policies (involving changes in taxes, public spending, interest rates or credit availability), and it is tempting to see the two phenomena as causally related. 'Fine tuning' the economy was an inexact science, however. The economic models used by the Treasury often failed to make adequate allowance for fluctuations in the marginal propensity to consume, for the time needed for multiplier effects to work through the economy, or for the trade effects of boosting aggregate demand. As a result, policy modifications designed to solve one economic problem (increasing unemployment, for example) would create another one (a trade deficit, for example). Governments, too, were tempted to use

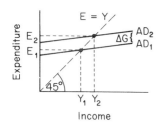

Figure 9.5 The effect of an increase in government expenditure on national income.

demand management policies to boost their chances of staying in power –
engineering a boom in the run up to an election, for example, and then
dealing with adverse balance of payments effects afterwards (or bequeath-
ing them to their successors).

R.C.O. Matthews, in a detailed study of the post-war period (1968),
suggested that the long boom was due more to sustained investment in the
private sector than to government policy, and that in most years fiscal
policy had been used to damp down aggregate demand rather than boost it.
It may be, of course, that government commitment to full employment as a
policy priority helped to boost business confidence and thus to sustain the
boom. Some businesses, however, faced considerable instability in demand
for their products as a result of shifts in government policy. Sales of
consumer durables like cars, for example, fluctuated considerably with
changes in purchase tax or hire purchase regulations. At the level of
macro-economic performance too, one study concluded that, far from
evening out economic cycles, Treasury policies had exaggerated them,
largely because they had underestimated the time lags between changes in
policy and their effect on output (Dow, 1964).

The balance of payments constraint and inflation

In the 1950s and 1960s, UK governments were committed to maintain
significant exports of capital, which had to be financed by surpluses on the
current account of the balance of payments. This was a period of booming
international trade, but when internal demand in the UK expanded
rapidly, so did imports, shifting the current account from a surplus to a
deficit. Governments were also committed to free trade and to a fixed
exchange rate, so they were unable to use import controls or devaluation to
restore balance of payments equilibrium. In this situation, the only way
they could maintain a surplus on the current account after aggregate
demand had risen was to use fiscal and monetary policy to deflate
aggregate demand (and thus demand for imports) again. One result of this
policy stance was a 'stop–go' cycle of economic activity, which, over time,
depressed the rate of growth of the UK relative to other industrial
economies.

A new problem which emerged in the post-war period was that of
permanent inflation (Key Concept 9.5). Before the war, prices would rise
in some periods, but fall in others. After the war, there was a continuous
rise in the general price level, though this was moderate at first. It seemed
to some economists that there was a direct relationship between high levels
of effective demand and inflation. A.W. Phillips (1958), for example,
studied the historical relationship in Britain between the percentage rate of
change in money wages (a measure of wage inflation) and the percentage
rate of unemployment (which, in Keynesian theory, is determined
primarily by the level of effective demand). The relationship he found
(relating to the period 1862–1958) is shown in Figure 9.6.

There has, over the post-war period, been little consensus among
economists as to either the effects or the causes of inflation. In the 1950s
and 1960s, modest inflation tended to be accepted as a lesser evil than that

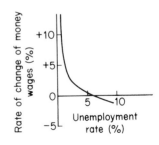

Figure 9.6 The Phillips curve.

KEY CONCEPT 9.5

**INFLATION AND THE
RETAIL PRICE INDEX**

Inflation is a rise in the general level of prices. To measure inflation, we need an index of prices. The index most commonly used in the UK is the Retail Price Index. Each month the Department of Employment notes the prices charged on 600 separate items, chosen to represent the expenditure patterns of most households (excluding older people mainly dependent on state benefits, and households with very high incomes). Each price change is weighted according to the importance of the item in a typical household expenditure budget, and then converted into an index which relates the general price level in the month to a reference date at which the value of the index has been set at 100 (January 1987, for example). Thus if the Retail Price Index in March 1988 is 104.1, compared with 100.6 in March 1987, this means that most people would have had to spend an extra 3.5% (104.1 ÷ 100.6) to repurchase the things they bought 12 months previously.

of unemployment, and most worries about inflation centred on its impact on income distribution, and particularly on the living standards of people dependent on fixed incomes. Some economists argued, on the basis of the Phillips curve, that governments could moderate inflation by deflating aggregate demand, and accepting increased unemployment as a consequence. (This is shown in Figure 9.7a by a move from P_1,U_1 to P_2,U_2.) Most 'Keynesian' economists, however, saw inflation as being caused by collective bargaining procedures which encouraged money wages to rise

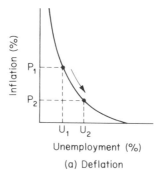

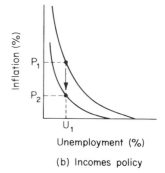

Figure 9.7 Alternative
counter-inflation policies.

(a) Deflation

(b) Incomes policy

faster than labour productivity, pushing up labour costs. As a result, regulation of growth in money wages would be the most effective counter-inflation policy. A successful incomes policy, they argued, would shift the Phillips curve to the left, enabling inflation to be reduced (from P_1 to P_2 in Figure 9.7b) without any rise in unemployment.

Stagflation

UK experience with incomes policies in the 1960s and 1970s was not very satisfactory. Most incomes policies established a 'norm' for pay increases, with some allowance for exceptional increases above the norm in special cases. There was often little consensus on what constituted a special case, however, and incomes policies often broke down because particular groups felt they had been unfairly treated by them. Although the first stages in an incomes policy were often accompanied by a reduction in money wage increases, when the policy broke down a 'catching-up' process often ensued. The end result was that incomes policies had more influence over the timing of pay increases (and thus of inflation) than over their long-term magnitude.

Even more serious for the operation of counter-inflation policy was the breakdown of the Phillips curve relationship in the 1970s. The stable inverse relationship between inflation and unemployment continued until the late 1960s, but then it broke down, with UK retail price increases averaging 13% per year in the 1970s, despite generally rising levels of unemployment.

Keynesian economists continued to focus on factors pushing up production costs as the main source of increased inflation, although they widened their analysis to include changes in world commodity markets, such as the impact of OPEC on oil prices (Kaldor, 1976). This focus on world commodity prices having a major effect on inflation is one for which there is considerable empirical support (Beckerman and Jenkinson, 1986). The policy that was most influential with governments from the late 1970s on was, however, the monetary policy associated with the work of Milton Friedman, and it is to this that we now turn.

Monetarist theory

There are many varieties of monetarist theory in existence. We concentrate here on the verion presented by Milton Friedman, because this has been the most influential in terms of UK government policy (though, as we shall see in the next section, Friedman's prescriptions have been considerably modified by the UK government in recent years). Friedman provides a distinctly non-Keynesian perspective on the relationship between inflation and unemployment, based on viewing inflation as an exclusively monetary phenomenon, caused by governments allowing the supply of money to grow faster than output.

Friedman's monetary approach to inflation is an updated version of the eighteenth century Quantity Theory of Money, according to which changes in the stock of money are directly related to changes in the general level of prices. Friedman's approach can be illustrated by the identity:

$$MV \equiv PT$$

(Money supply times the velocity at which it circulates is identical to the price level times the number of transactions. The 3-bar sign $\equiv$ indicates that MV and PT are identical *by definition*, in much the same way as 1000cc ≡ 1 litre.)

Friedman's argument, based on a rather idiosyncratic interpretation of historical data (Friedman and Schwartz, 1963 and 1982), is that the velocity of circulation (V) is constant over time. Because, historically, changes in money supply (M) precede changes in the value of transactions (PT), Friedman suggests that changes in the value of transactions (PT) are caused by changes in money supply (M).

An increase in the value of transactions (PT) can take the form of an increase in the volume of transactions (T), an increase in the price level (P), or a combination of the two. To analyse how an increase in the value of transactions is broken down between price increases and increases in real output, Friedman (1977) re-interprets the Phillips curve relationship between inflation and unemployment, to distinguish between unanticipated and anticipated inflation.

Assume that the economy starts at position A in Figure 9.8, with actual price inflation equal to expected price inflation at zero. For the actual inflation rate to equal the expected rate, Friedman argues, unemployment must be at what he calls its 'natural' rate (U_N). This 'natural' rate (sometimes called NAIRU, or the non-accelerating inflation rate of unemployment) is determined by competitive forces in the labour market (which require, for example, some workers to be frictionally unemployed as they switch jobs). Now suppose a government wishes to use Keynesian policies to bring unemployment down to the full employment level (U_F). Any attempt to boost aggregate demand will require an expansion in money supply, which will create an actual inflation rate of P_1. Inflation will increase (from P_0 to P_1), but in the short term inflationary expectations will remain at zero (P_0), so the economy will move along the Phillips curve from point A to point B.

Any reduction in unemployment below the 'natural' rate, Friedman argues, can only be sustained in the short term, when increased inflation is not anticipated. Eventually, people will come to expect an inflation rate of P_1, and the Phillips curve will shift outwards. The economy will move from point B to point C, where actual and expected inflation are again equal at U_N, but this time with a positive inflation rate P_1. If the government continues to try to achieve full employment, it will move along the new Phillips curve from C to D. This will increase the actual inflation rate to P_2, shifting the curve outwards again, and taking the economy from point D to point E, as people come to expect the new inflation rate P_2.

In Friedman's analysis, the long-term Phillips curve is vertical at the 'natural' rate of unemployment. It follows that monetary expansion can increase real output only in the short term, and that in the long term its sole effect is on inflation. Once inflation takes hold, people build expectations of inflation into their behaviour, causing the rate of inflation to accelerate. Any sustained attempt by a government to reduce unemployment below its 'natural' rate, Friedman argues, is doomed to failure, and can only result in accelerating inflation, the end point of which is a collapse in people's confidence in money.

Friedman goes on to suggest that although, in the long term,

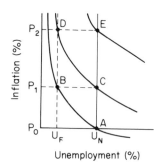

Figure 9.8 Expectations-augmented Phillips curve.

unemployment should fluctuate around its 'natural' rate, in the medium term accelerating inflation will bring about increased business uncertainty, causing unemployment to rise above its 'natural' rate.

Theoretically, many economists dispute whether money supply can be measured as precisely, or controlled as rigidly, as monetarist theory would suggest. As Kaldor (1980) pointed out, in a modern economy most 'money' consists of bank deposits created by commercial banks, whose supply is determined largely by private demand for loans. Part of this money supply consists of interest-bearing deposits, making a clear distinction between monetary and non-monetary financial assets difficult to make. This ensures that money supply is inherently difficult for any government to control – as soon as the government attempts to control a monetary aggregate, unsatisfied demand for money spills over into financial assets not included in the official definition. Another implication of Kaldor's analysis is that far from increases in money bringing about increases in expenditure, it is increases in expenditure which bring about increases in money.

There are considerable doubts, too, about the quality of the empirical evidence which has been put forward to support Friedman's theory. Desai, surveying the econometric literature in 1981, found little support for the monetarist propositions that the velocity of circulation of money is stable over time, or that real output in the long term is unaffected by monetary growth. Higham and Tomlinson (1982) found that Friedman's (1977) evidence on the positive links between inflation and unemployment was based on a selective interpretation of the available data. Even more seriously, the historical correlation between growth in money supply and inflation in the UK, supposedly 'established' by Friedman and Schwartz in 1982, has been shown to depend on a crude manipulation of the basic data to fit the hypothesis. This, and the use of dubious statistical techniques, leave Friedman and Schwartz conclusions 'stranded as assertions devoid of empirical support' (Hendry and Ericsson, 1983).

In the 1970s, many economists were convinced by the superficial plausibility of Friedman's monetary theory, and dissenting views were thin on the ground. Successive UK governments, from 1976 on, were influenced by this theory, and adopted more-or-less strict monetary controls to cure inflation. It is to these monetarist policies, and their effects on the economic environment of business, that we now turn.

Monetarist policies and their effect on business activity

In the mid-1970s, monetarist ideas became increasingly influential in the UK. The annual inflation rate peaked at 25% in 1975, and many economic journalists (like Peter Jay of the Times) felt that this was due more to high rates of monetary expansion and public borrowing than to the OPEC-induced oil price rises of 1974. Public expenditure had risen dramatically in the early 1970s, and successive governments had felt unable to finance the increase with higher taxes. This excess of public spending over taxation, though largely unplanned, was not unwelcome to Keynesians, who appreciated the boost it gave to effective demand, and thus jobs, in a

344344344344 of of of 272272272272272272272272272272272

In a modern economy, bank deposits form the main means of exchange. This makes any precise demarcation of what constitutes money impossible, because an increasing proportion of financial deposits are at the same time interest-earning assets and potential means of exchange.

KEY CONCEPT 9.7

MONETARY AGGREGATES

In practice, the UK monetary authorities employ a number of different measures of money supply. Four of the most widely used are defined and measured below.

Monetary aggregate	Definition	Size (£bn Dec 1987)
M0	Notes and coins in circulation *plus* banks' till money and operating balances with the Bank of England.	17
M1	Notes and coin in circulation *plus* private sector sight (i.e. current a/c) bank deposits.	92
M3	M1 *plus* private sector time (i.e. deposit a/c) bank deposits.	186
M4	M3 *plus* private sector holdings in building societies *minus* building society holdings of M3.	304

In the early 1980s, monetary targets were specified in terms of Sterling M3 (£M3, now simply called M3). This became increasingly unsatisfactory as the distinctions between banks and building societies became blurred, and as financial institutions began to offer customers interest-bearing sight deposits. Partly as a result of financial innovations such as these, the statistical relationship between £M3 and inflation broke down, and government attempts to control 'broad' money were circumvented as funds shifted between different assets, some regulated and some unregulated (Podolski, 1986).

By the late 1980s, monetary targets were specified only for the narrow M0 aggregate, and the behaviour of broader aggregates such as M3 and M4 was monitored on a less formal basis.

the conditions of the loan, it adopted target limits to growth in money supply, and a programme of public expenditure cuts. James Callaghan, the Labour Prime Minister, renounced Keynesian policies in a speech to the

Labour Party conference, quoted with approval by Friedman in his Nobel lecture 1977.

> We used to think [Callaghan argued] that you could just spend your way out of recession and increase employment by cutting taxes and boosting Government spending. I tell you, in all candour, that that option no longer exists, and that insofar as it ever did exist, it only worked by injecting bigger doses of inflation into the economy followed by higher levels of unemployment as the next step.

While it was the Callaghan government of 1976–79 (assisted by the IMF) which was responsible for introducing monetarist ideas to government policy-making in the UK, it was the Thatcher government elected in 1979 which adopted the most radical monetarist position. The new government announced that levels of output and employment were outside its control, and concentrated its macro-economic attention on target reductions in the rate of growth in £M3 (Key Concept 9.7) and in Public Sector Borrowing Requirement (PSBR – Key Concept 9.6). These reductions were projected ahead over a four-year period, in an attempt to reduce inflationary expectations.

The techniques of monetary control are complex, and beyond the scope of this book. Suffice it to say that the Bank of England in the early 1980s rejected direct controls, preferring instead to influence demand for money via interest rates. The calculation here was that if the authorities charged a higher rate when they lent cash to the banks, bank interest rates would rise, and this would restrain business and consumer borrowing, and hence the ability of the banks to create new deposit money. (In practice, the effect of higher interest rates on money supply was difficult to predict. Firms in financial difficulties, for example, had little choice but to increase their bank borrowing to meet higher interest payments on existing loans, so the rise in interest rates could have had the perverse effect of increasing bank lending.)

Policy in relation to public sector borrowing played a key supporting role here. Not only were there public expenditure cuts, to reduce the borrowing total, but the authorities attempted to finance as much of PSBR as possible from sales of long-term debt to the non-bank public (for example, by improving the attractiveness of National Savings certificates). In this way,

Table 9.2 Annual growth in £M3. 1980–87

Period	1980 target (%)	Updated targets (%)	Actual growth (%)
1980–81	7–11		19
1981–82	6–10		15
1982–83	5–9	8–12	11
1983–84	4–8	7–11	10
1984–85		6–10	12
1985–86		5–9	17
1986–87		11–15	18

Source: Financial Statement and Budget Report; *Bank of England Quarterly Bulletin.*

the government avoided expanding bank holdings of short-term securities which would form part of their liquid assets and thus increase their ability to create new deposit money (Key Concept 9.6).

PSBR, which was £12.7bn in 1979 (7.5% of national income), eventually reached zero in 1987. Monetary growth continued to exceed the official targets, however, as Table 9.2 shows.

Interest rates in the early 1980s were high, while inflation was falling (see Figure 9.9). This indicated to the authorities that monetary controls were working, despite the behaviour of £M3. By 1985, however, evidence was emerging that the most influential factor underlying the fall in inflation in the early 1980s was the fall in world commodity prices (Beckerman, 1985; Beckerman and Jenkinson, 1986). It is not clear whether or not the Treasury accepted this evidence, but it was around this time that the authorities abandoned the £M3 target, and replaced it with a target for a much narrower monetary aggregate, MO.

More significantly, however, the authorities began in the mid-1980s to adopt a target range for the exchange rate. This inevitably implied a relaxation of monetary targets, for the authorities could no longer ignore the effects of changes in interest rates on the exchange rate. High interest rates are a necessary concomitant of tight monetary control, but they also attract short-term capital into the country, pushing up the exchange value of the currency and making exports more expensive. If the government wishes to lower its exchange rate, to ease the burden on exporters, it can use its reserves to intervene in the foreign exchange markets, but at some point it will need to bring interest rates down so as to ease demand for its

——————— Per cent change in Retail Price Index

– – – – – Banks' base rate at end of year

Figure 9.9 Interest rates and inflation (1977–88).

currency, and indicate its intentions to speculators. For a short period after the mid-1980s, the Treasury became increasingly willing to allow interest rates to fall below the levels implied by its monetary targets, with the explicit aim of reducing the damaging effects of a high exchange rate on business. By 1988, however, the government was again allowing interest rates (and the exchange rate) to rise, in an attempt to reverse an upturn in inflation, and to attract capital inflows to counterbalance a record balance of payments deficit on current account.

While the impact of monetarist policies in the early 1980s on the rate of inflation was ambiguous, the outcome for output and jobs, particularly in the manufacturing sector, was not. High interest rates attracted short-term funds into sterling, raising its exchange rate and making it more difficult for UK businesses to maintain their share of export markets (already depressed as a result of the world recession). Domestic demand was hit by the public spending cuts, and low levels of product demand and high interest rates combined to discourage new investment. Company profitability hit a post-war low (Figure 6.1), and many firms went into liquidation. Manufacturing output fell by 15% between 1979 and 1982, and almost 1.5 million manufacturing jobs were lost. Registered unemployment rose from 4% to 10% of the working population (Figure 9.10), and in

UK registered unemployed (excluding school-leavers) in 3rd quarter (seasonally adjusted) as % of working population.

GB employees in employ ment in manufacturing sector in June.

Figure 9.10 Unemployment and manufacturing jobs, 1977–88.

1983, for the first time in centuries, the UK imported more manufactured goods than she exported.

After the early 1980s the government embarked on what has been termed a pragmatic approach to monetary control because inflationary pressure was easing. At one level it could be argued that these policies were beneficial to British industry. For example, in the cyclical recovery after 1983, company profitability recovered to a high level and manufacturing labour productivity growth hit an average level of 4% per year in the period 1983 to 1987.

However labour productivity was above the long-run trend because manufacturing output increased against a dramatic fall in labour employed in manufacturing. At a more general level there was some job growth, and the unemployment rate started to fall. In contrast to these positive indications of recovery, however, there are now a number of worrying aspects for UK business management particularly in relation to the deterioration in the UK's balance of trade in manufactures.

In the early 1980s, the implications of manufacturing decline for UK trade were masked by exports of North Sea oil, and by the restraining effect of the domestic recession on imports. It had been hoped that lower rates of inflation, coupled with greater exchange rate stability, would lead to improved competitive advantage for UK manufacturers. Many UK firms, however, were unable to produce goods with appropriate non-price characteristics (design quality, reliability, delivery, etc.), and their trading position continued to worsen. As oil markets became more depressed, and as consumer demand recovered, deficits on visible trade increased, exceeding £10bn per year by 1987.

Although the Conservative government has practised public expenditure restraint, the private sector has experienced a consumer spending boom which has been fuelled by the increase in consumer credit. This expansion in credit has been accompanied by distributional changes, where an increase in the share of national income has gone, through tax cuts, to upper income groups with a high propensity to consume imported goods. As a result, the imbalance between imports and exports of manufactures has widened, and the current account deficit has grown. In order to make the balance of payments balance, the government needs to attract capital investment on the capital account. This can be done by raising interest rates (as in 1988) making it more attractive for foreign investors to invest in the UK economy. In addition these higher interest rates should, in practice, make it more expensive for consumers to borrow credit and so dampen the demand for imports. But this tends to be indiscriminate, because it is also at the cost of domestic output and employment.

However, where interest rates rise to attract overseas capital investment into the UK there then takes place an increased demand for sterling investment funds and as a result the exchange rate rises. If the exchange rate increases from £1.00 = $1.50 to £1.00 = $1.80 exports from the UK become more expensive and imports become cheaper. So that although higher rates of interest may discourage credit borrowing and the demand for imports, this may be offset where the exchange rate effect on import prices is passed on to the consumer in the UK. As a result policy calculations designed to correct the imbalance on the current account can, in fact, have a contradictory adverse effect.

It is possible to restrict physically the level of credit available to individual consumers for the purchase of imports through credit restriction, either at the point of sale or at the financial institutions which extend credit facilities. This latter policy would be difficult to administer in practice where the definition of what constitutes credit could prove to be too narrow or too broad. That is, do you restrict bank and retail credit advances or should this be extended to building society mortgages? The former policy could be introduced but again the political repercussions might prove to be adverse where consumers argue that their freedom of choice is restricted. In addition where the object is to reduce the level of imports and substitute the domestic product there must *be* a domestic substitute, or at least a substitute with a low import content. In addition a policy of discriminatory credit would, by 1992, not be possible under the terms of a free internal European market.

Finally a balance of payments deficit could be corrected through physical quotas or financial tariffs which established a complete blanket on imports or some form of limited intervention through a policy of safeguarding the domestic market for a few industrial sectors which account for a large percentage of the manufactured trade deficit (A. Cutler *et al.*, 1987). Again, however, such national policies designed to encourage domestic manufacturing at the expense of imports would go against the terms of a free European market. Increasingly, therefore, firms will need to look to their own resources/calculations for survival in the face of intensified competition.

The limitations of macro-economic policy

As we have seen in this chapter, Keynesian policies centre around the use of budget deficits to sustain the economy at the full employment level. While this requires the existence of a substantial public sector, and a modest degree of income redistribution, Keynesians see the government's prime role as influencing the overall level of economic activity. Within that level, resources are to be allocated predominantly by market forces.

Monetarists view Keynesian demand management policies as inherently inflationary, and see the removal of inflationary expectations as a prime task for government. The government's role here is limited to controlling the money supply. If price signals are not distorted by inflation, monetarists argue, market forces will guarantee an ideal allocation of resources.

For all their manifest differences, Keynesians and monetarists agree on two fundamental points.

☐ That government has considerable power to improve (or worsen) the macro-economic environment of business.
☐ That, if the macro-economic environment is appropriate, market forces will encourage businesses to allocate resources in the most efficient way.

Constraints on macro-economic policy

While not denying the power of government to influence macro-economic variables, we would argue that governments are severely constrained by the environmental conditions we examined in Chapters 6 to 8. Financial institutions, for example, have enormous power to frustrate the ability of governments to finance a large budget deficit or to control the money supply. In the long term, too, ecological considerations place profound constraints on any economic strategy which is based on continued growth of resource-intensive industries.

Perhaps the most significant immediate constraint on UK macro-economic policy in the late 1980s is the international one. The UK economy is an unusually open one, and there is a deep-seated weakness in the international competitiveness of many UK businesses, particularly in the manufacturing sector. In this situation, macro-economic policies designed to improve the domestic economy could easily bring about a balance of payments crisis. Keynesian reflation in the UK economic context of the late 1980s, for example, would suck in huge quantities of manufacturing imports, and create even larger trade deficits. Monetarist policies are also constrained by the trade situation. It is sometimes argued by monetarists that the price competitiveness of UK business could be improved by tighter controls over monetary growth to bring about further reductions in the rate of domestic inflation. Intensified control over money supply would, however, require higher interest rates. These would increase the exchange value of sterling, thus limiting any price advantages for UK businesses in export markets, while making imports into the UK even more attractive to domestic consumers.

The efficacy of market forces

The international constraint on macro-economic policy in the UK is at root a constraint which results from UK business failure. This calls into question the assumption, shared by Keynesians and monetarists alike, that, if government macro-economic policies are appropriate, market forces will guarantee business success. As we saw in Chapters 1 to 5, business calculations cannot be reduced to straightforward responses to changed price stimuli. Business decisions are also influenced by the institutional and organizational context in which they are taken.

One of the key lessons of Chapter 1 is that, in many consumer goods markets nowadays, non-price factors, like quality and reliability, are critical in influencing consumers' choice of products. In these areas, however, the products of many UK businesses are judged unsatisfactory in relation to overseas competition, both in export markets and in the domestic market. To change the poor quality reputation of many British goods would require, in many cases, a complete re-structuring of management attitudes to product design, to production organization and changing technology, and to training and skills. It is difficult to see how 'market forces' could be relied upon to produce such a restructuring, particularly when the financial conditions under which UK businesses operate encourage them to give primacy to short-term calculations.

Government policies to ease the trade constraint could play a positive role here. In the 1970s, the Cambridge Economic Policy Group argued powerfully for general import controls which would enable the government to expand aggregate demand and reduce unemployment without running up a current account balance of payments deficit. The problem with general import controls, however, is that they would protect inefficiency, and invite retaliation by trading partners. A more feasible alternative might be selective controls, targeted on key sectors where the UK manufacturing base is under imminent threat of permanent collapse. As Cutler et al. (1986) argue, tax incentives to discourage the consumption of motor vehicles and consumer electronics products with a high proportion of value added originating outside the UK could be more readily justified, and would have a dramatic effect on the trade deficit. It is doubtful if EC rules would permit the UK government to take such independent initiatives after the achievement of a single market in 1992, yet, as we saw in Chapter

8, it is after 1992 that UK manufacturing industry is likely to be most vulnerable.

Whatever form trade policy might take, it would need to be supplemented by direct encouragement to business to produce the sort of products today's consumers demand. As we shall see later in this chapter, experience elsewhere in Europe and in Japan suggests that this might require active intervention by government in business policy-making to encourage greater international competitiveness. Governments in the UK have, however, been reluctant to intervene too directly in what is seen as the preserve of private business, and industrial policies have tended to be piecemeal in approach.

Industrial policies in the UK

Industrial policies in the UK have taken four main forms – regional policy, competition policy, industrial intervention, and privatization. In this section, we give a brief overview of each of these forms, before going on in the final section to contrast UK experience with that elsewhere in Europe and in Japan.

Regional policy

It has long been accepted in the UK that business location decisions involve significant externalities (Key Concept 8.1), and that government should attempt to reduce the regional inequalities in employment which result from shifts in business location. In the 1950s and 1960s, the main concern was about above-average levels of unemployment in 'peripheral' regions dominated by declining industries – particularly Wales, Scotland, Northern Ireland, and the North of England. More recently, this has been supplemented by concern about the disappearance of manufacturing jobs from inner city areas, in 'peripheral' and 'central' regions alike.

The late 1960s were the high point of regional policy in the UK. A range of incentives was available for all firms locating in regions of high unemployment, including building grants, investment grants, and labour subsidies, while in the more prosperous regions permission for new industrial or office development was made conditional on the government being satisfied that the business could not be re-located in a region of high unemployment.

Regional policies were pursued less energetically in the 1970s, while in the 1980s there was a radical shift in emphasis. The boundaries of assisted areas were redrawn to cover only those areas with very high local unemployment, funding of regional development grants was substantially reduced, and businesses were no longer required to apply to central government for permission to undertake new industrial or office developments. At the same time, the government has made selective assistance available to certain deprived inner city areas and to 'enterprise zones', small districts in older urban areas where firms are freed from certain government regulations, including the requirement to contribute to the financing of industrial training schemes. The main emphasis in the late 1980s has been to channel central government investment, in partnership with the private sector but bypassing local planning controls, into Urban Development Corporations to re-develop areas of urban dereliction, on the model of Docklands (London) and Merseyside (Liverpool).

Competition policy

Competition policy in the UK dates from the establishment of the Monopolies and Restrictive Practices Commission (now called the Monopolies and Mergers Commission) in 1948. The Commission is an independent statutory body which inquires into and reports on matters referred to it by government under the 1973 Fair Trading Act and the 1980 Competition Act.

References mainly relate to monopoly situations (where one firm supplies at least a quarter of a market), and mergers (involving either a potential monopoly or combined assets of over £30 million), but they also include 'anti-competitive practices', and the performance of public sector bodies. There is no assumption in the UK legislation that monopoly situations or mergers are inherently undesirable. Rather, each case is judged on its merits, to determine whether or not it is 'in the public interest'.

The criteria for determining the 'public interest' are vaguely formulated in the legislation, and their interpretation can vary from reference to reference. In practice, the Commission looks, in a monopoly situation inquiry, for evidence of practices like above-average profits, and then assesses whether this is justified on grounds other than abuse of monopoly position. In its 1977 investigation of petfoods, for example, it found Pedigree earning exceptionally high profits, but felt that this was a justifiable reward for their efficient use of new technology. In a merger inquiry, the Commission might attempt to assess whether possible disadvantages from reduced consumer choice might be outweighed by possible advantages from economies of scale.

The Commission's investigations of monopoly situations have generally taken a lenient approach, and where it has recommended remedial action, the government has almost always been satisfied with an informal undertaking by the firm concerned. In no case has the break-up of a monopoly been considered. Some mergers have been stopped as a result of the Commission's recommendations, and some allowed to proceed only after assurances have been given. Only a small proportion of eligible mergers are referred to the Commission, however, despite the research evidence we referred to in Chapter 6 on the generally adverse effects of merger activity on economic efficiency in the UK.

Restrictive trade practices, such as price-fixing agreements and resale price maintenance, are treated differently from monopolies and mergers. The presumption here is that such practices are against 'the public interest'. Restrictive trade practices are therefore illegal, unless the parties can establish a case for exemption before the Restrictive Practices Court, a specially constituted body with the status of a High Court.

Industrial intervention

Industrial intervention policy in the UK is more recent in origin, and has suffered severe discontinuities resulting from changes in the political philosophy of the government in power. Disillusion with the stop–go cycle of economic activity led the Conservative government in the early 1960s to form the National Economic Development Council (NEDC). This brought both sides of industry together, with government, in an attempt to identify obstacles to faster growth, and remove them. The NEDC spawned a number of industrial sub-committees which examined the specific problems for their industries of achieving an overall target of 4% growth in GDP per year, but there was little government commitment to implementing the target.

In 1964, the new Labour government set up a Department of Economic Affairs to demonstrate its commitment to economic growth. This published, in 1965, a National Plan which worked out the detailed implications for each industry and region of a 25% increase in national output over six years. The National Plan was an attempt at 'indicative planning', with the government hoping that businesses would expect targets to be achieved, and so take the actions which would ensure that they were. Because the plan was seen as a self-fulfilling prophecy, little attention was given to implementation. This was an important part of the plan's downfall. To pay for the raw material imports required by the growth targets, the growth rate of exports should have doubled, and this did not happen, The government, hit by waves of speculation against sterling, refused to devalue, and embarked instead on a deflationary package to defend the existing exchange rate. The National Plan was formally abandoned in 1966, less than a year after it was published.

After the abandonment of the National Plan, government attention shifted to the activities of the Industrial Reorganization Corporation (IRC). This body was set up in 1966 to promote industrial change, with the particular aims of improving productivity and the balance of payments. In practice, much of its effort went on promoting mergers like those forming GEC and British Leyland (Case Study 6.1). Mergers such as these, the IRC considered, would enable key British industries to benefit from economies of scale, and thus become more competitive in international markets. There was little analysis of the composition of those markets, or of the importance of non-price factors, however, and there is little evidence to suggest that the IRC's activities did much to improve international competitiveness.

The IRC was disbanded by the Conservative government in 1971, as part of a policy of disengaging from industry, but within a year that policy was reversed, and the same Conservative government introduced selective financial support for weak industrial sectors. The Labour Government effectively resurrected the IRC in 1975, renaming it the National Enterprise Board. The NEB was meant to channel finance for industrial investment to promote industrial efficiency, and some of its funds went on establishing new technology enterprises (most notably Inmos). Most of its funds, however, went into the financial rescue of loss-making enterprises like British Leyland. Despite attempts to formulate an Industrial Strategy under the auspices of the NEDC, there was little attempt to relate the ad hoc interventions of the NEB either to each other or to an overall strategic perspective.

The election of a new Conservative government in 1979 saw a return to, and intensification of, the 1970–72 philosophy of disengagement. Support for the rescue of 'lame ducks' declined dramatically, and new government financial support for industry in the early 1980s was concentrated on innovation and research and development. By the late 1980s, the main emphasis of government policy towards private industry had shifted to promoting 'enterprise', through measures such as exempting small businesses from 'unnecessary' regulations.

Privatization

As part of their philosophy of 'disengagement', Conservative governments in the 1980s embarked on a programme of selling off publicly-owned assets (chiefly nationalized industries like British Telecom and British Gas) to the private sector. The privatization programme involves a number of separate objectives, including improved economic efficiency, reductions in PSBR, and wider share ownership.

There is little evidence to support the idea that private sector organizations are inherently more efficient than those in the public sector. The research that has been done in this area suggests that it is competitive product markets, not private ownership, which promotes greater efficiency (Kay and Thompson, 1986). This raises interesting questions for the privatization programme, because it implies that the objectives of the programme are in conflict with each other. In practice, the monopolistic market situations of most privatized industries have been retained, reflecting government fears that a more competitive structure would be less attractive to private shareholders and achieve less income from asset sales.

Industrial policies in other countries

Negative attitudes to industrial intervention in the UK are linked to negative perceptions of centralized planning in the USSR and Eastern Europe. What is often not understood in the UK, however, is that competing capitalist economies in Western Europe and in Japan make extensive use of economic planning and industrial intervention to promote national economic objectives. We concentrate here on experience in France and Japan.

France

In France, post-war reconstruction was planned by a small group of government officials in the Planning Commission, who gave priority in spending Marshall Plan aid to the modernization of transport, energy, and iron and steel. When Marshall Aid came to an end, the Commission supervised a series of plans, drawn up after consultation with a wide range of business opinion, to re-structure the French economy in the direction of greater productivity and higher growth. The basic approach adopted was for the planners to extrapolate recent trends over the planning period, identifying possible sectoral imbalances. Alternative assumptions about government policies to resolve the inconsistencies were then fed into the projections, and the results shown to a range of business, trade union, and government representatives, in order to identify points of agreement. Resulting from this consultation, detailed projections were then made for each sector, to guide individual businesses in their investment planning.

This sort of approach to indicative planning was what the UK government had in mind when it decided in the mid-1960s to publish a National Plan. Unlike the UK government, however, the French planners paid great attention to the relationship between domestic growth and the balance of payments (even if at times they miscalculated the extent of the trade constraint), and they were not averse to controlling imports in support of their domestic strategy. The French plans were also used as a basis for extensive state intervention in industry. Successive French governments used their power as shareholders in business, as purchasers of equipment, and as owners of financial institutions, to further the priorities identified in the plans. The government used its influence with financial institutions, for example, to guide investment in a co-ordinated way and make funds available at concessionary rates for selected key investments.

Japan

Japan is, of course, the success story of the post-war capitalist world, yet the role of industrial intervention in that story is often inadequately recognized. The key institution here is MITI, the Ministry of International Trade and Industry. Back in 1949, when MITI was first established, the Bank of Japan expressed the view that it would be pointless for Japan to develop a car industry, because the comparative advantage lay with North American and West European firms. The MITI view, however, was that car industry development should be given high priority, and that the infant car industry should be protected from foreign investment and car imports. With these policies, they argued, the Japanese car industry could develop a competitive advantage in the long term, with positive knock-on effects for the capital equipment industry. The MITI view prevailed, with consequences that are familiar to us all.

MITI has continued over the years to identify development priorities in terms of long-term market (and value added) possibilities rather than short-term financial costs. The following quotation from Y. Ojima, a MITI vice-minister, is illuminating:

> MITI decided to establish in Japan industries which require intensive employment of capital and technology, industries that in consideration of comparative costs of production should be the most inappropriate for Japan, industries such as steel, oil refining, petrochemicals, automobiles, aircraft, industrial machinery of all sorts, and electronics, including electronic computers. From a short-run, static viewpoint, encouragement of such industries would seem to conflict with

economic rationalism. But from a long-range viewpoint, these are precisely the industries where income elasticity of demand is high, technological progress is rapid, and labour productivity rises fast (OECD, 1972).

MITI has been able, not only to determine priority sectors for long-term development, but also to co-ordinate private businesses towards these ends effectively. Its success in implementation has come largely from selective use of its powers to control imports and foreign investment, and to influence the allocation of bank loans. While there are many factors underlying Japanese business success, effective interventionist policy by MITI to promote long-term competitiveness is certainly a positive influence.

Lessons for the UK

Copying policies which have been successful in other countries is a dangerous exercise, because policies which may be appropriate in one environmental and institutional context will not be appropriate in another. There do seem, nonetheless, to be certain broad lessons which can be drawn for the UK from other countries' experiences with industrial policies.

One lesson is that market prices cannot be relied upon to provide an adequate guide for the investment planning of firms. If firms take investment decisions solely on the basis of current prices, those decisions are bound to be inconsistent with each other. Some form of co-ordination of investment plans is required, particularly if widespread re-structuring of the economy is envisaged.

It also seems clear that effective co-ordination requires some mechanism of implementation – it is not sufficient just to publish a plan and hope that businesses will follow it. Detailed production planning, on East European lines, would not be feasible in the UK, nor would it be desirable in terms of encouraging greater responsiveness to changing consumer demands. Finance and trade policies designed to give priority to industrial sectors with the best prospects of developing long-term competitive advantage would seem to be essential, however (Thompson, 1987).

Finally, *ad hoc* responses to immediate crises are unlikely to provide a sound foundation for long-term success. As C. Brown, concluding a study of Japanese and French experience (1980), put it: 'Perhaps the single most important lesson that can be learnt from Japanese and French experience is the importance of coherence and strategy in government intervention in the economy, elements which have been lacking in British policy.'

Conclusion

Macro-economics has been dominated in recent years by the debate between Keynesians and monetarists. Each side of the debate has exaggerated the ability of governments to control macro-economic variables, by underestimating both the power of financial institutions and the constraining effects of the UK's trade situation. Experience in other capitalist economies suggests that government industrial policies have a significant role to play in improving business performance. Such policies in the UK have, however, been characterized by inconsistency, discontinuity, and a failure to address the real problems.

Further reading

Andrew Dunnett's *Understanding the Economy* (Longman, 2nd edn, 1987) is a good basic macro-economics textbook, while a more advanced treatment will be found in Victoria Chick's *Macroeconomics after Keynes* (Philip Allan, 1983).

The shifting emphases in British macro-economic policies are traced by Jim Tomlinson in his *British Macroeconomic Policy since 1940* (Croom Helm, 1985). *Keynes, Beveridge and Beyond*, by Tony Cutler *et al.* (Routledge, 1986), highlights the foreign trade constraints on government policy in the UK, while Michael Stewart's *Controlling the Economic Future* (Wheatsheaf Books, 1983) is unusual in considering the long-term environmental implications of macro-economic policy.

The last four chapters of *An Introduction to Industrial Economics*, by P.J. Devine *et al.* (George Allen and Unwin, 4th edn, 1985), give a detailed account of UK micro-economic policies, while Paul Hare's *Planning the British Economy* (Macmillan, 1985) usefully compares British experience with that in other countries.

Exercises

(For exercises 1–6 you should refer to the most recent annual supplement of *Economic Trends*.)

1. Plot the relationship between real personal disposable income (on the vertical axis) and real consumers' expenditure (on the horizontal axis) in the UK for each of the years 1948 to 1982.
   (This can be done on graph paper, or using a suitable computer package.)

2. (a) Find the straight line which best fits the above points.
      (This is best done by using linear regression analysis – see our companion volume, *Quantitative Methods in a Business Context*.)
   (b) What are the values of a and b in the equation $C = a + bY$?

3. What is the correlation coefficient for these data?

4. Given the real personal disposable income in the years since 1982, what levels of real consumers' expenditure would you predict in those years, on the basis of the equation you identified in 2 (b)?

5. Compare your predicted values of real consumers' expenditure in the years since 1982 with the actual values.
   How would you account for your results?

6. Plot the relationship between growth in £M3 and growth in the retail price index for each of the past 15 years.
How would you interpret changes in this relationship over time?

7. What are the effects of a rise in UK interest rates on:
   (a) Business investment?
   (b) The exchange value of sterling?
   (c) Money supply?
   (d) The current account of the balance of payments?
   (e) Capital flows between the UK and other countries?
   (f) The retail price index?

8. In what ways might business in the UK benefit from a more interventionist industrial policy on the part of government?

References

Beckerman, W. (1985) How the battle against inflation was really won. *Lloyds Bank Review*, Jan.

Beckerman, W. and Jenkinson, T. (1986) What stopped the inflation? *Economic Journal*, March.

Beveridge, Lord (1944) *Full Employment in a Free Society*, Allen and Unwin, London.

Brown, C.J.F. (1980) Industrial policy and economic planning in Japan and France. *National Institute Economic Review*, August.

Cuthbertson, K. (1982) The measurement and behaviour of the UK saving ratio in the 1970s. *National Institute Economic Review*, Feb.

Cutler, T. *et al.* (1986) *Keynes, Beveridge and Beyond*, Routledge, London.

Desai, M. (1981) *Testing Monetarism*, Frances Pinter, London.

Dow, J.C.R. (1964) *The Management of the British Economy 1945–60*, Cambridge University Press, Cambridge.

Friedman, M. (1977) Inflation and unemployment. *Journal of Political Economy*, **85** (3) (also Institute of Economic Affairs Occasional Paper, no. 51, 1977).

Friedman, M. and Schwartz, A. (1963) *A Monetary History of the United States 1867–1960*, Princeton University Press, Princeton.

Friedman, M. and Schwartz, A. (1982) *Monetary Trends in the United States and the United Kingdom 1867–1975*, Chicago University Press, Chicago.

Hendry, D. and Ericsson, N. (1983) *Assertion without Empirical Basis: an econometric appraisal of 'Monetary trends in . . . the UK'*, Bank of England panel paper no. 22, Oct.

Higham, D. and Tomlinson, J. (1982) Why do governments worry about inflation? *National Westminster Quarterly Review*, May.

Kaldor, N. (1976) Inflation and recession in the world economy. *Economic Journal*, Dec.

Kaldor, N. (1980) Monetarism and UK monetary policy. *Cambridge Journal of Economics*, Dec.

Kay, J.A. and Thompson, D.J. (1986) Privatisation: a policy in search of a rationale. *Economic Journal*, March.

Keynes, J.M. (1936) *The General Theory of Employment Interest and Money*, Macmillan, London.

Keynes, J.M. (1943) The Long Term Problem of Full Employment. (Reprinted in *Collected Writings*, vol. XXVII, Macmillan, 1980).

Matthews, R.C.O. (1968) Why has Britain had full employment since the war? *Economic Journal*, Sept.

OECD (1972) *The Industrial Policy of Japan*, OECD, Paris.

Phillips, A.W. (1958) The relation between unemployment and the rate of change of money wage rates in the UK 1861–1957. *Economica.*

Podolski, T.M. (1986) *Financial Innovations and the Money Supply*, Basil Blackwell, Oxford.

Thompson, G. (1987) The American industrial policy debate: any lessons for the UK? *Economy and Society*, Feb.

Statistical appendix

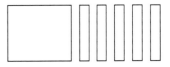

In this appendix, we present a range of official statistics to indicate some of the main trends, since the early 1970s, in the economic environment of UK business. In selecting the tables, our main criterion has been relevance to the analysis in the text. For a fuller picture, you should explore for yourself official publications such as *Economic Trends* and the *Annual Abstract of Statistics.*

Tables A.1–3 examine various aspects of the economic performance of the manufacturing industry in the UK, while Table A.4 concentrates on the service sector. Tables A.5–13 explore the UK's current account balance with those in other countries. The overall picture is summarized in Table A.5, while the subsequent tables focus in greater detail on aspects of this picture which are particularly significant. Tables A.10–13, for example, draw attention to the critical role of UK deficits in manufacturing trade with other members of the European Community, West Germany, France, Italy, and the Netherlands in particular. Finally, in Tables A.14–16, we present comparative data on trends in key macro-economic variables for the seven major OECD countries.

A useful exercise for any Business Economics student would be to update at least tables A.1, A.4, A.5, A.6, and A.7, using the latest issues of the sources cited. In doing this, you will encounter a number of potential pitfalls such as:

☐ Confusing UK figures with those for Great Britain only.
☐ Confusing balance of payments figures which are prepared on a 'balance of payments' basis with those prepared on an 'overseas trade statistics' basis. (The main difference is that import figures prepared for trade statistics include the cost of insurance and freight, while in the balance of payments accounts these items are deducted.)
☐ Confusing monetary values which are quoted in current prices with those in constant prices (i.e. discounting inflation).
☐ Not making allowance for the changes which statisticians make from time to time in their definitions, or in the base year from which their index numbers are calculated.
☐ Not incorporating revisions to the figures which statisticians make as new information becomes available (this applies particularly to the most recent balance of payments figures).

The ability to analyse official statistics, identifying and avoiding the pitfalls, but focussing on the most significant trends, is an important part of the skills of a business economist. To develop these skills, we would agree with Dudley Jackson (1982), that 'to find the statistics for yourself and to work with them is absolutely essential'.

Reference

Jackson, D. (1982) *Introduction to Economics: Theory and Data*, Macmillan, London.

Appendix tables

A.1   Capital formation, output, employment and labour productivity in the UK manufacturing industry

A.2   Value added in the UK manufacturing industry

A.3   Rates of return (before interest and tax) on capital employed by the UK manufacturing companies

A.4   Capital formation, output and employment in the UK service sector

A.5   The UK balance of payments current account (balance of payments basis, £m)

A.6   The UK current account transactions with other European Community members (balance of payments basis, £m)

A.7   Import penetration and exports/sales ratios in UK manufacturing

A.8   The UK balance of trade, by industry

A.9   Growth of UK manufacturing imports and exports (Index 1985 = 100)

A.10 The UK trade balance, manufacturing trade balance and manufacturing trade balance with other European Community members

A.11 Balance of UK manufacturing trade with other European Community members (£m)

A.12 UK manufacturing trade with West Germany and France, by industry

A.13 UK manufacturing trade with Italy and the Netherlands, by industry

A.14 Annual change in real national income and employment in the seven major OECD economies

A.15 Inflation and unemployment in the seven major OECD economies

A.16 Savings ratios and effective exchange rates in the seven major OECD economies

Table A.1 Capital formation, output, employment and labour productivity in the UK manufacturing industry

Year	Gross domestic fixed capital formation £m (1980 prices)	Gross domestic fixed capital formation Index 1980=100	Output at constant factor cost Index 1980=100	Employees in employment Thousands	Employees in employment Index 1980=100	Output per person hour Index 1980=100
1972	6344	97.9	104.5	7778	112.1	89.0
1973	6765	104.4	114.2	7828	112.8	95.2
1974	7397	114.2	112.8	7871	113.5	95.8
1975	6781	104.7	105.0	7488	107.9	94.0
1976	6475	99.9	106.9	7269	104.8	98.9
1977	6774	104.5	109.0	7317	105.4	99.8
1978	7221	111.5	109.7	7281	104.9	101.0
1979	7496	115.7	109.5	7253	104.5	101.5
1980	6478	100.0	100.0	6937	100.0	100.0
1981	4865	75.1	94.0	6222	89.7	104.8
1982	4704	72.6	94.2	5863	84.5	110.4
1983	4779	73.8	96.9	5525	79.6	118.9
1984	5752	88.8	100.8	5409	77.9	124.4
1985	6424	99.2	103.7	5366	77.4	128.1
1986	6329	97.7	104.7	5236	75.5	132.2
1987	6674	103.0	110.7	5145	74.2	141.1
1988						
1989						
1990						

Sources: *Annual Abstract of Statistics; Monthly Digest of Statistics; Economic Trends*
Note: Manufacturing, in this table and in Tables A.3 and A.7 includes all activities in Divisions 2 to 4 of the 1980 Standard Industrial Classification (SIC 1980); 2. Chemicals, metal manufacture, etc. 3. Engineering, vehicles, and metal goods. 4. Other manufacturing industries. Gross Domestic Fixed Capital Formation is expenditure on fixed capital (including depreciation costs) less expenditure on stocks.

Table A.2 Value added in the UK manufacturing industry

	Gross output (£ million)	Value added (£ million)	Value added as % of gross output	Labour's share of value added
1970	47 359	n/a	n/a	74.0
1971	50 325	n/a	n/a	74.0
1972	53 760	n/a	n/a	73.5
1973	63 340	23 731	37.5	73.1
1974	83 153	29 345	35.3	78.3
1975	93 048	32 390	34.8	81.5
1976	113 170	38 832	34.3	80.1
1977	132 030	43 992	33.3	74.8
1978	142 980	48 640	34.0	74.3
1979	165 386	56 418	34.1	77.6
1980	176 632	59 047	33.4	79.0
1981	178 351	59 609	33.4	78.7
1982	189 524	62 128	32.7	76.1
1983	203 702	67 277	33.0	73.8
1984	226 573	72 405	31.9	71.8
1985	242 894	78 021	32.1	n/a
1986	242 180	81 585	33.7	n/a

Sources: Census of Production PA 1002 (first three columns); United Nations National Accounts main aggregates and disaggregate tables (UN, New York) various years (last column).
Note: n/a not available. The first two columns are in current prices. The Census of Production data have been adjusted to correspond to the definition of manufacturing industry used in the 1968 Standard Industrial Classification (Orders III to XIX). Labour's share of value added includes social charges.

Table A.3 Rates of return (before interest and tax) on capital employed by the UK manufacturing companies

	Gross* (%)	Net† (%)
1960	12.2	14.8
1961	10.6	12.3
1962	9.8	11.1
1963	10.2	11.7
1964	10.5	12.1
1965	10.0	11.2
1966	9.0	9.7
1967	9.1	9.8
1968	8.9	9.5
1969	9.1	9.8
1970	8.0	8.1
1971	7.3	6.9
1972	8.0	8.1
1973	7.8	8.0
1974	5.3	4.3
1975	4.4	2.8
1976	4.7	3.2
1977	6.4	5.7
1978	6.5	6.0
1979	5.4	4.3
1980	4.7	3.0
1981	4.2	2.3
1982	5.2	4.0
1983	5.5	4.4
1984	5.9	5.1
1985	6.6	6.4
1986	7.3	7.5
1987	8.3	9.2

Sources: DTI; British Business.
Note:
* Gross operating surplus on UK operations (i.e. gross trading profits less stock appreciation plus rents received) as % of gross capital stock of fixed assets (excluding land) at current replacement cost plus book value of stock.
† Net operating surplus on UK operations (i.e. gross operating surplus less capital consumption at current replacement cost) as % of net capital stock of fixed assets (excluding land) at current replacement cost plus book value of stock.

Table A.4 Capital formation, output and employment in the UK service sector

| Year | Gross domestic fixed capital formation | | Output at constant factor cost | Employees in employment | |
	£m (1980 prices)	Index 1980=100	Index 1980=100	Thousands	Index 1980=100
1972	18 011	101.9	86.4	11 863	86.5
1973	19 852	112.4	90.1	12 299	89.7
1974	18 347	103.8	90.2	12 462	90.9
1975	16 300	92.2	91.2	12 788	93.3
1976	16 284	92.2	93.3	12 917	94.2
1977	16 194	91.7	94.6	12 990	94.7
1978	16 743	94.8	97.5	13 003	94.8
1979	18 002	101.9	100.4	13 581	99.1
1980	17 668	100.0	100.0	13 710	100.0
1981	16 592	93.9	100.3	13 466	98.2
1982	17 832	100.9	101.7	13 448	98.1
1983	18 579	105.2	105.0	13 500	98.5
1984	21 103	119.4	109.2	13 838	100.9
1985	22 942	129.9	113.3	14 188	103.5
1986	22 612	128.0	117.5	14 484	105.6
1987	24 122	136.5	123.3	14 844	108.3
1988					
1989					
1990					

Sources: *Annual Abstract of Statistics; Monthly Digest of Statistics; Economic Trends.*
Note: Services are all activities in Divisions 6–9 of SIC 1980. 6. Distribution, hotels, catering, repairs. 7. Transport and communication. 8. Banking, finance, insurance, etc. 9. Other services (mainly government). The increase in employees shown in this table exaggerates the increase in hours worked, as much of the increase has been in part-time employment (see Chapter 3).

Table A.5 The UK balance of payments current account (balance of payments basis, £m)

	1970	1971	1972	1973	1974	1975	1976
Visibles	−14	+210	−742	−2566	−5233	−3257	−3959
Oil	−497	−691	−666	−943	−3361	−3062	−3953
Non-oil	+483	+900	−76	−1623	−1872	−195	−6
Invisibles	+830	+901	+940	+1567	+2034	+1753	+3018
Current A/c	+816	+1111	+198	−999	−3199	−1504	−941

	1977	1978	1979	1980	1981	1982	1983
Visibles	−2324	−1593	−3398	+1353	+3350	+2218	−1076
Oil	−2775	−1989	−738	+308	+3105	+4639	+6972
Non-oil	+451	+396	−2660	+1045	+245	−2421	−8048
Invisibles	+2174	+2557	+2902	+1769	+3586	+2467	+4907
Current A/c	−150	+964	−496	+3122	+6936	+4685	+3831

	1984	1985	1986	1987	1988	1989	1990
Visibles	−4580	−2345	−8716	−10 162	−20 335		
Oil	+6932	+8101	+4056	+4184	+2344		
Non-oil	−11 512	−10 446	−12 772	−14346	−22 679		
Invisibles	+6602	+5683	+8541	+7475	+6065		
Current A/c	+2022	+3338	−198	−2504	−14 270		

Sources: UK Balance of Payments (pink book); British Business.
Note: Imports and exports, in this table and in Table A.6, are both calculated 'free on board' (i.e. excluding the cost of insurance and freight).

Table A.6 The UK current account transactions with other European Community members (balance of payments basis, £m)

	1977	1978	1979	1980	1981	1982	1983
Visible balance	−1809	−2486	−2709	+757	+85	−1175	−2460
Invisibles							
Services	−304	−369	−493	−720	−1113	−1818	−1884
Interest profits and dividends	+290	+610	+1075	+795	+2410	+3425	+4010
Transfers	−458	−903	−1057	−697	−409	−586	−614
Current A/c balance	−2281	−3148	−3184	+135	+973	−154	−948

	1984	1985	1986	1987
Visible balance	−3098	−2056	−8411	−9010
Invisibles				
Services	−2212	−2113	−2708	−2922
Interest profits and dividends	+3705	+3085	+2800	+395
Transfers	−712	−1772	−512	−1628
Current A/c balance	−2317	−2856	−8831	−13165

Source: UK Balance of Payments Pink Book.
Note: The other European Community members are listed in Table A.11.

Table A.7 Import penetration and export/sales ratios in UK manufacturing

Year	Imports as % of home demand	Exports as % of manufacturers' sales
1972	18.2	18.5
1973	21.4	19.6
1974	23.3	21.3
1975	22.0	22.6
1976	24.4	24.7
1977	25.1	25.7
1978	26.0	26.1
1979	26.9	25.1
1980	26.2	26.5
1981	27.8	27.2
1982	29.0	27.2
1983	31.1	26.6
1984	33.4	28.4
1985	34.3	30.2
1986	34.3	29.6
1987	35.2	30.3
1988		
1989		
1990		

Sources: *Annual Abstract of Statistics; Monthly Digest of Statistics.*
Note: 1972–74 figures are for Orders III to XIX of the 1968 Standard Industrial Classification, while for 1975 and after they are Divisions 2 to 4 of SIC 1980. Imports in this table, and in Tables A.8–A.13 include carriage, insurance and freight (c.i.f.), while exports are free on board (f.o.b.),

Table A.8 The UK balance of trade, by industry

a) *Exports (f.o.b.) less imports (c.i.f.) by SITC division (£m)*

	0–9	0+1	3	2+4	5–8	5+6	7+8
1970	−1012	−1514	−742	−1165	+2254	+290	+1964
1971	−713	−1567	−1016	−1056	+2799	+511	+2288
1972	−1471	−1678	−1007	−1060	+2134	+315	+1819
1973	−3635	−2189	−1361	−1626	+1375	+88	+1287
1974	−6726	−2647	−3865	−2093	+1620	−363	+1983
1975	−4433	−2852	−3495	−1776	+3467	+157	+3310
1976	−5893	−3239	−4409	−2678	+4128	+461	+3667
1977	−4235	−3631	−3166	−2997	+5116	+898	+4218
1978	−4161	−3150	−2435	−2717	+3651	+527	+3124
1979	−6311	−3495	−1464	−2964	+1173	−140	+1312
1980	−1864	−2837	−454	−2644	+3624	+457	+3176
1981	−32	−2856	+2443	−2739	+2637	+514	+2123
1982	−1310	−3235	+3824	−2638	+196	−36	+232
1983	−4991	−3579	+6023	−3228	−4854	−1091	−3763
1984	−8387	−4176	+4970	−3479	−6314	−1560	−4754
1985	−6641	−4299	+6128	−3313	−5812	−1414	−4398
1986	−12734	−4550	+2387	−2969	−8246	−1992	−6253
1987	−14164	−4533	+2648	−3445	−9947	−2883	−7064

b) *Exports (f.o.b.) as a % of imports (c.i.f.) by SITC division*

	0–9	0+1	3	2+4	5–8	5+6	7+8
1970	89	25	22	19	149	112	194
1971	93	27	19	21	157	121	193
1972	87	28	19	24	136	111	157
1973	77	29	21	21	116	102	127
1974	71	29	17	22	114	94	135
1975	81	33	19	24	128	103	149
1976	81	34	22	24	125	106	141
1977	88	38	40	25	125	110	137
1978	89	48	49	28	115	105	122
1979	86	46	75	31	104	99	108
1980	96	53	93	36	112	103	118
1981	100	56	134	33	108	104	111
1982	98	55	152	34	101	100	101
1983	92	54	185	34	89	94	87
1984	89	53	148	37	88	92	86
1985	92	54	158	40	90	93	88
1986	85	55	138	41	87	91	84
1987	85	55	143	39	86	89	85

Source: DTI.

Notes: (a) The industrial classification used in this table, and in Tables A.9–A.13, is the Standard Industrial Trade Classification (SITC). Sections 0,1, food, beverages and tobacco; Sections 2,4, basic materials; Section 3, fuels; Section 5, chemicals; Section 6, other semi-manufactured goods; Section 7, machinery and transport equipment; Section 8, other finished manufactured goods; Section 9, commodities and transactions not classified by kind. (b) Sections 5 and 6 are semi-manufactures; Sections 7 and 8 are finished manufactures.

Tables A.9 Growth of UK manufacturing imports and exports (Index 1985=100)

a) Value of exports and imports (current prices)

	Exports index	Imports index
1970	20	23
1971	21	24
1972	22	25
1973	24	30
1974	31	38
1975	38	44
1976	46	54
1977	54	63
1978	59	66
1979	64	69
1980	71	71
1981	75	75
1982	81	81
1983	87	88
1984	94	94
1985	100	100
1986	104	103
1987	108	106

b) Volume of exports and imports (constant prices)

	Volume index exports	Volume index imports
1970	61	29
1971	66	31
1972	65	37
1973	74	45
1974	79	48
1975	77	44
1976	83	48
1977	88	52
1978	90	60
1979	88	69
1980	87	65
1981	85	68
1982	85	76
1983	84	85
1984	93	95
1985	100	100
1986	101	106
1987	109	116

Sources: *DTI Monthly Review of External Trade Statistics* annual supplement; *Monthly Digest of Statistics.*
Note: The figures exclude erratic items, sometimes called SNAPS (Ships, North sea installations, Aircraft, Precious stones, and Silver).

Table A.10 The UK trade balance, manufacturing trade balance and manufacturing trade balance with other European Community members

	Trade balance (SITC 0–9)	of which manufacturing	of which other EC members
1975	−4233	+3660	−376
1976	−5422	+4403	−232
1977	−3647	+5501	−239
1978	−3548	+4026	−1445
1979	−5664	+1653	−2607
1980	−2409	+3641	−1723
1981	−170	+2905	−3000
1982	−1420	+198	−5004
1983	−5417	−4849	−8049
1984	−8194	−6308	−8863
1985	−6635	−5806	−9599
1986	−13188	−8245	−10925
1987	−14164	−9944	−11133

Source: DTI.

Note: Manufacturing, in this table and in Tables A.11–A.13, is SITC Sections 5–8.

Table A.11 Balance of UK manufacturing trade with other European Community members (£m)

	1975	1976	1977	1978	1979	1980	1981	1982	1983	1984	1985	1986	1987
Belgium/Luxembourg	+121	+227	+313	+346	+126	-168	-379	-525	-499	-559	-518	-357	-529
Denmark	+130	+234	+263	+180	+147	+114	-5	-1	-71	-81	-77	-91	-106
West Germany	-755	-1033	-1339	-1865	-2516	-2001	-2152	-3314	-4926	-5069	-5833	-6712	-7456
France	-157	-119	-293	-525	-726	-439	-595	-535	-1082	-1154	-1221	-1510	-1161
Greece	+81	+100	+165	+135	+184	+140	+136	+137	+172	+162	+167	+149	+152
Irish Republic	+285	+372	+497	+749	+959	+793	+690	+547	+471	+495	+548	+584	+488
Italy	-186	-190	-380	-669	-800	-368	-497	-826	-1175	-1307	-1387	-1590	-1554
Netherlands	+6	+33	+290	+161	+80	+184	-191	-466	-803	-876	-747	-1128	-1119
Portugal	-15	+21	+102	+54	+16	+79	+49	+39	-74	-236	-238	-216	-98
Spain	+114	+123	+143	-11	-77	-57	-56	-60	-62	-238	-293	-54	+250

Source: DTI.

Table A.12 UK manufacturing trade with West Germany and France, by industry

a) Exports (f.o.b.) less imports (c.i.f.), by SITC section (£m)

West Germany

SITC	1975	1976	1977	1978	1979	1980	1981	1982	1983	1984	1985	1986	1987
5	-107	-168	-200	-236	-258	-163	-224	-277	-332	-397	-406	-475	-547
6	-173	-157	-179	-277	-317	-506	-496	-688	-947	-1058	-1187	-1146	-1255
7	-422	-662	-921	-1285	-1807	-1274	-1252	-2065	-3296	-3179	-3728	-4458	-5051
8	-53	-46	-39	-66	-133	-58	-179	-283	-350	-435	-511	-634	-603

France

SITC	1975	1976	1977	1978	1979	1980	1981	1982	1983	1984	1985	1986	1987
5	-22	-32	-92	-175	-149	-101	-154	-165	-198	-244	-213	-468	-256
6	-20	+36	-2	-90	-107	-258	-200	-257	-416	-508	-529	-512	-537
7	-109	-136	-215	-275	-474	-109	-244	-181	-468	-422	-454	-543	-449
8	-6	+13	+16	+16	+4	+30	+4	+68	-1	-1	-26	+12	+81

b) Exports (f.o.b.) as a % of imports (c.i.f.), by SITC section

West Germany

SITC	1975	1976	1977	1978	1979	1980	1981	1982	1983	1984	1985	1986	1987
5	49	50	51	53	60	71	67	64	66	67	70	69	69
6	60	71	74	65	68	59	56	50	43	46	47	52	53
7	55	51	50	46	43	54	57	46	38	44	45	42	41
8	71	81	87	84	75	89	72	62	62	62	60	60	65

France

SITC	1975	1976	1977	1978	1979	1980	1981	1982	1983	1984	1985	1986	1987
5	83	83	71	60	72	79	72	73	72	74	79	62	79
6	91	113	99	82	82	67	70	66	53	52	55	59	62
7	83	85	79	77	69	92	83	88	75	79	80	79	85
8	95	108	108	106	101	107	101	116	100	100	96	102	110

Source: DTI.

Table A.13 UK manufacturing trade with Italy and the Netherlands, by industry

a) Exports (f.o.b.) less imports (c.i.f.) by SITC section (£m)

Italy

SITC	1975	1976	1977	1978	1979	1980	1981	1982	1983	1984	1985	1986	1987
5	+20	+23	+24	+58	+58	+86	+89	+121	+156	+142	+156	+203	+214
6	-50	-25	-64	-186	-164	-90	-211	-284	-342	-387	-439	-456	-503
7	-58	-50	-137	-259	-315	-58	-8	-185	-367	-327	-345	-472	-451
8	-97	-138	-203	-282	-380	-305	-367	-478	-569	-695	-758	-866	-815

Netherlands

SITC	1975	1976	1977	1978	1979	1980	1981	1982	1983	1984	1985	1986	1987
5	-20	-40	-19	-26	-20	+61	-15	-96	-190	-145	-123	-296	-398
6	-71	-58	+1	-14	-54	-75	-138	-219	-311	-345	-379	-386	-370
7	+76	+92	+231	+136	+86	+146	-17	-145	-282	-291	-171	-357	-277
8	+21	+41	+76	+65	+67	+52	-20	-6	-21	-63	-74	-90	-74

b) Exports (f.o.b.) as a % of imports (c.i.f.) by SITC section

Italy

SITC	1975	1976	1977	1978	1979	1980	1981	1982	1983	1984	1985	1986	1987
5	143	133	126	165	151	175	173	183	156	142	157	169	164
6	65	87	76	51	64	80	54	49	46	50	50	52	53
7	81	86	75	63	65	93	99	80	68	74	76	71	77
8	31	32	27	25	25	37	33	27	27	26	28	29	34

Netherlands

SITC	1975	1976	1977	1978	1979	1980	1981	1982	1983	1984	1985	1986	1987
5	90	87	95	93	97	112	97	86	77	85	89	74	70
6	71	83	100	96	88	85	72	60	52	53	57	59	64
7	125	125	154	128	114	123	97	83	74	77	88	78	84
8	133	141	154	138	132	123	93	98	94	85	85	84	88

Source: DTI.

Table A.14 Annual change in real national income and employment in the seven major OECD economies

a) % change in real national income

	1975	1976	1977	1978	1979	1980	1981	1982	1983	1984	1985	1986	1987
USA	-1.3	4.9	4.7	5.3	2.5	-0.2	1.9	-2.5	3.6	6.8	3.0	2.9	2.9
Japan	2.7	4.8	5.3	5.2	5.3	4.3	3.7	3.1	3.2	5.1	4.9	2.4	4.2
Germany	-1.4	5.6	2.7	3.3	4.0	1.5	0.0	-1.0	1.9	3.3	2.0	2.5	1.7
France	-0.3	4.2	3.2	3.4	3.2	1.6	1.2	2.5	0.7	1.4	1.7	2.1	1.9
UK	-1.1	2.9	2.2	3.6	2.7	-2.4	-1.2	1.6	3.3	2.6	3.6	3.3	4.5
Italy	-3.6	5.8	1.9	2.7	4.9	3.9	1.1	0.2	1.0	3.2	2.9	2.9	3.1
Canada	2.6	6.2	3.6	4.6	3.9	1.5	3.7	-3.2	3.2	6.3	4.3	3.3	3.9

b) % change in employment

	1975	1976	1977	1978	1979	1980	1981	1982	1983	1984	1985	1986	1987
USA	-1.1	3.4	3.7	4.4	2.9	0.5	1.1	-0.9	1.3	4.1	2.0	2.3	2.6
Japan	-0.3	0.9	1.3	1.3	1.3	1.0	0.8	1.0	1.7	0.6	0.7	0.8	1.0
Germany	-2.8	-0.8	-0.2	0.6	1.4	1.1	-0.7	-1.7	-1.5	0.1	0.7	1.0	0.7
France	-1.0	0.8	0.8	0.3	0.1	0.2	-0.7	0.3	-0.3	-1.0	-0.2	0.2	-0.1
UK	-0.6	-0.7	0.1	0.8	1.3	-1.0	-3.4	-1.9	-0.6	1.8	1.4	0.6	1.8
Italy	0.2	0.8	0.5	0.7	1.0	0.8	0.5	0.6	0.5	0.8	0.6	0.9	0.2
Canada	1.7	2.1	1.8	3.5	4.1	3.0	2.8	-3.3	0.8	2.5	2.8	2.9	2.8

Source: *OECD Economic Outlook*

Note: Some of the national data in this table, and in Tables A.15 and A.16, have been adjusted by the OECD to make them more comparable between countries. For details, see 'Sources and Methods' in the *OECD Economic Outlook*.

247

Table A.15 Inflation and unemployment in the seven major OECD economies

a) % change in consumer prices

	1975	1976	1977	1978	1979	1980	1981	1982	1983	1984	1985	1986	1987
USA	9.1	5.7	6.5	7.6	11.3	13.5	10.3	6.1	3.2	4.3	3.5	1.9	3.7
Japan	11.8	9.3	8.1	3.8	3.6	8.0	4.9	2.7	1.9	2.2	2.1	0.4	-0.2
Germany	6.0	4.5	3.7	2.7	4.1	5.5	6.3	5.3	3.3	2.4	2.2	-0.2	0.2
France	11.8	9.6	9.4	9.1	10.8	13.6	13.4	11.8	9.6	7.4	5.8	2.7	3.1
UK	24.2	16.5	15.8	8.3	13.4	18.0	11.9	8.6	4.6	5.0	6.1	3.4	4.2
Italy	17.2	16.5	18.1	12.4	15.7	21.1	18.7	16.3	15.0	10.6	8.6	6.1	4.6
Canada	10.8	7.5	8.0	8.9	9.2	10.2	12.5	10.8	5.8	4.3	4.0	4.2	4.4

b) % unemployment rate

	1975	1976	1977	1978	1979	1980	1981	1982	1983	1984	1985	1986	1987
USA	8.3	7.6	6.9	6.0	5.8	7.0	7.5	9.5	9.5	7.4	7.1	6.9	6.1
Japan	1.9	2.0	2.0	2.2	2.1	2.0	2.2	2.4	2.6	2.7	2.6	2.8	2.8
Germany	3.6	3.7	3.6	3.5	3.2	3.0	4.4	6.1	8.0	7.1	7.2	6.5	6.5
France	4.0	4.4	4.9	5.2	5.9	6.3	7.4	8.1	8.3	9.7	10.2	10.4	10.8
UK	4.3	5.6	6.0	5.9	5.0	6.4	9.8	11.3	12.5	11.7	11.2	11.2	10.3
Italy	5.8	6.6	7.0	7.1	7.6	7.5	8.3	9.0	9.8	10.2	10.5	–	–
Canada	6.9	7.1	8.0	8.3	7.4	7.4	7.5	10.9	11.8	11.2	10.4	9.5	8.8

Source: *OECD Economic Outlook.*

Table A.16 Savings ratios and effective exchange rates in the seven major OECD economies

a) net household savings as a % of disposable household income

	1975	1976	1977	1978	1979	1980	1981	1982	1983	1984	1985	1986	1987
USA	9.4	7.8	6.7	7.3	7.0	7.3	7.7	7.0	5.5	6.3	4.6	4.5	3.9
Japan	22.8	23.2	21.8	20.8	18.2	17.9	18.3	16.5	16.3	16.0	16.0	16.6	16.6
Germany	15.1	13.3	12.2	12.0	12.6	12.8	13.4	12.7	10.9	11.4	11.5	12.2	12.2
France	20.2	18.2	18.7	20.4	18.8	17.6	18.0	17.3	15.9	14.6	13.8	14.0	13.0
UK	12.3	12.0	10.4	11.8	13.0	14.2	13.1	12.2	10.6	10.7	9.3	7.4	5.6
Italy	30.6	30.1	28.6	29.3	29.2	28.0	26.7	25.9	24.7	24.6	24.2	24.4	23.5
Canada	12.7	11.8	11.4	12.6	13.2	13.6	15.4	18.2	14.8	15.0	14.1	11.7	9.4

b) effective exchange rates (average of daily rates), index 1970 Q1 = 100

	1975	1976	1977	1978	1979	1980	1981	1982	1983	1984	1985	1986	1987
USA	85.3	89.1	88.5	80.4	79.1	80.1	85.9	94.5	98.0	103.6	106.7	87.6	77.8
Japan	108.1	113.4	126.2	154.6	143.6	139.2	156.1	146.8	161.5	169.7	174.1	227.6	249.0
Germany	122.5	130.5	139.3	147.3	153.6	155.7	151.2	159.3	167.8	167.7	170.9	185.9	196.9
France	102.3	99.9	93.9	93.1	93.3	94.8	90.2	83.4	78.5	76.8	78.2	80.3	80.2
UK	75.2	64.9	61.8	62.4	65.6	72.5	74.8	71.9	67.3	64.6	65.3	59.8	58.9
Italy	73.7	61.8	56.6	53.0	51.0	49.6	45.4	42.6	41.7	40.2	38.5	39.4	39.5
Canada	101.3	106.8	98.5	89.0	85.7	85.8	85.8	85.8	87.2	83.8	80.1	74.2	75.4

Source: OECD Economic Outlook.

Index

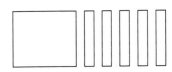